333 .78 Ev2n 1983 2202106
Everhart, William C.
The National Park Service /

THE NATIONAL PARK SERVICE

WESTVIEW LIBRARY OF FEDERAL DEPARTMENTS, AGENCIES, AND SYSTEMS

Ernest S. Griffith and Hugh L. Elsbree, General Editors

The Library of Congress, Second Edition, Charles A. Goodrum and Helen W. Dalrymple

The National Park Service, William C. Everhart

The Forest Service, Michael Frome

The Smithsonian Institution, Paul H. Oehser

The Bureau of Indian Affairs, Theodore W. Taylor

*Available in hardcover and paperback.

THE NATIONAL PARK SERVICE

William C. Everhart

Foreword by Russell E. Dickenson

Westview Press / Boulder, Colorado

Westview Library of Federal Departments, Agencies, and Systems

Published in 1983 in the United States of America by
Westview Press, Inc.
5500 Central Avenue
Boulder, Colorado 80301
Frederick A. Praeger, President and Publisher

Library of Congress Cataloging in Publication Data
Everhart, William C.
The National Park Service.
(Westview library of federal departments, agencies, and systems)
Bibliography: p.
Includes index.
1. United States. National Park Service. 2. National parks and reserves—United States. I. Title. II. Series.
SB482.A4E95 1982 353.0086′3 82-10884
ISBN 0-86531-130-7
ISBN 0-86531-498-5 (pbk.)

Printed and bound in the United States of America

CONTENTS

ILLUSTRATIONS

FOREWORD

In the decade that has passed since the publication of the first edition of this book, the National Park Service has seen the strongest period of growth in its history. Today the Service has responsibility for more than 330 areas and sites, now embracing nearly 50 million acres. There have been important, and sometimes controversial, departures in the development of the national park system, ranging from major urban recreation areas to intergovernmental cooperative ventures to the great wilderness parks of Alaska.

It is most welcome that Bill Everhart now chooses to completely rewrite the earlier volume. His credentials for commenting on the National Park Service are as good as a man can have, given his years of experience first as a field historian and then as chief of interpretation for the Service. Immediately before his retirement, Bill gained added insights as a close adviser to two directors. Those insights are now brought to bear on the past and present of the National Park Service at a time in the Service's history when opportunity and strain are combining to stretch minds and resources in a kind of sweet agony. With growth have come new levels of responsibility and new constituencies, amid the effects of inflation and a reduced staff.

As one reflects on the dimensions of the park system today, it is useful to remember that the concept of a *system* of places and structures to embrace the national patrimony is a relatively new idea. In the beginning the primary object was to set aside the greatest of the majestic "wonders" of the nation. Today that concept embraces a wide spectrum of resources—natural, historical, and recreational—that taken together share a remarkable similarity to the geographic and ethnic pluralism of our culture. It is hard to imagine how even a conscious plan could have achieved so much so well.

It seems probable that the immediate period ahead will be a time of consolidation and a time for nurturing the growth of the last several years in ways that insure the permanence of the values held in stewardship by the National Park Service and its highly dedicated staff. This volume will sharpen our understandings of the past and the present and, I hope, serve to further fuel the enthusiasm of people both inside the Service and among the public to push ahead with the great work now underway. Much remains to be done. Our proud past can be a powerful prologue.

Russell E. Dickenson
Director, National Park Service

PROLOGUE: "FOR THE GOOD OF THE SERVICE"

Park Service people, who are not loosely attached to their organization, know what Harold Nicholson meant when he said that his pulse quickened every time he saw the name Oxford, even on a jar of marmalade. At a time when it is fashionable to regard corporate loyalty as an amusing anachronism, nearly 200 members of the 1916 Society gathered in Washington, D.C., on August 25, 1981, for an evening of cocktails, dinner, and speechmaking by Park Service director Russ Dickenson and Interior Secretary James Watt. An easygoing fellowship with no bylaws, the society was formed by retired Park Service employees living in the Washington area for the sole purpose of holding a reunion every year on August 25, the date on which the National Park Service was created in 1916.

Convivial get-togethers of this kind are much favored by people who have lived and served together in U.S. national parks from Alaska to the Everglades. Park communities are often in remote locales where the winters are long and residents must ward off cabin fever. According to the wife of one Yellowstone superintendent, the surefire recipe for a rousing party is to set out a case of beer and casually mention the word "bear."

Predictably, the program for the society's 1981 meeting was heavy on nostalgia, including an exchange of telephone greetings with colleagues holding similar sessions in Omaha, Denver, Santa Fe, Seattle, and San Francisco. The highlight of the evening was a telephone hookup with Horace Albright, a legendary figure who links the Park Service with its past. As a young assistant to the secretary of the Interior in 1916, Albright helped lobby the Park Service legislation through Congress. When the U.S. cavalry turned Yellowstone over to the Park Service after guarding the park faithfully for thirty years, Albright became its first civilian superintendent in 1919. In 1929, he became the second director of the Park Service.

Now ninety-one, and still blessed with a renowned memory capable of recalling the exact details of a chance meeting with John Muir in 1912, Albright has been the elder statesman of the organization for nearly half a century. Generations of Park Service people, myself included, have relished the hearty friendship and benefited from the tart advice of an exceptional man who continues to convey encouragement to his numberless friends across the country. In 1980 President Jimmy Carter sent his personal representative to California to bestow upon Horace Albright the nation's highest civilian award, the Medal of Freedom, for his distinguished achievements in the field of conservation. One hopes this recognition will prove a good omen for the organization Horace has loved and served so well.

In case any reader may have overlooked the clues, the Park Service comes closer to being a tribal clan than a government agency. In its early years it was shaped by a resourceful group of gifted amateurs—Albright was one of them—for the craft of administering a park system, developing a guiding philosophy, and training a corps of rangers had to be learned from scratch. There were no examples to follow and no books on the subject.

Right from the beginning the Park Service seemed to attract more than its share of unconventional yet able personalities, who may well have been drawn by the rewarding and occasionally adventurous life in the parks. They added a distinctive flavor to an organization that happily developed a fond tolerance for eccentrics, allowing them a certain amount of running room. There were high standards, but they were gently imposed. The Park Service has remained a career organization from top to bottom; almost everyone, including director Dickenson, came aboard at the entry level and moved through the ranks. Defections to other organizations are almost unknown. Even the green ranger uniform with the familiar broad-brimmed stetson is a model of permanence. For close to fifty years the only change worth mentioning was the disappearance of the high cavalry boots in 1940.

Anyone who joins the Park Service must be prepared to move frequently (there is a fairly low tolerance for "homesteaders"). As you move from park to park you develop an ever-widening circle of friends and associates, and the result is the Park Service version of the "old-boy" network. The system has in the past produced skilled and uncommonly dedicated employees. It has also induced a parochial outlook: "But we've always done it this way in Yellowstone" is a frequently heard expression meant to be humorous. It may also be diagnostic.

Back in the glowing years of the Kennedy administration, when the Park Service was considerably more in charge of its own fortunes and had more than its share of fervor, an Interior assistant secretary made a speech that is now part of Service folklore. In it he denounced the agency for steadfastly maintaining its own traditions and its separate identity within the Department of the Interior. According to the ruthlessly unsentimental John Carver, the Park Service was suffering from a bad case of mystique. Since Carver's outburst was rated on a par with so many of his peevish pronouncements, the mystique was in no danger.

More recently the Park Service has experienced troubling changes, with the result that some of the vitality and the excitement of the earlier years seem to have worn away. There is general agreement that the organization's blood has grown thinner and that it takes an ungodly amount of time to get anything done or to get anyone to make a decision. It was not all that long ago that duties were far less constricted by administrative procedures, and the work seemed to matter more. The old mystique is nearly dormant, and anyone who today asked an employee to go the extra mile without overtime pay "for the good of the Service" might well receive a mocking response. The energy and idealism that have characterized the Park Service for so long have not vanished, but they do seem to be the victims of a slight recession.

With an annual budget large enough to earn it a place on *Fortune's* list of the largest American corporations, the Park Service is inevitably being transformed into a bureaucracy. This may not be the most shameful trend; there are strong indications that after being spared the application of partisan politics for so long, it is now in danger of being politicized.

Readers, however, should be ever mindful when confronted with such observations that, having but recently retired from the Park Service, I am often guilty of seeing perfection in the past and typical of my generation in being inordinately fond of keeping the legends and the tribal memories alive. In defense of this bias, there is something ineffably fine in having been a part of an organization entrusted with the care of the national parks, in having shared the experience with about as engaging a set of lively minded individualists as one could ever hope to encounter. Admittedly, this account of the nature and substance of the National Park Service comes from a touchable heart.

1

THE FIRST PARKS

Tracing the origin of the national park idea is like nailing jelly to the wall. The author of a recent study of the subject detected certain proclivities toward parks in the Greeks and Romans, not to mention the royal gardens of the Persians, but concluded that the national park concept, with its insistence upon both protection and public use, is a relatively modern invention.

It was the misfortune that blighted Niagara Falls, at one time the most famous and popular tourist attraction in the United States, that convinced a good many people the nation should take steps when one of its scenic marvels was being desecrated. Soon after 1800 the land around the falls began to slip into the hands of tourist promoters. Eventually the rim was almost filled with blocks of dreary and vulgar shops and catchpenny booths. Travelers were hustled and harassed and fleeced. By 1860 there was no point on the U.S. side from which the falls could be seen without paying some sharpie a fee. The commercialization and defacement of Niagara Falls became the country's first environmental disgrace.

Still missing, as Americans began to voice appreciation for nature and regret at the passing of the frontier, was a sense of purpose. It was supplied in part by acts of national vandalism. In California, frontier entrepreneurs in search of quick profits stripped the bark from a giant sequoia, exhibiting the reassembled specimen in eastern cities and, in 1854, at the Crystal Palace in London. There, ironically, disbelieving spectators accustomed to much smaller trees jeered the display as a fraud. The incident, widely reported in the U.S. press, angered many people who damned the wanton destruction of the 3,000-year-old tree for a shilling a show. The danger to these unique forest giants was reported by *Harper's Weekly,* which declared the tree had been cut and peeled "with as much neatness and industry as a troupe of jackals would display in cleaning the bones of a dead lion."

At the end of the eighteenth century the romantic movement in Europe began to articulate a new attitude toward nature, that it was beautiful and restorative rather than stern and oppressive. Witnessing the effects of industrialism in New England in the early nineteenth century, the conversion of once lovely villages into grimy factory towns, the prophets of transcendentalism, Thoreau and Emerson, found a receptive audience when they preached that a return to nature was the only remedy.

Also influencing the national park movement was the country's need to establish a national identity. Recognizing that the United States could not match the cultural achievements of the Old World, as manifested in its cathedrals and castles and ancient cities, Americans began to take pride in their own natural monuments, the awesome mountains and canyons of the West that far surpassed the more tranquil scenery of Europe. Landscape painters produced huge spectacular canvases; photographs taken by government surveys appeared in the press. It gave a young nation considerable self-assurance to realize it had something unique to contribute to world culture.

Yet in the mid-nineteenth century there was nothing resembling even an embryonic conservation movement, no organized sentiment for protecting scenic wonders in some systematic fashion, no mention anywhere in the world of setting aside outstanding landscapes as public parks. The prospectors, cattlemen, and lumber operators moving into the virgin lands of the West were followers of manifest destiny, not transcendentalism.

Then in the midst of the Civil War, on June 30, 1864, as Grant launched his Wilderness campaign against Lee, President Abraham Lincoln signed a bill transferring jurisdiction of Yosemite Valley and a grove of giant sequoias to the state of California. Yosemite was an important precursor; the argument is even advanced, mostly by Californians, that it was in fact the first national park. The valley had been discovered in 1851 by a volunteer brigade of soldiers in search of hostile Indians. Although Horace Greeley returned from an 1859 trip proclaiming it to be the most majestic natural feature on earth, the general public was barely aware of Yosemite in 1864. There is no evidence the Yosemite legislation was the result of careful planning or popular support or represented any considerable forethought.

It was in fact more curious than illustrious. The congressman who introduced the legislation explained only that "certain gentlemen in California, gentlemen of fortune, of taste, and of refinement" had suggested the measure. There being no one so churlish as to demand further details, the measure passed Congress without debate. Grants to the states from the federal government were not uncommon at the time, although the stipulation that the lands "shall be held for public use, resort and recreation" was significant and unprecedented. Had the valley remained in the public domain it would undoubtedly have been taken up by those recognizing its future tourist potential, perhaps preempting later national park designation. Even before the valley was ceded to the state, settlers had filed claims and a couple of primitive hotels had been erected.

Yellowstone

One of the spaces in the West that attracted early notice was that mysterious area lying at the headwaters of the Yellowstone River. John Colter, the legendary mountain man, is believed to have been the first white man to see that country during his astonishing 500-mile journey, in winter and alone, through the northern Rockies in 1807. Walled in by mountain ranges and far from the major travel routes, Yellowstone was inaccessible, which partially explains why it remained a shadowy province for so long. Fur trappers passed through Yellowstone almost every year, but they were a special breed, not much given to writing things down.

They regarded story telling as a form of camp fire entertainment, constantly embellishing favorite tales of deeds they had performed and sights they had seen. Jim Bridger was a master of this frontier drama, but his recitals only strengthened general disbelief among sober citizens as to the existence of a land where the earth shook and smoked from subterranean fires and exploding waterspouts. (Not to mention mountains of glass and petrified birds sitting on petrified trees singing petrified songs!)

Prospectors wandering through the Yellowstone country in the 1860s brought back reports, mostly hearsay, that excited the citizens of Montana Territory. There were several unsuccessful attempts to obtain more reliable information (one returning explorer told a welcoming committee "he was unwilling to risk his reputation for veracity by a full recital, in the presence of strangers, of the wonders he had seen"). Then, in 1870, a full-scale expedition was organized.

With packers, cooks, forty horses and mules, a dog named Booby, and rations for thirty days, the company of some twenty gentlemen-adventurers (mustered from the local business community plus a few townsmen temporarily between jobs) rode out from Helena in late August. It was under the command of Civil War general and former congressman Henry D. Washburn, the surveyor-general of the territory, who had arrived in Montana on a wagon train and heard tales of Yellowstone from Jim Bridger. A small cavalry detachment, under Lt.

Gustavus C. Doane, guarded the civilian explorers against the unpredictable tendencies of the Crow and Blackfeet.

A nine-day ride brought the party to the boundary of the present park. Yellowstone, they discovered, was a wonderland surpassing their most optimistic hopes, and they spent a month marveling at the curiosities: geysers and hot springs, waterfalls and canyons. Accounts written by several of the explorers bordered on the rhapsodic:

> I can scarcely realize that in the unbroken solitude of this majestic range of rocks, away from civilization and almost inaccessible to human approach, the Almighty has placed so many of the most wonderful and magnificent objects of His creation, and that I am to be one of the few first to bring them to the notice of the world.

One of the most memorable experiences for the party, as for most Yellowstone visitors since, took place almost at the end of the journey. As the horsemen rode along the Firehole River, they abruptly came out of a dense lodgepole pine forest. Only a few hundred yards away, in an open basin marked by rising clouds of vapor, a column of steam and water was shooting more than 100 feet into the sky. Displaying impeccable timing, the geyser that the party named "Old Faithful" emerged from fable to become the symbol of Yellowstone.

Returning expedition members wrote articles about their adventures, which were widely reported. Denver's *Rocky Mountain News* headed the Washburn story a "Mountain Romance," suggesting it might tax a reader's credulity, but the *New York Times* called its account "unpretentious eloquence." The publicity prompted the Geological and Geographical Survey of the Territories to send a party of scientists to Yellowstone the following summer. Included in the party were the pioneer photographer William Jackson and the artist Thomas Moran, whose pictures and sketches went on display in the nation's Capitol (Moran's most famous painting, "The Grand Canyon of the Yellowstone," was promptly purchased by Congress and hung in the Senate lobby). Lt. Doane's official report contained a prediction: "As a country for sightseers, it is without parallel; as a field for scientific research, it promises great results; in the branches of geology, mineralogy, botany, zoology, and ornithology, it is probably the greatest laboratory that nature furnishes on the surface of the globe."

On March 1, 1872, President Ulysses S. Grant signed the act establishing Yellowstone National Park, setting aside 2 million acres "as a public park or pleasuring ground for the benefit and enjoyment of the people." Reserving so large an expanse—larger than the two eastern states of Rhode Island and Delaware combined—with all of its potential wealth of water power, timber, and grazing lands barred from private use was so dramatic a departure from the public land policy of Congress that in retrospect it almost seems to smack of the miraculous.

The explanation is probably not all that complex. The public domain still seemed endless, no commercial interests were immediately threatened, and creating the preserve cost the government nothing. Agitation for the park came from a handful of enthusiasts, members of the several Yellowstone explorations, and a few individuals in Congress, including the far-sighted senator who warned that if Yellowstone were not protected some chiseler would "plant himself right across the only path that leads to these wonders, and charge every man that passes along between the gorges of these mountains a fee of a dollar or five dollars." Yellowstone was the work of a relatively small group of activists and Congressmen, supported by publishers and conservationists. The pattern hasn't changed much since 1872.

Yellowstone's early history was unpromising. Believing the park should somehow be self-supporting, Congress provided no appropriations, and the superintendent served without salary or staff. The purpose of the park was clearly defined by the enabling act, but the legislation did not include any legal means for protecting features or wildlife. When his appeals for funds and a set of regulations were ignored, the superintendent went back to his duties as a bank examiner in Minnesota.

Traveling through Yellowstone in 1875, the secretary of War found that poachers were roaming freely. With elk hides bringing six dollars, more than 4,000 animals had been slaughtered the previous winter, their antlers scattered along every hillside and meadow. The report of another military expedition the same year indicates vandalism in a national park is not a modern phenomenon. People who had made the difficult journey to Yellowstone were writing their names in the pools and chopping and hacking off ornamental work from the formations. Just in time, a woman was diverted as she was about to bring her ax down on the tip of a geyser cone. Few geyser formations escaped some multilation. Everyone who visited the park agreed that it could not survive unless someone was given authority to stop the devastation.

On the evening of August 17, 1886, Troop M, First United States Cavalry, jogged into Yellowstone, relieving the civilian superintendent of his duties. Orders were promptly issued—and enforced—against defacing or removing curiosities, hunting or trapping, commercial fishing, or stock grazing. Although Congress had been unwilling to provide funds to the secretary of the Interior, it now supported the military administration. For the next thirty years the army was responsible for Yellowstone. The Corps of Engineers was in charge of developments, including the construction of a road system. The thesis of a book entitled

How the U.S. Cavalry Saved Our National Parks (army management was also extended to other parks) may be slightly overblown, but the military supplied effective control of the parks at a critical time, earning a well-deserved tribute from John Muir: "Blessings on Uncle Sam's soldiers. They have done the job well, and every pine tree is waving its arms for joy."

The Beginnings of Conservation

Born in Scotland, Muir arrived in Yosemite in 1868. It was to become his personal sanctuary, and until his death in 1914 he was "great Nature's priest," the first of the conservation prophets, an explorer, advocate, and writer. Because the original Yosemite grant included only a few thousand acres, Muir led the fight to set aside a much larger area of the Sierra range, his beloved "mountains of light," and in 1890 Congress established a Yosemite park nearly the size of Yellowstone.

Congressional action next shifted to preservation of the giant sequoias. Logging of the great redwoods by hack and slash methods, typical of the callous disregard of the public interest during the period, had almost wiped out the accessible groves. Much of the destruction, in the words of the secretary of the Interior, was "useless, wasteful, lamentable." The wood of the giant sequoia (as opposed to that of the coastal redwood) is so brittle as to have only minimal commercial value. Much of the wood was lost when the giant trees were brought crashing down.

In the Converse Basin, one of the largest of all the giant sequoia groves, it is estimated that fewer than one half, probably only one third, of the trees that were felled ever reached the mills. Once as splendid as the Giant Forest in Sequoia National Park, the grove was completely gutted, with many of the trees left behind after they were blasted with gunpowder, sawed apart, and burned over. Perhaps the crew foreman had one final twinge of conscience; he left a single tree standing, named for himself, measuring more than 100 feet in circumference. Sequoia and General Grant (later part of Kings Canyon) National Parks, both created to protect the giant sequoias, were authorized in 1890.

In the early 1890s Congress did make an important distinction between national parks and national forests. The Forestry Reserve Act of 1891, consisting of only a few lines added to an omnibus public land bill, was one of the most far-reaching conservation measures ever enacted. It gave the president unilateral authority to establish national forests from the public domain; no congressional approval was required. This was a significant advantage, for each national park has required a separate act of Congress, dictating that parks would come along slowly. Before this executive authority was abolished by Congress in 1907, four presidents set aside 175 million acres of national forest lands, considerably more than twice th[illegible]e present national park system, even incl[illegible] Alaskan parks.

The orig[illegible]rably stimulated in 1906 by legislation th[illegible]be other than scenic values in the parks. Beginn[illegible] the 18[illegible], many people were outraged by the widespread lo[illegible]ng of the cliff dwellings and pueblo ruins of the Southwest, the remains of a civilization the Indians had abandoned—for reasons not yet clearly understood—about A.D. 1300. Discovered by cowboys, army officers, explorers, and, occasionally, ethnologists, the sites were looted to supply the demands of collectors. Major sites now in the park system were plundered and vandalized. Parties of pot hunters camped in Cliff Palace for several winters, blasting down the walls, using ceiling beams for firewood.

Mesa Verde National Park, set aside in 1906, established the precedent of historic preservation on the national level. It also gave permanent protection to that matchless tableland 2,000 feet above the surrounding country, broken by deep, winding canyons holding hundreds of cliff ruins, the largest concentration in the Southwest. Photographs by William Jackson, of Yellowstone fame, helped generate public support for the legislation.

The Antiquities Act was passed the same year and proved one of the most far-reaching pieces of park legislation ever enacted. For the first time, protection was given against removing or destroying any historic object or excavating any historic or prehistoric ruin on the public lands. Perhaps of even greater significance, the act empowered the president to declare as national monuments any sites on federal lands containing outstanding historic, scientific, or scenic values.

Before the year was out President Theodore Roosevelt created four national monuments: Devils Tower, Petrified Forest, Montezuma Castle, and El Morro. Between 1906 and 1970, eighty-seven monuments were established by eleven presidents; thirty-six were historical preserves and fifty-one were scientific. The Antiquities Act permitted a president to recognize a significant area as a national monument—which Roosevelt did at Grand Canyon—until Congress could be persuaded to make it a national park. The brief and vague phrase in the Act, "and other objects of historic or scientific interest" was liberally interpreted by the chief executives, perhaps beyond the imaginations of those who wrote the act (and who almost established a maximum limit of 640 acres). Glacier Bay and Katmai National Monuments in Alaska, each nearly 3 million acres, were larger than Yellowstone. And national monuments were proclaimed to preserve caves, forts, canyons, battlefields, pueblos, and the birthplaces of famous men.

As the nation moved into the twentieth century, there were some faint signs of a changing attitude toward natural reserves. The census of 1890 had sounded America's earliest environmental warning, announcing that for the first time the country no longer had a frontier—a term long synonymous with free land, abundant resources, and prosperity. After nearly 300 years the continent was conquered, but, as some people were beginning to realize, at considerable cost. The finest stands of virgin timber in the East and Midwest had been ravaged by lumber companies whose slogan was "cut and get out." Hundreds of millions of tons of coal and barrels of oil were being wasted each year by inefficient or reckless methods of extraction.

Theodore Roosevelt, the first president to make conservation a national goal, convened a Conference on Conservation at the White House in 1908 that brought together one of the most distinguished assemblages of national leaders ever gathered, including most of the members of Congress and the Supreme Court and the governors of thirty-four states. The president opened the proceedings with a disturbing declaration: "It seems to me time for the country to take account of its natural resources, and inquire how long they are likely to last."

His was a lone voice during an era when exploitation of the country's resources was the watchword and establishment of the early parks was a concession to a minority, rather than an expression of national purpose. The parks were little more than administrative stepchildren within the federal government, with operational responsibility scattered. Yellowstone, Sequoia, Yosemite, and General Grant were supervised by the War Department. Eight others, including Mt. Rainier, Crater Lake, Mesa Verde, and Glacier, were under the direct control of the Department of the Interior. National monuments were administered by the deparment that had jurisdiction over the lands, usually Interior or Agriculture. There was no defined, accepted policy to guide administration and no continuity of personnel. And so the parks came along, one by one, each the work of a relatively few people who saw the need. Congress did not contemplate there would ever be a need for a national park *system*, properly organized.

In contrast, utilitarian conservationists, headed by Gifford Pinchot, chief of the Forest Service, were at the height of their power during the progressive era of the early twentieth century. The utilitarians demanded an end to unplanned and uncontrolled exploitation of natural resources. They advocated a scientific approach and proposed giant multipurpose development projects that made full utilization of timber, grasslands, mineral deposits, and hydroelectric power sites.

Creation of the National Park Service

In 1912, a small band of national park enthusiasts convinced President William Howard Taft that the haphazard method of handling parks should be replaced by unified and professional direction. Taft sent a special message to the Congress that year that began, "I earnestly recommend the establishment of a Bureau of National Parks." Pinchot opposed the formation of a parks bureau, and the Forest Service launched an active lobbying campaign, arguing that the Forest Service was the logical agency to administer national parks.

The historic battle over the construction of the Hetch Hetchy dam in Yosemite National Park aroused national attention and polarized the conservation movement. Hetch Hetchy was a deep, glacier-carved valley whose towering granite walls, massive domes, and cascading waterfalls closely approached the grandeur of Yosemite Valley. In a search for a future water supply in the early 1900s, the city of San Francisco had selected Hetch Hetchy as the most feasible site for construction of a reservoir. Local politicians seemed undisturbed at the prospect of a dam destroying an incredibly lovely valley in a national park. However, John Muir and the Sierra Club, which he founded in 1892 and which had already proved its readiness to scrap with anyone, led a fight to preserve the integrity of Yosemite and in a surprising show of strength blocked congressional action. Pinchot persisted in supporting the project, saying "I will stand ready to render any assistance in my power."

The controversy dragged on for years until, in 1913, the bill authorizing the dam finally passed Congress. Supporters of the dam held that, wherever located, the natural resources of the country should serve the needs of the people. With fervent eloquence, Muir denounced this philosophy: "These temple destroyers, devotees of ravaging commercialism, seem to have a perfect contempt for nature, and, instead of lifting their eyes to the God of the Mountains, lift them to the almighty dollar." Muir took some consolation that, finally, "the conscience of the whole country has been aroused from sleep." Although similar dam proposals have been repeatedly advanced, most recently in Dinosaur and Grand Canyon, Hetch Hetchy is the only dam ever to be constructed in a national park.

Future success for a national park agency was assured the next year due to a remarkable chance incident, that has been retold perhaps too often. A Chicago borax manufacturer wrote to an old friend he had known thirty years earlier at the University of California, complaining about conditions in the national parks. The friend, Franklin K. Lane, happened to be secretary of the Interior, and he was looking for a man who could help bring some order into the management of Interior's national parks. The letter writer was Stephen T. Mather, descendant of a Mayflower Puritan, for a time a *New York Sun* reporter, later a high-powered salesman for Twenty Mule Team borax, and by then a self-made millionaire, philanthropist, and sometime mountain climber.

The letter of complaint, hardly a rare item for a secretary of the Interior then or now, described the deplorable conditions Mather had observed on a recent camping trip to Yosemite and Sequoia. Trails were poorly maintained, often impassable; trespass cattle were numerous; and enterprising lumbermen had acquired choice sequoia groves based upon the intriguing premise that because the ground was soggy in the spring from melting snow, they qualified for cutting under the Swamp Land Act, a measure designed to unburden the government of bog land. Mather's protest brought a quick—and historic—reply: "Dear Steve, If you don't like the way the national parks are being run, come on down to Washington and run them yourself."

Reluctantly, for he already had more interests than most people could handle, Mather agreed to meet with Lane and discuss the matter. The secretary made an eloquent appeal, pointing out that the parks desperately needed public and congressional support and that Mather could provide the right kind of dynamic leadership. Knowing Mather's reputation as a freewheeler and anticipating that he would be unwilling to exchange this freedom for the numbing procedures of the federal bureaucracy, Lane shrewdly offered the services of Horace Albright as Mather's chief assistant to help him cut through the red tape.

But as Mather and Albright exchanged confidences, they agreed that someone must do battle for the parks, for both shared a profound love of the wild country. Albright had grown up in the midst of the High Sierra; Mather had climbed Mt. Rainier in 1905 with fellow members of the Sierra Club. Mather's ingrained enthusiasm soon surfaced, and he began to picture the contribution they could make in creating a top-notch, professional organization to administer the parks. Albright, who had already planned to return to California in a few months, felt his resolve weakening. "I couldn't resist him," he recalled later.

In January 1915, Mather was sworn in as an assistant to the secretary of the Interior in charge of the national parks. Mather's credentials for the job were hard to beat. Most likely, Lane could have searched America thoroughly without finding a better man for the job—even allowing for the fact that, to some considerable degree, the man has been obscured by his legend. Certainly, the vigor and charm of his personality and his talent for quick action impressed Washington politicians. When he moved in public, a contemporary wrote, every eye seemed to be attracted to him: a man then forty-seven years old, an inch over six feet, with broad shoulders, prematurely white hair, a handsome ruddy face, and notably blue eyes. He had a knack for salesmanship: "Something about his eyes and the way his face changed color when he talked. If he was out to make a convert, the subject never knew what hit him."

But the task awaiting Mather and the equally indefatigable Albright was enormous. Everything hinged on getting a bill through Congress to establish a parks bureau, which would then have to be organized, funded, and staffed. Substantial increases in appropriations would be needed for the existing parks and monuments; a nationwide publicity campaign must be launched to generate public interest and support; concessioners must be stimulated to improve hotels, camps, and other facilities. Congress must also be persuaded to establish new parks and defeat bills to set aside substandard areas. It shouldn't take more than a year, Mather decided.

Parks are good for the country, and incidentally good for business, was Mather's message. Editors and publishers were favored with special attention, although governors, mayors, civic leaders, and the few identifiable conservationists also received the Mather treatment. He traveled constantly, and parks began to attract headlines for the first time.

As his promotional schemes multiplied, he hit upon a real winner, one that has never failed to gain friends for the parks. In the summer of 1915 he invited a carefully chosen group of citizens to a camping trip through Sequoia and Yosemite. Joining him were such well-known figures as Burton Holmes, the travel lecturer of lantern slide memory; Henry Fairfield Osborne, president of the American Museum of Natural History; Emerson Hough, popular western writer and author of *The Covered Wagon;* Frederick H. Gillett, member, and later Speaker, of the House of Representatives; and Gilbert H. Grosvenor, editor of *National Geographic* magazine.

Among the first to appreciate the persuasive value of a junket, Mather wisely chose not to subject his guests to excessive privations. The lavish arrangements, for which he personally paid the bill, included a new sleeping bag and air mattress for each pioneer and a famed Chinese camp cook borrowed from the Geological Survey. Meals were "an Oriental dream," recalled one saddle-sore traveler; at day's end dinner was accompanied by freshly baked bread and served on a white linen tablecloth. On Mather's carefully selected itinerary was the Giant Forest, a private inholding within Sequoia National Park that was superior to anything in the park. Through contacts made on the trip Mather convinced Congress to appropriate half the purchase price; then he turned to Grosvenor. The National Geographic Society supplied the remaining funds to acquire the sequoia grove, the first of many subsequent gifts to the parks.

Following the mountain trip, Mather and Albright set out to review field operations, crisscrossing most of the West by railroad, switching to automobile and traversing primitive roads as they visited Crater Lake and Mt. Rainier—where Mather talked a group of Seattle and Tacoma businessmen into forming a Rainier concession and building the landmark Paradise Inn. They made a quick trip to the Olympic Peninsula to promote an extension of boundaries and park status for the national monument set aside by Roosevelt (it would take twenty-three more years and an epic battle pitting conservationists against the lumber interests and Park Service against Forest Service before Olympic National Park was established). After the dedication of Rocky Mountain National Park, they tested the new policy of allowing cars in Yellowstone and pushed on to Glacier. Halted by heavy snow, they ignored local warnings, mounted horses, and set out, spending two nights in backcountry cabins while crossing the mountains.

Despite the killing pace—Mather alone had covered 30,000 miles—and the considerable public interest Mather generated, no action was taken on the Park Service bill in 1915, but the following year Mather organized national park defenders for a major lobbying campaign. The popular *Saturday Evening Post* joined the campaign; *National Geographic* devoted an entire issue to the scenic wonderlands; the railroads paid for a handsome *National Parks Portfolio* publication, which a corps of volunteers from the General Federation of Women's Clubs addressed and mailed free to a quarter of a million people. The promotion campaign paid off; on August 25, 1916, President Woodrow Wilson signed the bill establishing a National Park Service.

The National Parks Act spoke in only the most general terms of the way in which the new organization should provide for public use while protecting park resources, but it has proved an enduring and oft-quoted statement that has never been improved upon. The Park Service was established to promote and regulate the use of the national parks and monuments, taking such measures as conform to the fundamental purpose of these preserves: "Which purpose is to conserve the scenery and the natural and historic objects and the wildlife therein, and to provide for the enjoyment of the same in such manner and by such means as will leave them unimpaired for the enjoyment of future generations."

2

THE NEW BUREAU

For some time the new Park Service was an organization in name only. Mather soon proved he had a genius for bringing together talented men and women and focusing their efforts on the parks, but he had to start from scratch. In the early years, park superintendents and rangers were not under Civil Service; some of the parks had been regarded virtually as fiefdoms by congressmen who injected themselves into daily operations and controlled staff appointments. Glacier was a sorry example of the results of political patronage; the superintendents were often lightweights and the rangers incompetent, if that. Albright, who tirelessly reviewed field operations, doubted that many of the Glacier rangers patrolled a mile beyond their stations; some were lazy, others probably fearful of getting lost.

Just a few days after Congress declared war on Germany in April 1917, it authorized an appropriation to organize the new bureau. Circumstances were hardly favorable; wartime priorities not only curtailed budgets for nonessential agencies but also brought charges that critically needed resources were being "locked up" in the parks. The pressure on the parks was considerable. One patriotic group worked hard to have the Yellowstone elk slaughtered to provide canned treats for the doughboys in France. Eager to place his department on the firing line, Interior Secretary Lane himself proposed that Yosemite be opened to sheep grazing. Eventually cattle and sheep were grazed in a number of the parks, but the short duration of the war prevented much damage.

The Mather Style

Creating a professional corps of rangers was one of Mather's first priorities. Army troops were withdrawn from the parks during the war; they had been in charge of Yellowstone since 1886. Military operation had come at an opportune time for the parks; although final administrative authority remained with the secretary of the Interior, the soldiers did a capable, conscientious job. They were the forerunners of the rangers who replaced them (a few soldiers chose to resign from the army and join the ranger ranks), and they protected the wildlife when there was no other protection, put out forest fires, and helped tourists who got themselves into difficulties. Even today there are clear reminders of army ways in the tradecraft of the rangers. Facilities constructed by the military were a great help. The Fort Yellowstone complex of several dozen buildings continues to serve as administrative headquarters for the park.

Beginning with a special appropriation in the summer of 1918, the Service was able to hire a qualified force of rangers for the parks. Speaking recently to a Park Service gathering, John Davis, a ranger employed at Mt. Rainier in those early days, recalled Mather's visits to the park, "a friendly person, easy to talk to and very personable." Of the rudimentary nature of the organization in its formative years, Davis said: "To many of you it may seem like these were the golden years of the service. This was not entirely true. We had very little in the way of operating funds, equipment, or personnel." Advancement through the ranks was unknown; in a period of twelve years, he pointed out, "only one person had been promoted or transferred from Rainier to another park or location. [It was Davis, who later served as superintendent of both Sequoia–Kings Canyon and Yosemite.] We expected to remain in the park for our entire career." Competition with the Forest Service began early: "We longed for stature and recognition such as had been accorded to the Forest Service. I might add they were not always very nice to the young upstarts who had carved large chunks out of the national forests to make national parks. While they were quite quick to ridicule us for our ignorance and blunders, they really didn't know what to think of us."

In 1916 the Park Service had had responsibility for fourteen national parks and twenty-one national monuments, but its budget was meager, about $30,000 a year for each of the parks—badly needing funds for facilities development—and only $166 a year for each of the monuments. Mather could not hire even a skeleton crew for his Washington operation; Congress had placed a $19,500 limit on salaries for the director and his entire staff. Compared to other agencies, the Park Service was barely operational. Still, in its first annual report the young agency showed its spunk, calling for the establishment of new parks and the enlargement of existing areas—with most of the acreage coming from the Forest Service.

The report also proposed that tourism be actively encouraged in the parks. In view of recent recriminations by those blessed with hindsight, the reasons for the campaign to increase the number of park visitors and to accelerate the construction of roads, trails, and accommodations need to be examined. It was a deliberate joint decision reached by Mather and the conservationists, who had come to realize during the Hetch Hetchy battle that the national parks could not be defended on scenic merit alone. They had learned that they must rely on economic arguments as well as emotional ones. The political climate of the time demanded that the parks be used, or there would be no appropriations from Congress. Seeking political and financial help, the park defenders formed a "pragmatic alliance" with the railroads to promote park travel. The prestigious American Civic Association, which had led the fight to establish a parks bureau, endorsed tourism as a "dignified exploitation of our national parks." The result of the tourist promotion campaign was the construction of many facilities that are now the target of conservationists with short memories who condemn their presence and demand their removal.

Railroads had already provided the first access to many parks: the Great Northern to Glacier; the Northern Pacific to Yellowstone; the Union Pacific to Zion, Bryce, and the North Rim of Grand Canyon; and the Santa Fe to the South Rim. To attract passengers the companies developed some of the great resort hotels of the West, including Yellowstone's Old Faithful Inn (1903) and Grand Canyon's El Tovar (1904). Handsome and rustic, they were built by craftsmen using native materials and, all in all, are forgivable intrusions on the landscape. They also provide an intriguing historical record of people's use of the parks.

Automobiles had also come early to the parks, admitted to Mt. Rainier in 1908. Within a few years the new inventions were reliable enough, or so their owners thought, for cross-country touring. Nevertheless, in 1924, the year that Henry Ford turned out No. 10,000,000 in his unending line of black tin lizzies, there were only twelve miles of paved road in all of the national parks. Mather, a person who went along with progress, took delight that automobiles would enable many more Americans to enjoy the parks, and he was confident that the experience would convert them into certified park boosters. When a friend reported complaints about "tin-canners" who were less than careful about their litter, Mather replied, "They own as much of the parks as anybody else. We can pick up the tin cans. It's a cheap way to make better citizens."

While he worked hard at democratizing the parks, Mather was no less insistent that they must be preserved unimpaired at a time when national park integrity was not yet an established national policy. It took seventeen pages of the annual report for 1920 to list proposed commercial raids on the parks; the report was titled, "A Crisis in National Conservation." A scheme to build dams and canals in Yellowstone for the purpose of supplying water to Idaho potato farmers had been approved by the secretary of the Interior, who helped prepare the legislation and ordered the Park Service to prepare a favorable recommendation. In his annual report, Mather took a stand against "desecration of the people's playground for the benefit of a few individuals or corporations," and he appealed for public support: "Is there not some place in this great nation of ours where lakes can be preserved in their natural state; where we and all generations to follow us can enjoy the beauty and charm of mountain waters in the midst of primeval forests?" Fortunately, the resignation of the secretary and the reversal of the decision by his successor blocked the project, releasing Mather and Albright from their pledge to resign rather than support the bill.

Under Mather, the parks had no publicity problem. Wearing his Park Service uniform and riding in his big Packard touring car with the license plate USNPS-1, Mather became a popular figure, the rich man who gave the rest of his life and part of his fortune to the parks. Mather anecdotes abound, many of which are verifiable. When the Great Northern railroad was given permission to put up a sawmill during construction of the Many Glacier Hotel in Glacier National Park, Mather pressed for prompt removal after the hotel was completed. The Great Northern asking for one too many delays, Mather commandeered a Park Service trail crew and personally lit the fuse of the dynamite charge that blew up the sawmill.

He was also prone to lighthearted, almost sophomoric, enthusiasms that sometimes belied his keen mind and sound organizational abilities. His biographer describes a national park conference in Washington at which the program, stage directed by Mather, suggested he had an almost limitless capacity for tomfoolery. The dinner was a dignified affair, which attracted Cabinet officers, members of Congress, and lesser notables. Mather led off the program with an act he had put together and insisted upon presenting at camp fire programs in the parks: a colleague disguised behind a beard, greasy hat, antique rifle, and broken-down boots telling improbable yarns about Yellowstone lifted from the chronicles of Liver-Eatin' Johnson. There followed, among other highlights, two Alaskan brown bear cubs, an extended program of lantern slides, a myna bird trained by a Washington Zoo curator to ask the congressmen "What about the appropriations?," and a fawn named "Chummy," the pet of a Grand Canyon ranger, that strolled into the formal ballroom and browsed on Herbert Hoover's salad.

Born on July 4 (an appropriate date for a fervent patriot), Mather was sixty years old in 1927; his bureau was beginning to function well, and he seemed as full of drive and ideas as ever. Most recently he had convinced Congress of the wisdom of extending the national park concept into the East, and in 1926 Shenandoah and Great Smoky Mountains national parks were authorized. But in 1928 he suffered a paralytic stroke, an ironic fate. Mather's epitaph was spoken in a congressional eulogy, "There will never come an end to the good that he has done." As a memorial to him those words were inscribed, with his profile, on bronze plaques placed in many of the national parks—despite his known aversion to such intrusions on the park scene.

Albright and Historic Preservation

Mather's successor was his trusted friend and closest associate, Horace Albright, who in 1919, at age twenty-nine, had been appointed superintendent of Yellowstone and field director of the Service. It was said, during Albright's years in the park when he entertained princes and presidents, that Albright and his rangers believed the Park Service was doing the Lord's work. His administrative talent set a pattern for all the parks, and his attractive personality earned him a wide circle of friends, many of whom happened to be in Congress. Hardworking and self-confident, he candidly confessed to the habit of having about 500 irons in the fire at once.

When Albright became director in 1929, there were twenty-one national parks, thirty-three national monuments, and a budget of $9 million. A practical man—most park people became pragmatists—he realized that the unstructured, spur-of-the-moment methods of Mather must now be replaced by a more orderly approach. Albright brought cohesion to the inner workings of the Service but continued what has been called the Mather style: dynamic, high-minded, opportunistic, if occasionally impetuous, administration.

Growth of the park system and professionalization of personnel were two Albright objectives, and he succeeded in elevating his agency to an equal station with the other resource agencies. However, his most valuable contribution was in the field of historic preservation. Although the Park Service had jurisdiction over a few Indian sites in the West, its primary function was considered to be the preservation of natural areas. When Congress began to establish national military parks to commemorate Civil War battles, beginning with Chickamauga-Chattanooga in 1890, it placed them under the War Department. Albright, a longtime history buff, believed they were worthy of more enlightened stewardship. As early as 1917, when he wrote the first annual report of the Park Service, he called for all such historical areas to be administered as part of the national park system.

The conservation movement in those days had almost no interest in historic preservation, but Albright and his colleagues held that as the American heritage was made up in equal parts of the unique grandeur of its geography and the heroic deeds of the people, it was just as important to preserve historic sites as to set aside places of natural beauty. Both were essential components of true conservation. To an up-and-coming agency like the Park Service, the idea of including all parks, whether natural or historical, in one federal organization was particularly attractive. And the fact that most of the historical preserves were located in the more heavily populated East, which would give the Park Service a nationwide image and considerably more political support, may not have been overlooked.

The celebration in 1932 of the 200th anniversary of the birth of George Washington provided Albright with a splendid opportunity. When a private campaign to reconstruct Washington's birthplace failed to raise the necessary funds, he judged correctly that Congress would hardly turn its back on the Father of our Country during the bicentennial year. At the same time the massive restoration project at Williamsburg, begun by John D. Rockefeller several years earlier, helped to focus attention on the desirability of preserving nearby sites: Jamestown Island, where the first British colony was established, and Yorktown, where British rule over her American colonies ended on Surrender Field. Congress added the Washington birthplace, Jamestown, and Yorktown to the national park system, partly as the result of some skillful lobbying by Albright, thus enlarging the original park idea to include the preservation of historic places.

Albright soon capitalized on a rare chance to argue his case for Park Service administration of federal historic parks. A few weeks after Franklin D. Roosevelt's inauguration in 1933, Albright was invited to accompany the president on an inspection trip to Camp Hoover, a presidential retreat Herbert Hoover had built adjacent to Shenandoah National Park and then donated to the Park Service. The camp setting beside a trout stream was particularly magnificent in April with the dogwood in full bloom, but Roosevelt was unable to navigate with his crutches over the broken terrain.

There is an interesting footnote to this incident. At Roosevelt's request the Service found a more appropriate site in its Catoctin Recreational Demonstration Area, sixty miles north of Washington, and there built a comfortable but unpretentious hideaway, which FDR called Shangri-La and used frequently. President Dwight Eisenhower changed the name to Camp David (after his grandson), and it was here in 1978 that Egyptian President Anwar Sadat, Israeli Prime Minister Menachem

Begin, and President Jimmy Carter reached their historic agreement for peace in the Middle East.

On the drive back to Washington from Camp Hoover, Roosevelt invited Albright into his car, and the talk, somehow, turned to parks. Both were students of American history, and as they passed through the Manassas battlefield they discussed Civil War strategy—and the advisability of transferring all such military parks from the War Department to the National Park Service. "I knew before we got to Washington that night that I had my foot not only in the door for historic preservation, but that I had it in the White House," Albright recalled.

Two months later Roosevelt signed an executive order that consolidated all federally owned parks, memorials, national cemeteries, and the parks in Washington, D.C., into a single system. The reorganization of 1933 added twelve natural areas in nine western states and fifty-seven historical areas in seventeen predominantly eastern states to the national park system. The system was transformed into a truly national one. The action also significantly broadened the national park idea, for joining such illustrious wilderness places as Glacier, Rocky Mountain, and Yellowstone were equally famous names from the American past: Gettysburg, Fort McHenry, and Appomattox Court House.

The New Deal Brings New Kinds of Parks

His goals accomplished, Albright retired later in the year and began a successful business career. As the country sank deeper into the Great Depression, it seemed likely that the expansion of the Park Service was over. Recreation travel dwindled away, park concessioners were forced to curtail services and close many of their hotels, and appropriations for the parks were slashed. Yet many New Deal emergency relief programs were conservation oriented, for there was general agreement that the nation's plight could be traced, in part, to the ruinous waste of its natural resources and that massive federal programs would be required if the land were to recover from years of abuse.

Perhaps remembering his concerns of thirty years earlier, when he served as chairman of the Forest, Fish, and Game Committee of the New York state senate, President Roosevelt conceived the idea of a Civilian Conservation Corps (CCC) that would occupy the nation's jobless youth while conserving its resources. During his first day in office he scrawled out and signed an organization plan, noting "I want personally to check the location, scope, etc. of the camps, size, work to be done, etc.—FDR."

Within three months, 1,500 CCC camps were in operation and more than 250,000 young men enrolled, a miraculous achievement for the federal bureaucracy. The Park Service administered more than 400 camps in state, county, and municipal parks. The CCC program enabled the Service to catch up on badly needed construction and rehabilitation work: campgrounds, trails, and bridges were built; utility systems installed; roads repaired; historic buildings and sites restored; and visitor facilities constructed. By the time World War II ended the CCC program, the Park Service had supervised the work of more than 3 million young men and received appropriations of nearly $500 million. For the CCC portion of its overall operations alone, the Service had hired an additional 7,000 employees; the permanent personnel of the entire organization did not reach that level until the mid-1970s.

Work relief funds of diverse kinds and huge quantities were channeled to the Park Service. It was to be a long time before the organization would see that kind of money again or be heading at top speed in so many directions at once. Division and branch chiefs carried responsibilities rivaling those of the director only a few years earlier. Field and central office employees moved up to higher classifications, accelerating the development of a bureau capable of executing large-scale programs. One of the casualties of the frenzied pace was Arno B. Cammerer, who had replaced Albright as director in 1933. A workhorse administrator who had taken less than two weeks' leave in five years, Cammerer was forced to step down in 1940 when his health failed.

The barrage of New Deal social and political legislation included programs authorizing the Park Service to carry out nationwide resource surveys. The Historic Sites Act of 1935 directed the Service to conduct a survey of nationally significant historic sites; under the provisions of the Park, Parkway, and Recreation Study Act of 1936, it conducted an inventory of the outdoor recreation needs of the country. Providing technical and planning assistance to state and local agencies became a major and continuing activity.

Other legislation of the 1930s brought new kinds of parks into the system. The Blue Ridge Parkway, first of the scenic roadways, was begun. It now extends for 500 miles along the crest of the Blue Ridge Mountains, connecting the Shenandoah and Great Smoky Mountain parks. It is a road of harmonious design in a parklike setting; one traveler suggested that driving along it was like browsing in a bookstore, "stopping every little while to look upon a scene that has no counterpart in America."

Lake Meade, behind Hoover Dam, was the first of the national recreation areas, a place for water activities set within nearly 2 million acres of desert environment. Park Service administration of reservoirs formed by the giant reclamation dams followed. Lake Powell, created by the most recent dam, Glen Canyon, flooded a glorious landscape worthy of national park status until the arrival of the dam builders.

Cape Hatteras National Seashore, an enchanting and little-developed chain of barrier islands extending seventy miles north and south of the famous headland, pioneered the establishment of a dozen seashores and lakeshores that have been set aside along the Atlantic, Pacific, and Gulf coasts and the Great Lakes.

The new parks had their skeptics as well as their supporters. Some conservationists argued that the Park Service should restrict its efforts to the preservation of unspoiled wilderness and charged the agency with the unforgivable sin of embracing recreation. The National Parks Association led the attack. "Park Service Leader Abandons National Park Standards" was a typical headline in a series of articles it ran that rebuked the director for his position that it would be better to add Glacier Bay to the system, even with minimal mining activity permitted, than to exclude it. At the same time the association vigorously opposed the Park Service drive to establish Grand Teton National Park—a bitter battle that took several decades. It described the Jackson Hole area, with disdain, as "a Biological Service game preserve, three irrigation reservoirs, large areas of national forests, commercial traffic ways, dude ranches and plain desert."

Mission 66

From its establishment in 1916 until Pearl Harbor in 1941, the Park Service enjoyed twenty-five years of almost uninterrupted growth, but World War II nearly closed the agency down. Vacation travel was almost at a standstill due to gas rationing and a moratorium on automobile production. If Congress had been agreeable, many of the concessioners would have been glad to sell their empty facilities to the nation at bargain prices. All except essential park operations were discontinued, the agency lost two-thirds of its employees, and the Park Service headquarters was moved to Chicago to make room for more important wartime functions in Washington.

In activities reminiscent of those during World War I, entrepreneurs eager to support the war effort at a profit made a few inroads on the parks. A shortage of Sitka spruce for airplane construction threatened the forests in Olympic for a time, but other sources were found; a few mines were opened, including one at a tungsten deposit in Yosemite; and many hundreds of permits were issued to the military to use the parks for arctic, mountain, and desert warfare training.

Immediately after World War II there was an explosive growth in tourist travel. The parks were soon overrun, for they were still operating on an austere war-time level budget, lacking even minimal staffs or funds. As the years passed there was no relief.

In 1940 the secretary of the Interior, for the first time, had gone beyond the ranks of the career Park Service to choose a director. Newton B. Drury proved one of the best. For many years head of the Save-the-Redwoods League in California, Drury was an articulate preservationist who thoroughly understood the parks. In 1949 he issued a report, "The Dilemma of Our Parks," that documented the deterioration: roads and trails wearing out; campgrounds, museums, and concessioner accommodations badly in need of repair and replacement; insufficient numbers of rangers to serve visitors and protect the resources. Ten years had passed without appreciable maintenance of facilities; as a result of this neglect, the cost of upgrading the parks was estimated to be $300 million. The appropriation for 1949 was less than $14 million.

The outbreak of the Korean War in 1950 reduced appropriations even further, yet tourist travel continued to increase. By 1954 the parks were receiving 54 million visitors a year, using the same run-down facilities that had served only 15 million visitors before the war. Working conditions for park people seemed a test of their commitment, for 60 percent lived in one-bedroom houses or worse, including CCC barracks hastily built in the 1930s and intended to last only a few years. A *New York Times* editorial observed that unless funds were forthcoming, the park system was threatened with ruin: "In fact, just about everything concerning the parks is inadequate except their magnificent scenic or historic values and the dedication of the men and women of the National Park Service, whose morale remains, on the whole, unshaken despite the shabby treatment sometimes accorded them."

A brilliant solution to the quandary was devised by Conrad L. Wirth, who became director in 1951, following the one-year incumbency of Arthur Demaray. A landscape architect by training—his father was a distinguished city park administrator—Wirth entered the Service in 1931 and earned a reputation for carrying off difficult assignments, including supervision of the CCC program. A realistic planner, with an engaging, outgoing personality and a shrewd knowledge of how things are done in Washington, Wirth understood that yearly appeals to the Appropriation Committees could bring only temporary relief. He foresaw the political attractiveness of putting all the Park Service's needs together in a single package: every project in every park identified and cost estimates supplied.

Selection of a name for an enterprise of this scale may have been the most important factor, and here Wirth struck gold. In 1966 the Park Service was to celebrate its 50th anniversary. He used that date as the target for the end of a ten-year restoration program he called "Mission

66." At a meeting arranged with President Eisenhower and his cabinet, Wirth presented the Mission 66 program. Eisenhower warmly responded by pledging his support. It was generally agreed by observers of the session that a color slide showing a long line of visitors in front of a battered old outhouse may have been the most decisive piece of evidence.

Shown the need and the cost, and with something nice in the package for the many members of Congress who had parks in their districts, Congress bought Mission 66 completely. It provided appropriations totaling more than a billion dollars for the ten-year period.

Always wary of "development" in the parks, conservationists were less enthusiastic about Mission 66 than the 2,000 park families who moved into new residences. There were criticisms that Mission 66 was primarily a construction program and that better facilities would encourage more people to come to the parks—an accurate prediction, if a philosophical dilemma. The Mission 66 program brought nearly 150 new museums and visitor centers to strengthen park interpretation; it also built the handsome training centers at Harpers Ferry and the Grand Canyon that provide Service employees with one of the most extensive training programs in government. Of considerable consequence, there was a rejuvenation in the spirit of park people who could—for a few years at least—hold things together with something more serviceable than paper clips and baling wire.

The Up-and-Down Years

The decade of the 1960s, which encompassed the administrations of John F. Kennedy and Lyndon B. Johnson, was a time when conservation moved to the front page at the national level. People were no longer willing to accept the spread of air pollution into their own neighborhoods or to live with the consequences of offshore oil spills. The "New Conservation" moved beyond partial solutions for resource problems and dealt with the total environment. Stewart L. Udall articulated the new philosophy better than anyone else, and until Congress established the Council on Environmental Quality and the Environmental Protection Agency, the secretary of the Interior became the acknowledged federal spokesman on environmental matters.

On the Park Service level, this period is often referred to as the Hartzog era. The seventh director, George B. Hartzog, Jr., who served from 1964 through 1972, was among all directors the closest to Mather in style. Not at all slavish about following established procedures, he refreshed the outlook of a tradition-loving organization with a constant stream of fresh ideas. Perhaps more important, he knew how to make the ideas work. Trained in the law, he had a sure knowledge of the ways of politics and politicians that helped him achieve legislation and appropriations from Congress on an unprecedented scale. During his regime sixty-two new parks were established, the most accelerated growth in Park Service history.

Congressional acts during the 1960s had a great effect on future park designations. When Congress established Cape Cod National Seashore in 1961, for the first time it also provided the funds to purchase the land. Until that time, all new parks were either carved out of the public domain or donated by states or private philanthropists. Significantly, the Cape Cod legislation also authorized the secretary of the Interior to allow private landowners to retain their property, so long as the towns adopted satisfactory zoning regulations to prevent unsightly intrusions. It was an important precedent. There were not many undeveloped tracts of land of park quality remaining in the continental United States. Many parks established since 1961 have contained extensive private holdings, and the continuation of these occupancies under various arrangements is often essential.

The Land and Water Conservation Fund, created by Congress in 1964, provided matching grants to states and municipalities for the purchase and development of new parklands. The fund also distributed land acquisition money to federal agencies; under this program Park Service acquisition funds, which had previously amounted to a few million dollars a year, soon passed $100 million annually. But the cost of buying parklands was also skyrocketing. The acquisition of Redwood National Park and Big Cypress National Preserve (established to protect Everglades National Park) bore a price tag of more than $500 million.

The historic preservation movement was massively strengthened in 1966 by the Historic Preservation Act. For the first time federal matching grants were provided to the states for the care and restoration of local sites and buildings. The Park Service was given responsibility for the administration of this program, which included the development of a National Register of Historic Places and the administration of the grants to the states. The transfer of this responsibility to another agency and its return to the Park Service under the Reagan administration are described in Chapter 4.

The Park Service was never held in higher esteem than in 1972, the 100th anniversary of Yellowstone. A presidential Commission sponsored a series of commemorative events, and representatives from eighty-three nations paid homage to the first national park when they gathered at Yellowstone for a World Conference on National Parks. The U.S. Park Service was host to the 1,200 delegates, and Director Hartzog presided over the most estimable meeting of the world park community ever held. It was the last panoply of the Park Service. Less than two months later, having earned a spot on President Richard Nixon's personal list of enemies, Hartzog was summarily fired.

Since 1972 the organization has passed through the most disquieting period of its history. In a stretch of nine years it has had five directors, four of whom were fired. In an agency that had never known political manipulation and had received consistently impressive and tenured leadership, the rapid turnovers have had a paralyzing effect on the once unshakable commitment and high morale of park people. The impact of the events since 1972 will be discussed at length in Chapter 10, which deals with the Service's drift toward politicization.

There has recently been, however, one hopeful sign. Shortly after he was sworn in as Interior secretary, James Watt announced that he would replace every agency head in the department except Park Service Director Russell Dickenson. The two men had worked closely together in the early 1970s when Watt was director of the Bureau of Outdoor Recreation and Dickenson was deputy director of the Park Service. Watt had come away with a high regard for Dickenson's capabilities. Named director the previous year, after the Carter administration had gone through two directors in three years, Dickenson was a consensus choice. He began his career as a ranger in Grand Canyon, moved steadily through the ranks, and was immensely popular with his colleagues. At the time of his appointment, Interior Secretary Cecil Andrus had called him "a consummate professional."

Other Watt pronouncements were less comforting. He proposed to shut down the Land and Water Conservation Fund, which would virtually prohibit the establishment of future parks. This would have required Congressional approval, however. Watt told concessioners that he favored granting them greater management responsibilities, a suggestion regarded by many people as a particularly chilling notion of how to improve the parks. His declaration, "I do not believe the national park system should run urban parks," sent the New York and California congressional delegations to the barricades to protect the Gateway and Golden Gate national recreation areas. Watt's policies sharply increased the membership rolls of conservation organizations, which promptly geared up to do battle.

Despite the clamor, Russ Dickenson's confidence remained unshaken. During a recent conversation with an old friend he said, "In all my thirty-four years in the Park Service I have never been more optimistic about the parks. It is evident the broad base of public support for them has never been more firm." At least for the present, the organization remains in capable hands, but it is a measure of the tension in the job of a Park Service director that one day he takes his policy direction from a Cecil Andrus, the next day from a James Watt. The ideals of park people are also subjected to considerable stress. No one has better described their special calling than Mather's biographer, Robert Shankland, when he observed that although the last of Mather's colleagues has long since retired, "The Mather tradition lives on: men and women are working, planning, maneuvering, doing everything humanly possible to save and protect America's great natural wonders. It is a grinding and often heartbreaking job, but few jobs are worthier."

3

THE ORGANIZATION AND ITS PEOPLE

On August 29, 1980, the *Anchorage Daily News* reported an exploit believed to be unequaled in recorded history: by visiting Katmai National Monument, a resident of New York City had just completed a tour of all 377 units (by his count) of the national park system. At a press conference the marathon tourist said "It's literally been a process of following the dots on a map," noting that 180 of the dots were crossed off on his honeymoon. The curious adventure, perhaps facilitated by the traveler's position as an executive of Trans World Airlines (TWA), took twenty-five years and covered a network of parks with outer limits extending from Alaska to Hawaii and American Samoa and to Puerto Rico and the Virgin Islands.

The national park system, which does contain a majority of the outstanding tourist attractions in the United States, is constantly expanding. Each year new parks are added. In one recent session of Congress the House considered 108 new park proposals and the Senate 51; 13 were authorized. Proposals are made periodically—generally during Republican administrations—that the system should be considered "rounded out" and complete, but a presidential veto of park legislation is almost unknown. It is typical that within a few weeks of the eruption of the Mt. St. Helens volcano, a bill was introduced in Congress, recommended by the Sierra Club, to make the mountain a part of the park system.

There have been occasional efforts to standardize the names given by Congress to the units of the system, but, despite a few improvements, confusion over terminology continues. The more than twenty Civil War sites bear the following titles: National Historical Park, National Military Park, National Battlefield, National Battlefield Park, National Battlefield Site, National Historical Site, and National Monument. Park Service people routinely refer to them all as "parks" and when necessary look up the official name in the directory.

The term "national monument" is also disconcerting because it is a title given to historic and prehistoric sites as well as to wilderness and geologic curiosities. The term originated in Europe, where it was applied to great historic and architectural edifices. It was used in the Antiquities Act of 1906 to make a distinction between national parks, of vast size and scenic grandeur, and sites of more modest proportions. There is one other important distinction between parks and monuments. With rare exceptions, the national parks are free from commercial exploitation. Some monuments would fully qualify for national park status except that they are subject to mining claims or other commercial development.

At one time all units of the system were divided into the three categories of natural, historical, and recreational. This was a justifiable classification, except that most parks contain all three elements. For a time a "cultural" classification was adopted, to fit areas such as Wolf Trap Farm Park for the performing arts and the Kennedy Center, but in recent years there have been additions to the system that seem to defy classification. Despite popular belief that most properties administered by the Park Service contain wilderness and bears, there are many more historical parks than there are natural and recreational parks combined.

The park system can be likened to a checklist of the nation's outstanding landscapes—called America's Wonderlands in the National Geographic Society's popular book—and a full representation of the significant historical sites of American history. At one extreme is Federal Hall National Memorial, where George Washington was inaugurated president in 1789, located on bustling Wall Street in downtown New York City. At the other is the pristine solitude of Canyonlands National Park in southeast Utah, an all-but-roadless labyrinth of sandstone chasms and arches that explorer John Wesley Powell termed "ten thousand strangely carved forms . . . and beyond them mountains blending with the clouds."

The system presently consists of 333 parks under more than twenty separate categories plus 26 affiliated areas that are not federally owned but do receive Park Service technical and financial support. A helpful publication, *National Park System and Related Areas,* is available through the Government Printing Office.

Despite the energy crunch, travel to the system continues to grow. In 1970 the number of visits passed 200 million; in 1980 the figure topped 300 million. (The totals, it should be pointed out, include a great many repeat visitors; in the course of a vacation a family of four visiting five parks would rack up twenty "visits".) Statistics on park travel, frequently quoted to prove the parks are being loved to death, can be deceiving. The yearly increase is not evenly distributed throughout the system, and many of the famous parks experience only modest gains. Yellowstone reached the 2 million mark in 1965, yet recorded exactly the same total fifteen years later in 1980—influenced no doubt by rising gasoline prices.

It should be noted also that a few of the areas, particularly the urban parks and parkways, are responsible for a disproportionately large percentage of the total travel figure. In 1980 the seven most visited parks in the system were Blue Ridge Parkway (16.7 million visits), Gateway National Recreation Area (9.3 million), Golden Gate National Recreation Area (18.4 million), Great Smoky Mountains National Park (11.9 million), Natchez Trace Parkway (15.9 million), Rock Creek Park in Washington, D.C. (18.2 million), and Valley Forge National Historical Park (11.5 million). They accounted for 102 million visits or one-third of all the visits to the national park system.

Organizational Relationships

As is typical of most federal agencies, the Park Service operates on three levels of management: the central headquarters in Washington from which policy originates, the regional offices responsible for field coordination, and the parks (see Figure 1). Although the parks come in many sizes and descriptions, their administrative organization reflects the fact that they all have essentially similar functions: protection of park resources and visitors, interpretation and visitor services, maintenance and repair of physical facilities, and financial and personnel chores. In the larger parks each of these functions requires a substantial staff, augmented by several hundred seasonal people, and a budget of several million dollars. In a small park there may be only one staff person for each activity—a good place to learn the trade, everyone agrees.

A great many occupational specialities are needed. Rangers (who hold degrees in a broad range of subjects) must be skilled in a variety of activities and be able to handle horses, snowmobiles, boats, and scuba gear. Interpreters have professional backgrounds in the natural sciences, history, or archeology; research biologists, museum curators and restoration architects are all experts in their fields. In addition there are fiscal, personnel, and purchasing officers; landscape architects and construction engineers; and maintenance crews equipped to repair buildings, roads, trails, and utility systems.

The park organization is headed by a park superintendent, and

FIGURE 1 The Organization of the National Park Service

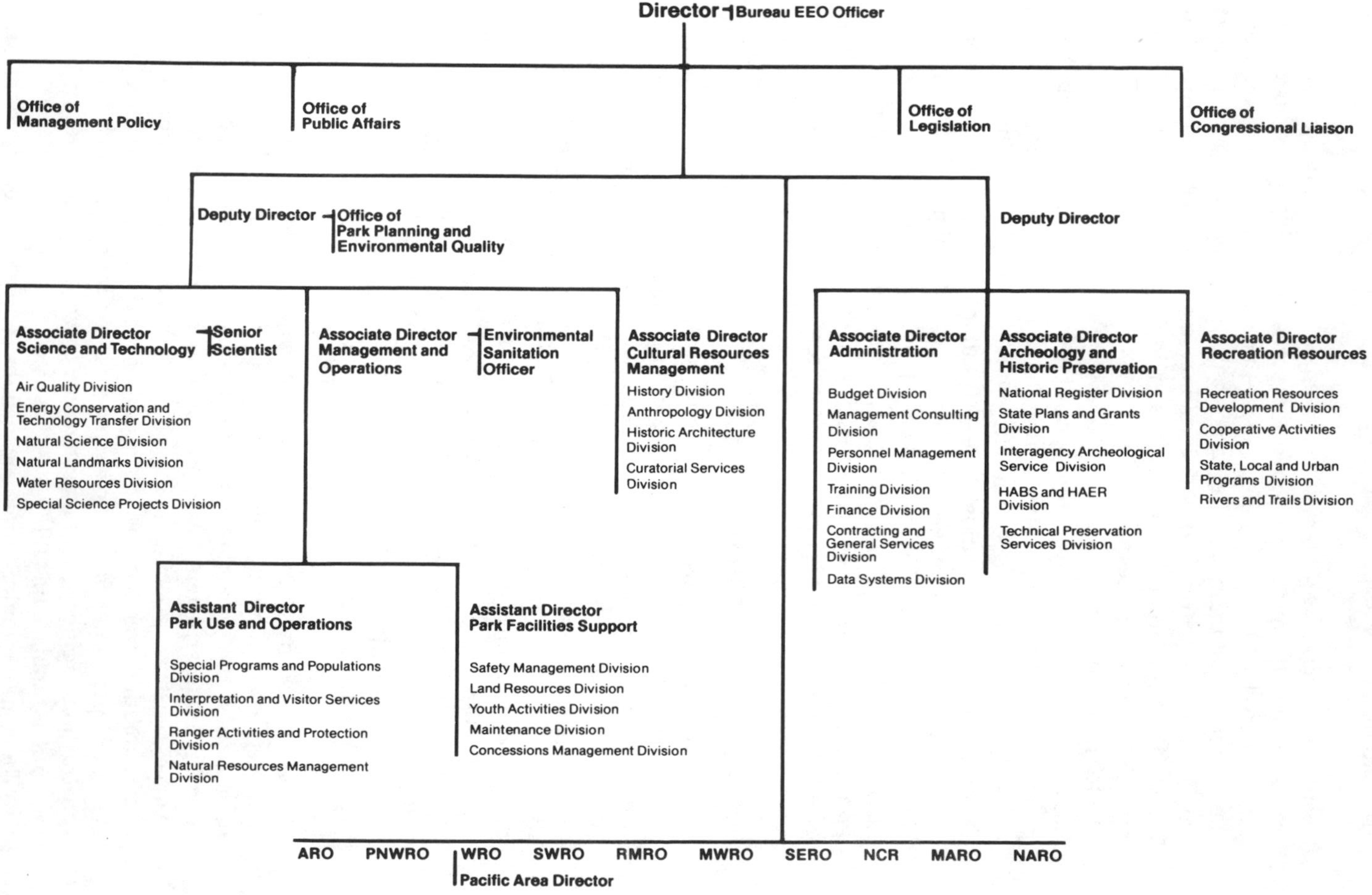

Director — Bureau EEO Officer

Office of Management Policy

Office of Public Affairs

Office of Legislation

Office of Congressional Liaison

Deputy Director — Office of Park Planning and Environmental Quality

Associate Director Science and Technology — Senior Scientist
- Air Quality Division
- Energy Conservation and Technology Transfer Division
- Natural Science Division
- Natural Landmarks Division
- Water Resources Division
- Special Science Projects Division

Associate Director Management and Operations — Environmental Sanitation Officer

Assistant Director Park Use and Operations
- Special Programs and Populations Division
- Interpretation and Visitor Services Division
- Ranger Activities and Protection Division
- Natural Resources Management Division

Assistant Director Park Facilities Support
- Safety Management Division
- Land Resources Division
- Youth Activities Division
- Maintenance Division
- Concessions Management Division

Associate Director Cultural Resources Management
- History Division
- Anthropology Division
- Historic Architecture Division
- Curatorial Services Division

Deputy Director

Associate Director Administration
- Budget Division
- Management Consulting Division
- Personnel Management Division
- Training Division
- Finance Division
- Contracting and General Services Division
- Data Systems Division

Associate Director Archeology and Historic Preservation
- National Register Division
- State Plans and Grants Division
- Interagency Archeological Service Division
- HABS and HAER Division
- Technical Preservation Services Division

Associate Director Recreation Resources
- Recreation Resources Development Division
- Cooperative Activities Division
- State, Local and Urban Programs Division
- Rivers and Trails Division

ARO PNWRO WRO SWRO RMRO MWRO SERO NCR MARO NARO

WRO — Pacific Area Director

perhaps it is the nature of the job that has attracted so many colorful characters. Unfortunately the superintendents' freedom and flexibility have been curtailed in recent years as the measurers and quantifiers have imposed their dismal rules. Formerly the authority of the superintendent was said to have been much like that of the captain of a ship, although intrepid superintendents were occasionally reminded that a navy is also supplied with admirals. Nevertheless, a superintendency is still the most sought-after assignment in the Park Service.

Park superintendents report to regional offices located in Boston, Philadelphia, Washington, D.C., Atlanta, Omaha, Santa Fe, Denver, San Francisco, Seattle, and Anchorage. The precise role of regional offices in any organization has long defied explanation by even the less obtuse of the organization and management practitioners. Presumably they exist in the Park Service because the central office cannot keep close tabs on the far-flung system nor supply the small areas with technical assistance, advice, and comfort. Staff people in the larger areas, including the "Great Western Parks," recognize no source of wisdom or experience comparable to their own.

From the point of view of regional office personnel, it must seem that their position, like that of the governor of North Carolina, lies between two mountains of conceit. The conceit of the park staff is its conviction that no one else remotely understands the hardships under which it is forced to operate, while the conceit of Washington is its attitude that its policy directives are of divine inspiration. One park superintendent, whose freewheeling style provoked repressive tactics from his regional superiors, was frequently heard to remark that only a eunuch would work in a regional office. Not long afterwards, when he became director and was enlisting support for his policy directives, he would announce, solemnly, that the regional office was the "cutting edge" of his administration.

The degree to which the authority of the director is delegated to the regional directors and park superintendents has varied with the individual style, or capability, of each director. The founding fathers, Mather and Albright, were strong administrators, and they set a pattern that has continued. The Forest Service, for example, has always delegated far more responsibility to its field offices than has the Park Service. Most directors, including the present incumbent, begin their administrations by announcing an intention to delegate authority to the regions, but when it begins to appear that each region is going to go off on its own, the director starts to tighten the reins.

By law there must now be public review of all planning and development projects and changes in basic policy, which requires the director to invite interested parties into the decision-making process, thus effectively reducing his freedom to make independent decisions. The sheer size and diversity of the system also prevents tight control from the Washington office, which increasingly must defer to the regional offices on day-to-day operational matters.

In carrying out its design and construction responsibilities, the Park Service tries to make a clear separation between the management staff, which determines what services are required, and the professional staff, which decides how the problems will be solved. The arrangement is similar to that between an architectural firm and a client. The Denver Service Center handles the planning, design, and construction of roads, trails, campgrounds, buildings, and utility systems and the restoration of historic sites. With a staff of 500 that includes architects, landscape architects and engineers, historians, economists, social scientists, naturalists, graphic artists, topographers, photographers, and energy specialists, along with clerical and administrative people, the center is able to design anything from garbage cans to hospitals or to restore structures that range from Fort Laramie on the Oregon Trail to Independence Hall in downtown Philadelphia.

The Harpers Ferry Center is housed in a handsome modern building, overlooking the Shenandoah River, that provides studios for artists, sculptors, cabinet makers, cartographers, cinematographers, writers, and film and book editors. Its staff produces interpretive program materials for the parks—films and slide shows, publications, and museum exhibits. The center also operates conservation laboratories for preserving historic artifacts and art works.

Two other centers provide for the specialized training needs of employees. At Grand Canyon, new rangers, interpreters, and administrative and professional employees spend eight weeks studying all phases of Park Service operations. Harpers Ferry specializes in the field of interpretation, but both centers offer a variety of courses covering most elements of park work. The staffs of the training centers are recruited from Park Service people with extensive experience as well as the necessary teaching ability.

Seasonals

Because most travel to the parks occurs during the traditional summer vacation months, from Memorial Day through the Labor Day weekend, both the Park Service and concessioners retain a relatively small year-round core staff that is considerably augmented by the summer "seasonals." The total employment of the Park Service doubles during this period as thousands of temporary rangers, naturalists, historians, and archeologists come aboard, along with maintenance and trail crew workers. A park that has a permanent staff of several naturalists and twenty rangers may hire several dozen seasonal naturalists and a hundred seasonal rangers. A single concessioner may hire a thousand or more employees, mostly from college campuses, for a ten-week season and then close down for the remainder of the year.

The contribution of Park Service seasonals can be simply stated: they operate the parks in the travel season. To the visitor they *are* the Park Service, for nearly every uniformed person encountered—in the historic houses and visitor centers, at entrance stations and on guided walks—is a seasonal. They are college professors, high school instructors, graduate students, and the unsettled young who have not yet found or sought permanent careers. Seasonals are notable for their verve and idealism, in-house purists who are intensely committed to the preservation ethic. They bring a welcome freshness that helps recharge the batteries of permanent employees who may get a bit jaded. Some, particularly the college teachers, remain in the same park throughout their professional careers. Bill Lewis, a slightly built, bearded communication teacher at the University of Vermont, has been returning to Yellowstone every summer since 1949. He describes his seasonal colleagues as "a happy crew of super-outstanding people." Lewis helps the seasonals improve their oral communication skills and recently published a handbook for seasonals, *Interpreting for Park Visitors.*

A considerable number of Park Service employees began their careers as seasonals, and this route is currently the preferred method of getting into the Service. A recent survey of new employees indicated that two-thirds had worked an average of four years as seasonals before receiving their coveted permanent appointments. The competition for seasonal jobs with the Park Service can only be described as ferocious.

Living in a Park

"When the Morfield Canyon campground is full," the superintendent of Mesa Verde once observed, "I'm the mayor of the second largest city in this section of the state." The 450-site campground alone holds a couple of thousand people. If the considerable number of visitors who stay overnight in lodges and cabins is added to the total, along with concessioner and Park Service employees and their families, the superintendent's claim is persuasive. The larger parks may have an overnight population of more than 20,000 people.

Living and working in a national park reverses traditional life styles. Vacationers leave the conveniences of the city behind; they want to get away. As a result, park employees often lack even the basics of modern life. Supermarkets, drug stores, banks, or even the services of a doctor or dentist may be far distant. Schools can be a real problem. A few of the parks have their own schools, but long bus rides for students are the rule. One alternative, used in remote locations such as Big Bend in western Texas, is to board the children at the nearest community, 125 miles away. Another alternative is the standard practice of sending young employees, whose children have not yet reached school age, to the most distant outposts. They seem to cherish this period of their lives and will reminisce about it with scarcely any urging.

Although located in picture-book settings, park housing is mostly uninspired. Congress has placed a stringent ceiling on the amount of money that can be spent on an employee residence, forcing Park Service architects to develop a standard-plan, rambler design, with the result that park residential areas have somewhat the look of suburbia. Rents are generally reasonable—the rate becomes proportionally lower the farther the occupant is removed from civilization—but after a career spent living in rental housing, a Park Service employee has no equity, only a shoe box full of rent receipts. Employees in parks located within driving distance of a town are beginning to buy houses, enjoying the amenities and commuting to their jobs in the parks.

Hospitality is one of the most common characteristics of the park community, a trait that has permeated the entire organization. Employees who have been in the Service for a few years have friends in many places, and a Park Service family on vacation invariably heads for the parks and a reunion with former associates. The practice is not without drawbacks; a succession of houseguests through much of the summer can make the lonely winters seem much more attractive. The travel season is also marked by the arrival of dignitaries on official business from the Washington and regional offices, as well as a plentiful supply of prominent public figures, congressmen, conservationists, and the ubiquitous *National Geographic* photographers.

There is not much variation in the subject of discussion at Park Service gatherings: shop, shop, shop. The recent appointment of a popular colleague to be a regional director is approved; the latest example of bureaucratic ineptitude in the personnel office is deplored; the new policy of allowing park superintendents to decide whether snowmobiles will be permitted is questioned. Park people regard their occupation as a way of life. Assigned to the Washington office and living in a city after a good many years in the parks, an associate observed that for the first time in his career he was living among people who didn't talk Park Service business all the time. It was a welcome change, he conceded, and one he intended to enjoy thoroughly—until he wangled a transfer back to the field.

All Park Service people do not, of course, work in the large western parks. They may live in a historic farmhouse on the Gettysburg battlefield or in the crumbling brick citadel of Fort Jefferson on a tiny island in the Dry Tortugas off Key West. At the latter they have ample time to watch a spectacular wildlife show when great numbers of sooty terns gather on a neighboring key for the nesting season. Wherever they are stationed, they are bound to move soon. Those who successfully resist transfers are referred to, often with envy, as "homesteaders," but if they choose to remain in one park their opportunities for promotion are scant.

Becky Griffin, profiled in a recent issue of the Park Service newsletter, characterizes her Park Service career as "rich and very, very diverse." In the seven years since she graduated from the University of Montana with a degree in resource conservation, she has served in the Pacific Northwest regional office in Seattle; Mt. Rainier National Park, Washington; Sitka National Historical Park, Alaska; Gateway National Recreation Area, New York; and Shenandoah National Park, Virginia. Presently she is the public information officer at Grand Teton National Park in Wyoming.

The Rangers

"An image of competence, fairness, and friendliness as protectors, rather than of employees who flaunt their authority, affects profoundly the behavior of visitors," a Park Service official concluded recently, commenting on the law enforcement role of the rangers. If the Park Service does communicate a positive image, much of the credit belongs to the rangers, who possess an extensive assortment of skills, from fire fighting to scuba diving to wildlife management. Interpreters—naturalists, historians, and archeologists—carry on educational activities, operate the visitor centers, give the talks and walks, and plan the museums, publications, and audiovisual programs. Rangers, who are not so specialized, spend considerable time on law enforcement and road patrols, plus a variety of resource management and visitor protection duties. Such experience must be broadening: the present director and more than half of his regional directors began their careers as buck rangers.

Regrettably, the craft of rangering has changed considerably over the years. The traditional administrative title of the ranger organization has been the Division of Resource Management and Visitor Protection. Many rangers have remarked it would be more accurate if the name were changed to Resource Protection and Visitor Management. Certainly a ranger now spends the majority of his or her time responding to visitor problems and has little time for wildlife surveys and back country patrols.

A city hires firemen, policemen, and paramedic rescue squads, but in the parks the rangers do it all. "Get the rangers!" is the urgent call when a boat is overturned, a child is lost, or a climbing party is stranded in a storm. The rangers have given the organization much of its distinctive flavor and some of its most extravagant tales. When they get together—and they have formed an Association of National Park Rangers to help retain their traditions and determine their appropriate role in the organization—stories abound of old times and old timers.

One such yarn comes from a tape in the Yellowstone archives, recorded at a ranger retirement party by a veteran who described one of the many escapades of two legendary Yellowstone rangers:

> I'll never forget the trip Harry Liek and Harry Trischman made to countin' buffalo up the head of Lamar. They were runnin' out of grub, they were gettin' down low, and one mornin' they built up a lot of pancakes and Trischman said "Harry, do you want any more of this syrup?" as he kept puttin' it on the hotcakes, just had the top of the can open, you know, just pourin' it on and Harry said, "Sure, I'll take a little more syrup." So Trischman said, "Alright, I'll shake her down, she's gettin' a little light on top." Finally, he shook her down and out came a mouse's head. Harry was sick all day; he couldn't make it up over the hill.

One of the more colorful of the early rangers, Trischman had been a scout with the army in Yellowstone from 1909 until its departure in 1918, whereupon he joined the rangers and served as chief buffalo keeper and assistant chief ranger until his retirement in 1946. Accounts of his physical stamina, including his 100-mile nonstop ski tours, tend to be cut from the same cloth as stories of furbearing trout and jackalopes, but Trischman broke in a lot of young rangers during his twenty-eight years on the force. The story is told that he once took two ranger recruits, probably fresh out of college, on a ski patrol through the park to show them the country. When they stopped the first night at a patrol cabin, they complained the blankets were dirty. "Boys," Harry told them, "sleep in these blankets tonight and when you wake up tomorrow you'll smell like rangers."

The nature of the ranger's job in the early days, with much hard physical labor and lonely patrols in remote and difficult terrain, was a strong factor in making the Park Service an almost exclusively male organization. Attitudes—and hiring practices—have changed considerably in recent times, but not all that long ago when an old-line Yosemite ranger was asked how he and his wife split the domestic chores during their many years of living in backcountry quarters he replied, bluntly: "Everything for fifty feet around a cabin is woman's work."

Even though women do not figure in ranger stories, they were serving in the uniformed ranks as early as the 1920s. Isobel Bassett, a geologist, visited Yellowstone with a tour group in 1919. Her voluntary lectures on the park's geologic formations so impressed superintendent Horace Albright that she was appointed a seasonal park ranger the following year, making her in all probability the first woman to hold a park ranger job. She assisted the park naturalist—appointed the same year—to initiate one of the first Park Service interpretive programs and was succeeded by another woman who worked for several summers and wrote a children's book on the national parks.

The enterprising Marguerite Lindsley also began working as a seasonal ranger in the Yellowstone interpretive program in the early 1920s, while attending Montana State University. In 1928, having received her master's degree in bacteriology from Bryn Mawr, she rode her motorcycle from Philadelphia to Yellowstone, a feat that must have impressed even Harry Trischman. Lindsley is believed to have been the first year-round woman park ranger in the Park Service, continuing to serve for several years after her marriage to a fellow Yellowstone ranger. It would doubtless impress Trischman even more if he knew that in 1981 there were twenty-five women serving as park superintendents and the superintendent of Yellowstone was reporting to a female regional director.

The Friends of the Service

The Park Service is mightily served by people and groups that do not appear on the organizational charts. "Friends of the Service" are highly esteemed; they support the Service in many ways. In what must be one of the more productive relationships between a government agency and the private sector, cooperating associations have been formed to sell educational materials in the parks. They are major contributors to park interpretation, particularly in publishing. Most of the guides—trail, bird, tree, and wildlife—and many of the other publications visitors obtain in the parks are produced by the associations. They also provide the personnel, uniforms, and equipment for many of the living-history and craft demonstrations. All profits from their activities are donated to the parks to support interpretive programs. Over a period of more than fifty years the associations, now operating in nearly 250 sites, have returned many millions of dollars to the Park Service.

Many parks exist today only because of the generosity of individual donors, who have received little notice. The splendid bequests of John D. Rockefeller, Jr., and his family, are of a special dimension. Rockefeller philanthropy made possible the establishment of Great Smoky Mountains, Grand Teton, Acadia, and Virgin Islands national parks and acquired critical lands in Sequoia, Yosemite, and the Blue Ridge Parkway. Through the Mellon Foundations, Paul Mellon has also made notable contributions, sharing the land acquisition costs for Cape Hatteras National Seashore and funding the surveys of the Atlantic, Pacific, and Gulf Coasts and the Great Lakes that led to the establishment of a dozen seashores and lakeshores. The Mellon donation to establish Cumberland Island National Seashore, one of the largest single such grants, was made through the National Park Foundation, a charitable corporation chartered by Congress to accept gifts and acquire lands, by purchase or donation, for inclusion in the system.

When the parks were in dire need during the early days, Steve Mather contributed from his personal fortune. In 1915 the Tioga Road, the only entrance to Yosemite from the east side, was a 56-mile dirt track built by Chinese laborers before 1900 in a failing venture by the Great Sierra Consolidated Silver Mining Company. Mather raised half the purchase price of the roadway from private sources, including the Sierra Club, and paid the rest himself. Among his many benefactions were the purchase of a headquarters site for Glacier, help in buying Pipe Spring National Monument, and construction of the Ranger Club House in Yosemite to house bachelor rangers.

Often the efforts of individual citizens have been responsible for creating parks, not by providing funds but by generating the necessary public support. Fresh from Kansas in 1885, William Gladstone Steel decided on the spot, when he first saw Crater Lake, that it deserved the same recognition given Yellowstone thirteen years earlier. He was soon able to have the area withdrawn from settlement, but it took him seventeen years of hard work to drum up support for creation of a national park. Addressing the first national park conference in 1911, he noted that when the park was established in 1902 he thought the U.S. government would step in and provide the visitor facilities. "In this, I found that I was mistaken, so I had to go to work again," Steel told the assembled superintendents. "All the money I have is in the park, and if I had more, it would go there too. This is my life's work, and I propose to see it through."

Many people support the parks by donating their services under the provisions of the Volunteers in Parks (VIP) Act. It authorizes the Service to pay the incidental expenses—transportation costs, meals, and uniforms—for volunteers who serve without salary. Each year several thousand VIPs perform a wide range of activities, mostly associated with the work of the interpreters and rangers.

No private citizens have better earned the title "Friends of the Service" than those eminent historians, archeologists, architects, and experts in "human geography" who have served on the national park system Advisory Board since it was established by the Historic Sites Act in 1935. Originally intended to advise the secretary on historical and archeological matters, the scope of board involvement was soon expanded, and members were appointed from a variety of disciplines. Every secretary has turned to the Advisory Board for advice before making policy decisions, and it has become customary for the secretary to obtain Advisory Board review before proposing new park legislation to Congress.

At the conclusion of their six-year terms, retiring board members automatically become members of the Advisory Council. In effect this allows them to continue their participation in board deliberations and field inspections as nonvoting affiliates. Some council members have been returning to the fall and spring meetings for more than twenty years, sharing their long experience with board newcomers. None have been more faithful in attendance or more perceptive in their observations than the sprightly quartet of Dr. Ned Danson, formerly director of the Museum of Northern Arizona; Frank Masland, former president of the Masland Carpet Company in Carlisle, Pennsylvania; Dr. Emil Haury, professor emeritus of anthropology at the University of Arizona; and Dr. Joe Brew, former director of Harvard's Peabody Museum. Their fidelity is evidence that once people become involved with the parks and the Park Service, they do not easily or willingly disassociate themselves.

During his tenure on the Advisory Board, Alfred A. Knopf traveled widely in the parks and came to know many park people. The urbane and respected publisher, who fought many battles to protect park integrity, always carried a case of his favorite wine, should there be any problem with the local water. Park Service people found Alfred Knopf a charming and unpretentious companion. Apparently the affection was returned. "It is hard to imagine more dedicated people than those who run the parks," he once wrote. "I have never met a single one whom I would not be glad to meet again, and I have invariably regretted the time to say goodbye. The range of their interests, their high intelligence, their devotion, make them a separate and wonderful breed."

4

PARK SERVICE FUNCTIONS AND ACTIVITIES

Long before anyone knew much about the practical details of running parks, there were people able to define their purpose. "The first thing to be kept in mind then," Frederick Law Olmsted, chairman of the board of commissioners for Yosemite, said in 1865, the year after the valley was ceded to California, "is the preservation and maintenance as exactly as is possible of the natural scenery."

Seven years before the establishment of Yellowstone, Olmsted, America's most notable landscape designer, formulated a distinctive theory of the role national parks should play in a democratic society that is wholly valid today: "In permitting the sacrifice of anything that would be of the slightest value to future visitors to the convenience, bad taste, playfulness, carelessness, or wanton destructiveness of present visitors, we probably yield in each case the interest of uncounted millions to the selfishness of a few individuals."

There were doubtless many who shared Olmsted's philosophy, but no one knew how to achieve his goal of determining the acceptable ways to encourage visitor use while preserving the natural scene. There were no models to follow anywhere in the world. Congress had generally left practical operational problems to the Park Service, and the enabling act (written by Olmsted's son, Frederick Law Olmsted, Jr.) did not go into details nor provide answers to the perennial problems facing park administrators: should concessioner facilities stay within the parks or be moved outside; should the Park Service build more roads, trails, and campgrounds to accommodate the increased numbers of people using the parks or should access be limited to insure an uncrowded experience for fewer people; if automobiles are permitted on park roads in the summer, why shouldn't snowmobiles be allowed in the winter. By 1923, the president of the National Parks Association concluded, "The law has never clearly defined a national park."

Every year Congress debates the merits of establishing proposed new parks, yet it spends little time on policy matters. One of the more knowledgeable authorities on the parks, Joseph L. Sax, recently observed that the most likely place to look for guidance on questions involving appropriate use of the parks should be in the congressional enactments establishing the parks, where presumably Congress would have laid down policy guidelines. Such search, Sax pointed out, would be fruitless, for Congress has never come to grips with the tough questions in all the years since Yosemite.

In its formative years the Park Service was led by what might be termed gifted amateurs. Some were professionals in the sense that they had degrees in the traditional disciplines—history, forestry, biology, archeology—but they had no training in park administration. They took a pragmatic approach, seeking a fair and supportable balance between the demands of preservation and use. Their approach reflected the commonly held attitudes of the times. Popular sentiment supported the idea of wildlife preserves, but the public and the Park Service alike separated animals into "good" and "bad" species. The bad animals were the predators, the coyotes, wolves, bobcats, and mountain lions who preyed upon elk, deer, buffalo, and antelope. In 1918 a well-known naturalist captioned a photograph of two mountain lions killed in Glacier National Park: "The only good mountain lions are those gathered in by hunters and trappers. Some effective means should be taken for their destruction." Rangers in those days routinely carried rifles to kill off coyotes.

Until 1941, there were "bear shows" in Yellowstone every evening where a couple of dozen grizzlies would forage through a garbage pile, while spectators safely seated behind a chain link fence were guarded by an armed ranger (when future president Jerry Ford worked as a seasonal in the summer of 1936, he was assigned to this duty). It was not until the 1960s that the Park Service finally ended the most incongruous spectacle in any national park, the nightly "fire fall" in Yosemite, in which the glowing embers from a roaring bonfire were pushed over the high valley rim. It was a decision much too long delayed, largely because of the intransigence of the Yosemite Park and Curry Company, sponsor of the pyrotechnical marvel.

The Fatal Flaw

Most people would argue that preservation versus use is the classic unsolvable dilemma, the fatal flaw in the national park idea. When Congress established the parks bureau it directed that the scenery, the natural and historic objects, and the wildlife were to be preserved, but that these resources were to be made available for people to enjoy. The instruction to preserve the parks unimpaired, while at the same time building facilities for public use, does seem contradictory. Building a road that allows people to enter a park obviously does cause damage to the landscape.

Almost every decision affecting the parks involves the balancing of preservation and use values: What should be done with cantankerous, food-begging (but popular) bears? Should backcountry lakes be stocked for fishermen? Can a boardwalk trail be developed through a swamp without affecting the vegetation? In the end, these are judgment calls, but then so is each decision of the Supreme Court. As there is no way to quantify all of the factors involved, from scientific to psychological, each decision is the product of the best-informed judgment of knowledgeable people, framed with a mindful consideration of the attitudes and opinions of the visiting public. (Perhaps the preservation-use debates explain why Park Service people use the expression "between a rock and a hard spot" so frequently.)

Often the Park Service is under fire for its stands; equally thoughtful people may arrive at different conclusions. *Man and Nature in the National Parks,* by Sir Frank Fraser Darling, the noted British ecologist, and Noel D. Eichhorn, was a study to determine whether the Park Service is even-handed in its stewardship. The authors concluded that the Service is guilty of a generous, if misguided, tendency to permit excessive use. "We ourselves have often had the uncomfortable feeling that the philanthropic ethos of the National Park Service has overshadowed the primary necessity to conserve the habitat."

One of the wisest observers of parks and park people, Freeman Tilden, once suggested with characteristic candor that the congressional mandate is a worthy aspiration, but one that will never be totally attainable.

> We may agree that it is a counsel of perfection, for even the discreet use of a wilderness area cannot help being in some degree an impairment. But why split hairs about it? The intent of Congress was high and good, and the very difficulty of fulfilling the injunction has been one of the fruitful challenges that has reached down through the personnel of the National Park Service to the loneliest laborer in the most remote spot.

That people can take almost opposite positions on fundamental questions is demonstrated by the reactions of two men, one a famous writer of western novels and the other a president of the United States, upon first viewing a superlative scene.

Early in this century Zane Grey became one of the first white men to reach Rainbow Bridge, the earth's largest such formation, located in the canyon country of southern Utah. It took him days of rugged horseback travel. Grey camped under the great stone arch that the Navajos call Nonnezoshie, and one morning at dawn he took up his notebook to express the hope that this sight would always be reserved for the few who earned the privilege: "The tourist, the leisurely traveler, the comfort-loving motorist would never behold it. Only by toil, sweat, endurance, and pain could any man ever look at Nonnezoshie. It seemed well to realize that the great things of life had to be earned."

Despite the protection seemingly granted to Rainbow Bridge when it was designated a national monument in 1910, the waters of Lake Powell, created by the Bureau of Reclamation's Glen Canyon dam, now extend to the base of the arch. The Park Service, which administers Lake Powell as a national recreation area, has built a dock a few hundred yards from Rainbow Bridge, making it easily accessible to the casual boating tourist.

Shortly after Herbert Hoover was inaugurated president in 1929, he built a fishing camp close by Shenandoah National Park and used it frequently to escape from Washington. One weekend he invited Park Service director Horace Albright, who had helped select the campsite, to join him. On Sunday morning the two rode horseback to the top of the Blue Ridge. As they moved along the crest of the range, Hoover remarked to Albright how wonderful it would be if more people could share such a marvelous view. "Albright," said the former engineer, looking over the contours of the ridge, "there ought to be a highway up here, a parkway. It's just a natural." The result of that conversation was the construction of the Skyline Drive in Shenandoah National Park with funds—and frequent suggestions—provided by President Hoover.

Most conservationists regard the Rainbow Bridge boat dock as a regrettable intrusion (which it is) and the Skyline Drive as a delight ("glorious" according to Darling and Eichhorn), even though unlike the boat dock, the parkway inflicts a substantial and permanent scar on the landscape. One suspects that had the Skyline Drive not been built in the 1930s, it would be impossible today to obtain public support for its construction.

In a somewhat similar context Ansel Adams tells of a comment made by a friend many years ago when both were looking down from a vantage point into Yosemite Valley: "Wouldn't it be wonderful if a million people could see what we're seeing today, and have the experience without damaging it." Adams points out that an almost unlimited number of people gathered along the rim could have an unobstructed view of the valley—but the experience wouldn't be worth much.

One of the most intriguing elements of the eternal debate is that persons with seemingly unbending convictions will occasionally switch sides. Even Darling and Eichhorn, staunchly preservationist on most matters, went haywire on others. They proposed that portions of the Appalachian Trail be blacktopped and that congestion in Great Smoky Mountains National Park be solved by replacing the existing two-lane road with a four-lane highway. Conservation through development indeed!

As Seen by the Press

Public controversy over park policy is continuous; it is a tradition in the Department of Interior that the number of letters received on park issues exceeds the total mail received by all other bureaus combined. To keep its widely scattered employees informed on current conflicts, the Park Service twice monthly collected and distributed to all field offices a representative sample of newspaper and magazine articles under the title "The National Park Service As Seen By The Nation's Press." Stories included in the March 17, 1981, issue contain a typical assortment that appeared in the *Fairbanks News-Miner,* the *Los Angeles Times,* the *Christian Science Monitor,* the *Anchorage Times,* the *Washington Star, Backpacker* magazine, and the *New York Daily News.* (Unfortunately this excellent and informative service has been one of the casualties of the Reagan austerity program.) It is evident from this sample that public criticism of Park Service operations is never in short supply.

Headlined "Denali Park Chief Agrees To Change Rules For Climbers," the *News-Miner* story reported a public meeting attended by the superintendent of Denali (formerly Mt. McKinley) National Park. It was called by members of the Alaskan Alpine Club who opposed restrictions on their freedom to climb, particularly the requirement that all climbers must register. Registration had been imposed to help rangers identify climbers who littered the mountain with garbage, explained the superintendent, who agreed the requirement had done little to improve the problem. (Many climbing parties discard surprising amounts of gear, rather than carry it out.) He conceded that Park Service funds spent on regulating mountaineers might better have been spent hiring people to clean up the litter. "Obviously you are an angry group, and you've raised some of the best points I've seen," said the embattled superintendent, who promised to consult with club members before drafting any more climbing regulations.

One of the results of the initial Reagan budget reductions was the elimination of land acquisition funds for the newly established Santa Monica National Recreation Area, with an implied threat that the entire project might be scrapped. Speaking to a *Los Angeles Times* reporter, the local congressman who had introduced the park legislation vowed that he would battle to restore the funds. He argued that while he fully supported efforts to reduce federal expenditures, "we will save large amounts of money in the long run by purchasing these lands now before their cost escalates," noting that land costs were rising at a rate of from 15 percent to 35 percent a year. The delay poses other problems, according to the park superintendent. A key tract of land slated for purchase, donated by actor Marlon Brando to a group of Indians, is now owned by a builder who plans a luxury housing development.

A contributor to the "Speaking Out, A Citizen's View" column in the *Monitor* had recently visited both the Galapagos Islands and Buck Island Reef National Monument in the Virgin Islands. "The Ecuadorian government appreciates its unique national treasure and enforces strict rules to keep the islands the way they are," declared the writer, a snorkeling enthusiast disappointed with the congregation of tour boats at Buck Island. The Park Service underwater nature trail there has been generally praised, but to this observer it was "cement block, billboards-sign pollution at its worst."

Invited to appear before the Alaska House and Senate Resources Committees, the executive director of the National Park Inholders Association told the lawmakers, "The Park Service has steamrollered inholders" (those who own property within the parks) elsewhere in the country and now has "almost absolute authority" over more than 100 million acres of Alaska in the newly established parks. According to the *Anchorage Times*, the head of the lobbying organization—who owns land in Yosemite—urged the Alaska legislature to take action immediately to protect citizens against the Alaska Lands Bill.

The conversion of Washington's Union Station to a National Visitor Center will undoubtedly be remembered as one of the most embarrassing and costly ventures in Park Service history. There was unanimous support for the idea in the 1960s when the railroads abandoned the deteriorating structure because of declining passenger traffic, but the ambitious project simply came apart at the seams, becoming an object of national ridicule for its horrendous cost overruns. The *Washington Star* reported that despite $51 million already spent (and with rain pouring through holes in the station ceiling), an Interior spokesman had told a House committee that the visitor center concept would be abandoned and Union Station returned to its original function as a railroad station, at a total cost of perhaps $120 million. Said the Interior official, sorrowfully, "The original intent of the National Visitor Center has been overtaken by events."

According to an editorial in *Backpacker* magazine, the Park Service doesn't even know how to pick good rangers, passing over candidates who have worked for years as seasonals in favor of applicants who do well on written exams but have had no field experience in the parks and "probably don't know a bald eagle from a bald pate." However, a recent analysis of newly selected rangers showed that, on the average, they had previously worked for several years as seasonals, so there is some doubt as to where the *Backpacker* writer obtained his information.

Congressman James Scheuer was characterized by a *New York Daily News* reporter as a "furious U.S. representative who wants skinny-dippers to wear fig leaves," after Scheuer fired off a letter to the superintendent of Gateway National Recreation Area demanding that nude sunbathing on one of the park beaches, "which continues to scandalize the community," be prohibited. "I urge that this immediate nudity ban be enforced with the vigor and professionalism that is characteristic of the Park Service," wrote Scheuer. Noting that nude sunbathing was a tradition long before Gateway was established, but that rangers would closely monitor "any lewd and provocative behavior," the superintendent responded with bureaucratic vigor: "We are studying the problem to see how best to resolve it."

Interpretation

Freeman Tilden took a whimsical view of many subjects that customarily receive sober treatment, once expressing sympathy for people who have made it a rule to dodge museums. "It is really bewildering to find a letter from Napoleon to Josephine reposing beside a stuffed albino squirrel," said the discerning man who wrote the standard work on Park Service interpretation, meanwhile assuring his audience that there are no Park Service museum exhibits of that kind.

The Park Service can take considerable credit for its pioneer work in the field of interpretation. Even before the turn of the century, efforts were being made to explain nature to visitors—and to develop embryonic museums. "I'll interpret the rocks, learn the language of flood, storm and the avalanche," John Muir had exclaimed, and in the 1880s soldiers in Yellowstone were giving geyser talks. By 1904 Yosemite soldiers were labeling plants and trees along what may have been the first nature trails. In his annual report for 1917, director Mather declared "one of the chief functions of the national parks and monuments is to serve educational purposes." In 1920, the year that Yellowstone appointed the first year-round naturalist in the Park Service, Mather arranged (with his own funds) for the first nature-guiding experiments in Yosemite. They drew more than 25,000 visitors to the evening camp fire lectures. Attractive museums built in several national parks in the 1920s with

Rockefeller funds are still in operation. More than 300 visitor centers and museums have followed—all designed to popularize knowledge, which is after all what a good museum should try to do.

The word "interpretation" replaced the original term "education" in Park Service usage, in part no doubt to avoid any suggestion that the modest appetite for knowledge of the average visitor would be submerged in a tide of completely accurate but exquisitely boring facts. Interpretation also seemed a better term to describe the function of dealing with subjects unfamiliar to most people, such as geology, biology, and botany. It was almost like learning a new language, and the process of translating this language of the earth came to be called interpretation.

In his book *Interpreting Our Heritage,* Tilden (who served an apprenticeship as a ranger historian at an advanced age, in order to get the feel of the job) quotes a choice sign written by a friend as an example of how a few well chosen words can tell a full and memorable story:

I am an Old Time Country Lane
Now I have been
Officially Vacated and Closed
(I never liked automobiles anyway)
I invite you to walk—as folks
have walked for generations
and be friendly with my trees
my flowers and my wild creatures

Undismayed by his friend's confession that the inscription was composed "mit beer," Tilden thought the inspiration might also be attributed to a great many years of genuine affection for, and a keen understanding of, human emotions. Still, mused Tilden, who held that good interpreters developed the skill of investing the most commonplace facts with interest, "There is something about Nature's stark reality that would ennoble a troglodyte."

Research

At the time the first historical parks were added to the system in the early 1930s, the Park Service did not yet have a research staff worthy of the name in either cultural history or natural history. When Rockefeller undertook the restoration of Williamsburg in 1927, there was no other project in the United States large enough to provide full-time employment for a research historian or a restoration architect. The Park Service did not fully appreciate the vital role of research in any restoration project until, with the establishment of the George Washington Birthplace National Monument in 1930, it acquired the birthplace home of Washington.

The structure had been built by a patriotic association and was supposedly an exact duplicate of the original built in 1725 and destroyed by fire in 1779. Among other miscalculations, as it turned out, the association had accepted a location marker erected by Washington's adopted son in 1815 to mark the home site. It was unaware that in the middle of the nineteenth century, the sign had been moved by a farmer when it got in the way of his operations. Soon the authenticity of the reconstruction became a matter of public speculation.

The Park Service was able to assemble a competent research staff after acquiring the historical parks in 1933. It then carried out a comprehensive historical and archeological study of the Wakefield structure. The study, completed in 1941, was a shocker. Notwithstanding that 600,000 people had already toured the monument and been told that the home was a faithful replica down to the last brick, the researchers found the house was actually a conjectural restoration, a building typical of the period—and located at some distance from the original site. (Apparently the architect had even first designed a building of frame construction, but changed this to brick to reduce maintenance costs.) Had it not been for the outbreak of World War II and the curtailment of Park Service funding, an irate secretary of the Interior, Harold Ickes, might have insisted the structure either be torn down or moved to the correct location.

Mindful of Wakefield and one or two similar experiences (the birthplace cabin of Abraham Lincoln, which was also donated by a private association as a national historic site, may or may not be authentic), the Park Service has taken a consistently dim view of reconstructions. This attitude was summed up in an observation that received wide circulation in Park Service offices after the Wakefield incident: "The curse of most historical restorations, reconstructions, or re-creations is an almost irresistible urge to gild the lily." On rare occasions a complete reconstruction will be approved, but only if sufficiently detailed information exists to do an accurate job. Despite strong arguments in favor of reconstructing the Benjamin Franklin home as a Bicentennial project, adequate information was lacking, so the Service settled for the interesting alternative of representing the exterior outline of the building with a framework of metal beams—a "ghost" restoration.

The Park Service has always had more success in getting funds from Congress for historical and archeological research than for the necessary scientific studies in natural areas. A milestone was passed in

1962, at a time when wildlife populations were a source of controversy, when Interior Secretary Udall appointed a special advisory committee on wildlife management, headed by Dr. Starker Leopold, to review conditions in the parks. Observing that significant ecological changes had taken place in many national parks—such as logging or grazing before the area was set aside, or elimination of predators—the committee concluded "A national park should represent a vignette of primitive America." Where the environment has been altered, the committee recommended that, to the extent it is practicable and based upon sound research, the area should be returned to its original condition. This counsel from the Leopold Committee has provided a sound guideline, but it is, admittedly, a concept of enormous complexity.

Many natural areas now have at least one staff scientist engaged in research that will help the superintendent make sound resource management decisions. The largest such staff is at Everglades, which for many years has been in a precarious position, plagued by insidious water problems. A vast network of ever-changing sloughs and waterways, once incredibly rich in aquatic life, the Everglades is at the end of the south Florida watershed. The park's life-giving water supply is now curtailed by drainage canals, variable rainfall, and farms and housing developments occupying one-third of the original glades. Wildlife has diminished, birds have vanished, and fish populations are threatened. A dozen scientists are studying the impact of these changes on plant and animal life. The leader of the project has commented, "Everglades is an ecosystem that we may lose if we fail to understand it."

Today park superintendents can call upon the services of biologists, geologists, zoologists, or even archeologists well-versed in magnetometry and aerial photography who can place the park area within a larger physiographic, climatic, and cultural context. A complete survey of a park containing Indian sites may take only a fraction of the thirteen years that were required to make a laborious survey of the sites in Mesa Verde. High technology is useful; remote sensing has revealed details hitherto undiscovered, including evidence of an ancient Anasazi road system at Chaco Canyon. A series of aerial photographs of Valley Forge, taken over a span of nearly half a century, shows that ground disturbances caused by a long series of Boy Scout jamborees now make it all but impossible to detect evidence of the Continental Army's original winter encampment site in 1777–78.

Resource Management and Law Enforcement

In Park Service terminology, utilizing research findings and taking appropriate action is called resource management. The most widely discussed such practice in recent years has been the policy of allowing natural fires to burn freely. At first rangers had considerable difficulty explaining the theory. A fire that burned and smoldered for months in Grand Teton, covering Jackson Hole with a smoke haze, so infuriated local citizens that they dispatched a petition to Washington demanding that the director remove the park superintendent and send in the fire fighters. "I understand biology but I don't understand politics," one ranger commented.

Applying the "let-burn" policy to lightning-caused fires but not to man-made ones may seem an unnecessarily fine distinction. It is an attempt to replicate the number and location of fires that have burned historically. Part of this is the phenomenon that lightning fires tend to start on top of a ridge and burn down slowly, whereas man-made fires more often start in low ground.

Every inch of wilderness has, of course, been burned and reburned ever since the emergence of forests on the North American continent some 250 million years ago, as ancient fires recycled mature forests and regenerated healthy new growth. Throughout this time areas that are now national parks were completely burned over countless times. The "beauty" of the national parks is the result of many forces—volcanic eruptions, glaciers, rivers, erosion, and fire. Those who still want the Park Service to put out fires might ask themselves how the wilderness managed to survive for so many millions of years without rangers.

Much is yet to be learned about the role of fire, although there are several premises that underscore John Muir's belief that everything in the universe is hitched together. Forest fires may be important in maintaining healthy fish populations: rain falling on the ashes in a burned-over area leaches out minerals that enter the drainage system and are carried by streams into lakes, where they raise the nutrient content of the water. Areas that suffer the most intensive fires seem to be those in which fire has been suppressed for a long time, allowing a heavy accumulation of dry fuel on the forest floor. In his book *Where The Grizzly Walks,* Bill Schneider suggests that fires may be essential to grizzly habitat by providing a new growth of succulent plants and that overzealous fire control may be the reason the vast Selway-Bitterroot Wilderness of Idaho and Montana lost its grizzlies. "Wouldn't it be ironical," Schneider speculates, "if one of the grizzly's biggest problems turned out to be another bear—Smokey Bear?"

Whether Smokey should exchange his shovel for a pistol, whether the park ranger should concentrate on law enforcement duties rather than on resource management tasks, is a matter of intense concern to the Park Service. Perhaps because crime in a national park is regarded as newsworthy, stories appear frequently; a UPI account in January 1981, datelined Gatlinburg, Tennessee, was typically ominous: "From the Great Smoky Mountains in Tennessee to Yosemite in California officials are raising a red flag on a skyrocketing crime increase in the national parks."

The statistics quoted in the article seem impressive—in 1979 there were 8,600 felony crimes committed in the parks, including murders, rapes, and armed robberies—but hardly on a scale to justify the assertion that "crime in the national parks, as in any crowded area, is common." Four of the parks accounted for more than 40 percent of the total, and FBI data show that a city of 50,000 people has a crime rate more serious than all of the parks combined with their 300 million annual visitors. Actually, the majority of the crimes are petty thefts of property worth less than fifty dollars, although that may be scant comfort to the owners of the 220 automobiles that were stolen in Great Smoky Mountains National Park in 1979.

Undeniably, the threat of crime has caused a substantial shift of emphasis toward the direction of law enforcement. Rangers now receive 400 hours of intensive law enforcement training at the Federal Law Enforcement Training Center, plus periodic refresher courses. Nevertheless, there is a continuing dialogue on the question of whether law enforcement duties, particularly in parks with the most serious problems, should be handled by policemen who have some ranger indoctrination or by rangers trained to handle police work. While the sentiment is heavily against replacing rangers with policemen, some people believe the emphasis on law enforcement cannot help but influence attitudes. For a ranger, a parked car along a remote road suggests its occupants are in need of assistance; for a policeman, the situation is potentially dangerous and should be so regarded.

At a conference of park superintendents, the moderator of a session on law enforcement noted that "hardly anything has been more talked about" within the Park Service, concluding that "our people are undertrained in resource management and overtrained in law enforcement. A tremendous imbalance has been created." The fact that the Yosemite pistol team regularly outshoots all other police organizations in California is a matter of some pride, but it may be too much to ask that rangers who wear guns and are professionally competent in conducting criminal investigations be equally proficient on bird identifications and the niceties of forest ecology.

Planning

The best treatment for park development problems is an application of practical common sense. It is to be hoped that this has been the function of the master plan, the Park Service instrument for reconciling preservation and use problems. The document had its origins in the 1920s, shortly after a field engineering office was established in Portland, Oregon to design and supervise construction projects in the parks. It soon became apparent that building facilities in the parks must take place with a special sensitivity for environmental concerns and for the impact of the developments on the park scene. The solution was the creation of a division of landscape architecture, probably unique at that time in the federal government. Landscape architects were assigned responsibility for determining how campgrounds should be sited for minimal encroachment or how roads should be located to cause the least possible damage to park features. A policy of strict landscape control over physical improvements was formulated. Beginning in 1926, documents were prepared for each park that marked out the areas in which development would be permitted.

These master plans—now called general management plans to eliminate the suggestion that they are fixed in concrete—are guided by several principles: planning requires a multi-discipline approach; no action will be taken in a park without an approved plan; participation of the public in the planning process is mandatory. "Public involvement," as it is called, has become an important, almost a controlling, factor in federal planning.

Even before publication of *The Greening of America* made him a controversial prophet, Charles A. Reich had published a report for the Center for the Study of Democratic Institutions entitled *Bureaucracy and the Forests.* Holding that any government agency is following a perilous course when it decides it knows what is best for people, Reich declared "In a democracy the 'public interest' has no objective meaning except insofar as the people have defined it; the question cannot be what is 'best' for the people, but what the people, adequately informed, decide they want." The flaw in this otherwise unarguable sermon is that many people are not "adequately informed." Another inherent problem in public planning meetings is that they are mostly held in the locale of the park, where there are sure to be strong economic interests represented.

Many of the national parks contain examples of spectacularly bad planning, but in most cases the pattern was set early by park administrators who could not possibly have foreseen that visitors would one day come in automobiles and be counted in the millions. Given the difficulty of stagecoach travel and the limited funds available, it is understandable that tourist facilities were clustered near the popular features and that support facilities later were added to the original complex. As travel increased and more facilities were required, the developed areas grew like Topsy.

A prime example of this unplanned chaos, the South Rim of Grand Canyon, overlooks one of the stupendous vistas of the world; it also contains a motley collection of hotels, motels, restaurants, stores, gas stations, offices, warehouses, maintenance yards, and residential areas for Park Service and concessioner families, all differing markedly in age, architectural design, and state of repair. Planners would like to start over on the South Rim of Grand Canyon.

Passage of the National Environmental Protection Act in 1970 radically changed the federal approach to planning, previously done behind closed doors. The present system of thoroughgoing public involvement has made the process almost interminable. During preparation of the Yosemite plan, the Park Service went public with a perhaps unnecessarily elaborate procedure for obtaining public sentiment, holding hearings in major cities from San Francisco to Washington, D.C., and distributing 50,000 "Work Books" which contained hundreds of questions. Computerized results and the expenditure of a great deal of money indicated that people did not want extreme changes in Yosemite. The majority preferred a modest reduction in facilities in the valley and a gradual scaling down of automobile traffic. The public has generally taken a middle-of-the-road position on park plans, with a slight partiality for the preservation viewpoint.

Historic Preservation

In his exhaustive and scholarly survey of the historic preservation movement in the United States, *Preservation Comes of Age,* Charles B. Hosmer, Jr., notes that the first two directors of the Park Service were responsible for the entry of the federal government into the preservation field, when they put together a nationwide program for administering historic sites. They started almost from scratch. One day in the mid-1920s when the two men attempted to drive from Washington to Yorktown, their car bogged down in the mud. "The picture of Horace Albright and Stephen Mather standing next to a roadster on an unpaved road in Virginia near Fredericksburg," Hosmer comments, "tells us a great deal about the problems that faced the preservationists of 1926." The two principal officers of the federal park agency couldn't make their way to the battlefield where Americans had won their independence.

Mather and Albright were convinced the Park Service should move into historic preservation, but at that time the organization was western oriented from top to bottom. About the only eastern installation was the Washington headquarters. Creation of the Civilian Conservation Corps in 1933 provided the manpower and funds that enabled the Park Service to broaden its mission. In 1932 its entire history staff consisted of the chief historian in Washington and two historians in the field, but the following year expansion began. By the end of 1933 there were 800 young men in four CCC camps at Yorktown alone, restoring the French, British, and American earthworks and batteries, carrying out archeological excavations, restoring colonial buildings, and constructing educational models. There were dozens of CCC camps in the historical parks transferred to the Park Service by the reorganization of 1933, and each camp needed historians and archeologists to direct the work programs.

When the head of the history department at the University of Minnesota received word from a former student, who had become the chief historian of the Park Service, that jobs were available in the parks, he immediately notified his six top graduate students. Employment opportunities being almost nonexistent during the Depression, the students pooled their resources and sent a telegram accepting the positions offered. It was an unusually gifted group, including two future chief historians of the Park Service. One was Ronald F. Lee, who upon his arrival at the Civil War battlefield of Shiloh hired twenty more historians under Civil Works Administration authority. A towering figure in the historical wing of the Park Service, Lee "was destined to become the central figure of the preservation movement in the United States during the 1940s," in the estimation of Hosmer.

Herbert Kahler, who later succeeded Lee as chief historian, found that the parks were not always grateful for the appearance of academic types. "We don't need any historians down here," he was told on his arrival at the Chickamauga-Chattanooga park by the superintendent, an army officer. Casting around for a worthy project, Kahler set out on horseback to record all of the inscriptions on the battlefield markers and monuments. A couple of weeks into the survey, Kahler discovered that the superintendent already had the inscription inventory in a desk drawer. Nevertheless, as a large number of college-trained people chose government service during the Depression years of the 1930s, the Park Service received an invaluable transfusion of professional talents. By World War II it had become the largest employer of historians and archeologists in the country.

The availability of New Deal funds and the desperate condition of the architectural profession in the early 1930s inspired a young Park Service architect, Charles E. Peterson, to write a letter to the director on November 13, 1933, noting that the considerable number of unemployed architects was a potentially valuable work force. They could be hired by the federal government to photograph and prepare measured drawings of buildings with significant architectural and historical values. Four days later Secretary of the Interior Ickes approved the ambitious scheme, and before the end of the month 1,200 architects were at work, recording forts, barns, bridges, residences, churches, mills, and public buildings. The Historic American Buildings Survey (HABS), now approaching its 50th anniversary, is a cooperative effort of three bodies: the Park Service, which administers the program; the Library of Congress, which houses the collection and makes it available to researchers; and the American Institute of Architects, which provides professional supervision. (In 1958 a companion program covering engineering feats, the Historic American Engineering Survey, was launched.) One of the largest such archives in the world, HABS now contains drawings, photographs, and historical data on more than 20,000 structures.

The Historic Preservation Act of 1966 greatly expanded federal involvement, extending financial aid for the first time to sites of local significance that were not in federal ownership. Nearly 25,000 properties have been nominated by the states to the National Register of Historic Places, a standing that gives them special protection against damage by any federally funded project. The President's Council on Historic Preservation, created by the act, has become a powerful voice that has halted major projects threatening important historic sites and districts. A grants-in-aid provision of the act has enabled the states to hire professional staffs and to undertake the restoration of thousands of structures.

In 1977 the Carter administration transferred the historic preservation functions of the Park Service to the Bureau of Outdoor Recreation. In recognition of the agency's considerably enhanced status, it was renamed the Heritage Conservation and Recreation Service (HCRS, which prompted the derisive, if apt, nickname "Hookers"). HCRS had a faltering start and by all accounts there was confusion and discontent in the ranks of federal, state, and local preservationists. Proving himself capable of statesmanship, Interior Secretary Watt, who had been director of the Bureau of Outdoor Recreation in the early 1970s, abolished HCRS in 1981 and transferred its responsibilities to the Park Service.

5

HAS SUCCESS SPOILED THE NATIONAL PARKS?

The Park Service celebrated its 50th anniversary in 1966 with banquets, ceremonies, and, perhaps the highest honor of all, a spread in *National Geographic* magazine. The introduction was written by National Geographic Society president, Dr. Melville Bell Grosvenor, who had known every Park Service director since 1916.

Quoting the first director, Steve Mather, who said the parks "belong to everyone—now and always," Dr. Grosvenor observed that 130 million visitors would use and enjoy the national parks during the golden anniversary year. "In hundreds of articles dealing with the natural and historic treasures of our parks, the *Geographic* has always emphasized their use and enjoyment," said the magazine's editor. "I stress 'use and enjoy'; that after all, is the fundamental purpose of our parks as Congress established them." Noting that he was a lifelong wilderness enthusiast who knew "no greater pleasure than a pack trip into the solitude of timbered mountains," Dr. Grosvenor said, "I cannot agree with those who maintain that any improvement of a park—an access road, a modest lodge—violates the principles of conservation." Under the inspired leadership of two of the country's greatest conservationists, President and Mrs. Lyndon B. Johnson, he concluded, "the beauty of America rests secure."

National Geographic diligently avoids controversy, but in Dr. Grosvenor's emphasis upon park use he was challenging a prevailing theme in the national press. The previous month the *Wall Street Journal* had run a story on its front page under the headline, "Ah Wilderness; Severe Overcrowding Brings Ills of the City to Scenic Yosemite," in which it charged the Park Service with failing to protect Yosemite Valley from calamitous overuse: "The damp night air, heavy with a pall of eyewatering smoke, is cut by the blare of transistor radios, the clatter of pots and pans, the roar of a motorcycle, and the squeals of teenagers. Except for hundreds of shiny aluminum trailers and multicolored tents squeezed into camping areas, this might be any city after dark." On an average summer day, the story claimed, the valley contained three times the number of people per square mile of Los Angeles County.

Shortly, the *Christian Science Monitor,* hardly given to sensationalism, published a full page article by the naturalist Peter Farb. "Six years from now representatives of dozens of nations will converge on Yellowstone for a World Conference on Parks," he warned. "Instead of a remote wilderness, they will see before them a national slum, the disgrace of the American national park system." Dr. Grosvenor was gratified that 130 million visitors would have the opportunity to enjoy the parks during 1966; that level of use, Farb declared, would insure "the destruction of the national parks in our time."

What can be said of extravagant rhetoric of this stripe, of Farb's surly indictment of Park Service management as "an act of official vandalism"? Printing embellished descriptions of Yellowstone Lake, stating that it has been "practically destroyed" by thousands of motorboats and that almost all the wildlife and the great flocks of birds "have largely fled," undoubtedly sells newspapers, but in politics it would be placed in that special category of hyperbole known as campaign oratory.

Farb's diatribe was followed by a series of articles, some thoughtful and informed, some superficial and sensational, but all expressing variations on the same theme: the parks are being loved to death. In 1972, the 100th anniversary of Yellowstone, the *Saturday Review* coined one of the more catchy headlines for its cover: "National Parks: Pristine Preserves or Popcorn Playgrounds?" The litany of wrongdoing echoed Farb:

> Favored portions of many parks have become "wilderness slums," with trailers jammed cheek by jowl, clothesline displays like those outside tenements, and litter blanketing the ground—the welkin rent not by birdsong but by the blare of radios . . . visitors stumbling over each other, falling into hot springs, getting themselves chewed by bears. . . . How do we stop the national parks from withering into an obscenity that may soon be shunned alike by taxpayers and visitors from abroad?

By the Bicentennial year of 1976, criticism of conditions in the parks was undiminished, but the blame was now assigned to the Ford administration for its failure to adequately fund or staff the Park Service. "The Shame of the Parks," according to a *Newsweek* article, was a prolonged budget squeeze: "Beset by galloping growth, inadequate funds, and manpower shortages, many of the National Park Service's 285 parks, recreation areas, and historic sites are rapidly deteriorating." It was a matter of "More People, Less Priority, National Parks Near Collapse" in an *Audubon* magazine report that placed the blame on "economic niggardliness." Even Congress, in an unprecedented move, accepted some of the blame for shortcomings in the parks. The House Committee on Government Operations, in a report entitled *The Degradation of Our National Parks,* acknowledged, "The degradation of America's National Parks can be halted most quickly and economically by immediately increasing the budget and personnel ceilings of the National Park Service."

Interestingly, the delegates from eighty-three nations who assembled at Yellowstone in 1972 for a World Conference on National Parks did not, as Farb feared, regard the park as a disgrace. The delegate from Belgium, Prof. Jean-Paul Harroy, chairman of the International Commission on National Parks, who delivered a paper on the growth of the national park concept, said of Yellowstone: "It is still a model because its organization most certainly places it among the best managed of the world's national parks; from this point of view, managers of national parks throughout the world can use it as an example and visit it to take lessons and obtain ideas."

Democracy and the Parks

People problems in the parks, if one is to believe a famous British writer, can be traced back to the democratic leanings of early national park authorities who opened the gates to people of all classes. "Today I am in Yellowstone Park and I wish I were dead," exclaimed Rudyard Kipling on July 4, 1889. A reporter with seven years experience, although only twenty-three, Kipling was financing his first trip to the United States by writing travel accounts for his newspaper, the *Allahabad Pioneer* in India. The brash young Englishman with the fierce black mustache affected a tone of mock horror in his reports, but it is evident that he was alternately delighted and exasperated by the uncouth good humor and "ghastly vulgarity" of American tourists.

The unruly excursionists who pelted out of the train and shoved their way into Kipling's stagecoach were in an Independence Day mood: the horses wore American flags in their bridles, girls wore flags in their sashes, and all but the peevish Englishman sang patriotic songs and yelled the name of their home state when they passed other stages. Kipling damned the unruly trippers as they jumped from the stage at the hotel: "The tourists—may their master die an evil death at the hand of a mad locomotive—poured into that place with a joyful whoop, and, scarce washing the dust from themselves, began to celebrate the

4th of July." To Kipling's feigned horror, the minister elected by his companions to lead the exercises "rose up and told them they were the greatest, freest, sublimest, most chivalrous and richest people on the face of the earth, and they all said Amen."

At the time of Kipling's journey, a significant change was taking place in the travel habits of affluent Americans, made possible by completion of the transcontinental railroads and the rising prosperity that followed the Civil War. Pullman trains running daily from coast to coast advertised the advantages of associating with a refined and cultivated class, yet appearances could be deceiving. A tourist might lack the wardrobe or the social graces so highly esteemed by Kipling, but to his banker he was a gentleman.

The symbolism of the Independence Day festivities he witnessed in Yellowstone was overlooked by Kipling. It has been argued that the national park idea is a direct legacy of the spirit of democracy expressed in the Declaration of Independence. Because of the expense of travel, however, during Yellowstone's first fifty years it catered largely to the first class trade, and the park became a semiexclusive resort for the wealthy. It was operated in a way to discourage the less favored who, unable to afford train and stagecoach fares, arrived in their own wagons and buggies and economized by cooking their meals and camping along the roadsides. They were disdainfully called "sagebrushers" and regarded as a nuisance by the hotel and restaurant establishment, which derived little profit from them.

In 1903, when President Theodore Roosevelt spent two weeks camping in Yellowstone, he was asked to dedicate the imposing new entrance arch built opposite the Northern Pacific depot to provide a more formal entrance for railroad passengers. Generally remembered as a big game hunter who relished blood sports, Roosevelt was also an accomplished field naturalist who entered Harvard already decided upon a career in science and was a nationally recognized ornithologist while still a teenager. Roosevelt used the dedication occasion to speak to the genius of the Yellowstone Act. "I cannot too often repeat that the essential feature in the present management of the Yellowstone Park, as in all similar places, is its essential democracy," said the president, who arrived at the ceremony riding a spirited horse and escorted by two troops of cavalry from Fort Yellowstone. "It is the preservation of the scenery, of the forests, of the wilderness life and the wilderness game for the people as a whole, instead of leaving the enjoyment thereof to be confined to the very rich who can control private reserves."

American technology, at the time of Roosevelt's speech, was providing the means of making his democratic goal a reality. That same year the Olds Motor Works in Detroit turned out 5,000 automobiles on its new assembly line. By 1910, newly established automobile associations were promoting the construction of cross-country highways. The first cars entered Mr. Rainier National Park in 1908, Crater Lake in 1911, and Glacier in 1912, but despite appeals from motorists, automobiles continued to be banned from Yellowstone and Yosemite.

There was considerable opposition to automobiles in these parks. It came from the railroads, fearful of losing passenger traffic; from the park concessioners with substantial investments in horse transportation (the Yellowstone system required nearly 1,500 horses, 400 coaches, wagons and surreys, and 250 drivers); and from a few far-sighted wilderness defenders who feared the automobiles would forever destroy solitude in the parks. The British ambassador, Lord James Bryce, issued a prophetic warning before cars were permitted in Yosemite. "If Adam had known what harm the serpent was going to work, he would have tried to prevent him from finding lodgment in Eden; and if you were to realize what the result of the automobile will be in that wonderful, that incomparable Valley, you will keep it out."

The automobile was, of course, more than a new exhibit of technology; it immediately began to transform the American life style by bringing the faraway places within reach. On August 1, 1915, the ban on automobiles was lifted in Yellowstone (Yosemite had begun admitting cars in 1913); in the few remaining weeks of the season, nearly 1,000 motorized vehicles were admitted, following a schedule calculated to keep machines and horse-drawn vehicles thirty minutes apart. Their predictions of economic disaster forgotten, the concessioners sold their horses and mules to the British army fighting in France and purchased more than 100 motor buses: the democratization of Yellowstone was underway.

Yellowstone admitted 10,000 automobiles by 1920, many piled high with tents, blankets, and food, "everything but their own scenery," said an observer. "I had a few days after I got my wheat out," remarked a farmer from Kansas, "so I just loaded my family in the old bus and lit out." Viewing the merrymaking of the "great unwashed," some who remembered the carriage-trade days of Yellowstone shared the view of cowboy artist J. M. Moore. He told a journalist, "A fellow used to meet people worth knowing in the old days, now he meets a lot of eighth graders and housemaids dressed up to kill and nothing to back it up. A forty dollar saddle on a five dollar pony. I wonder if you've got the guts to put this in print."

As early as the 1920s there were many who sided with Lord Bryce. The only difference between Yosemite Valley and downtown Los Angeles, one wag remarked, was that Yosemite had trees and no traffic cops while Los Angeles had traffic cops and no trees. Yet the only tenable position a Park Service director could have taken was to open the parks to all citizens. Today the Roosevelt Arch, as it is now called, is no longer on the main entrance road, and only a few visitors drive by to take pictures of the handsome stone structure and read the credo of the Yellowstone Act carved above the keystone: FOR THE BENEFIT AND ENJOYMENT OF THE PEOPLE. Few realize that through this gateway passed the millions of automobiles, in the years between the two world wars, that were the instrument for democratizing Yellowstone.

The Zion Solution

Critics who believe decisive steps must be taken to protect parks against the "hordes" generally direct their demands to the Park Service. "Do something!" they implore the director, under the mistaken assumption that, should he so decide, he could immediately place restrictions on the number of people allowed in the parks. Policy decisions of any importance are never formulated and carried out by the director unilaterally, for he is appointed by and serves at the pleasure of the secretary of the Interior. Matters of substance are routinely cleared first through the Department of the Interior and discussed with public groups and in most cases with the key members of the Interior committees on the Hill. Any action taken in a park that might affect local economic interests can galvanize a powerful counterattack. If constituent pressure builds up, congressional intervention can follow, as in the case of a concession squabble in Zion National Park a few years ago.

At stake was the one issue on which the general public, politicians, and conservationists cannot seem to agree: should concession facilities remain in the parks or be moved outside. During 1972, the Yellowstone Centennial year, the Park Service and the Centennial Commission sponsored an exhaustive analysis of park problems by private citizens. The task force on Preservation of National Park Values opened its review of concession policy with the declaration, "Entrenched concessionaries constitute a vested interest and a potential threat to the preservation function of the National Park Service." The task force, a blue ribbon panel representing conservation organizations, writers, scientists, and university professors, presented a single recommendation: "The National Park Service should work toward the elimination of private ownership of buildings and facilities by concessionaries preliminary to the movement of all such facilities outside the parks."

The Park Service has always taken the position that although general policies can be applied to all parks, thoughtful consideration of local differences is required. For example, the boundaries of Yellowstone and

Grand Teton are only a few miles apart, yet their concession problems are completely different. Most Yellowstone facilities are ancient, requiring extensive repair and replacement on a scale beyond the financial capability of a private entrepreneur—and visitor complaints are constant. At Grand Teton, established in 1950, a Rockefeller nonprofit corporation built and operates facilities that are modern, attractive, and well run—and there are few complaints.

At Zion, the Park Service agreed with conservationists that the overnight accommodations contributed to an already crowded area and should be removed. More than a million people were congregating in a single narrow canyon during the summer season, a situation resembling Yosemite. The facilities were nearly worn out, and when Union Pacific abandoned its unprofitable operation and donated its holdings to the government, the Park Service obtained general agreement that they should be phased out. At the request of the Utah congressional delegation, to allow the neighboring communities time to gear up, the Park Service leased the facilities to TWA Services, Inc., for five years, with the stipulation that when the lease expired in 1975, the buildings would be razed.

However, as the time for termination of the Zion concession approached, opposition began to develop. To suspicious observers there were elements of a well-orchestrated campaign involving TWA Services, Inc., the Utah congressional delegation, and the governor of Utah. Senator Jake Garn declared the Park Service policy was being influenced by a tiny minority of purists: "It has been our feeling that the in-park experience should be a part of everyone's heritage and not restricted only to those young and hardy enough to backpack and camp out." Governor Calvin Rampton spoke of a "devastating" economic impact, predicting the traveling public would bypass the region, threatening the solvency of motel, restaurant, and service station owners.

Members of the Conference of Concessioners chose to regard the Zion action as a threat to all park concessioners and consulted with their friends in Congress. Somehow the controversy was escalated into a debate over the sanctity of private enterprise in the parks. When director Gary Everhardt read a speech in the *Congressional Record* by Henry ("Scoop") Jackson, powerful chairman of the Senate Interior Committee, denouncing the Zion proposal as the beginning of a Park Service scheme to evict other concessioners and to reverse congressional policy, he knew the battle was lost.

Everhardt received his comeuppance formally when he was summoned to a meeting in the office of Senator Frank Moss, where the members of the Utah delegation and Governor Rampton were gathered to receive the final Park Service decision. The discussion was gentlemanly;

it was not necessary to mention that should the director fail to abandon his Zion plan, retribution in the form of massive retaliation against the Park Service legislative program would be inflicted. Everhardt made a last effort to bargain, inserting in the draft press release a statement that although the Park Service had decided to extend the Zion concession contract for seven years, the facilities ultimately were to be phased out. Senator Moss promptly struck the offending sentence, announcing to the press that the Park Service had reached "a good solution."

In the aftermath, the conservationists who had watched the hostilities from the sidelines and urged director Everhardt to stand tall, now accused him of caving in to political pressure. He was heard to say that their comments reminded him of a similar experience when he was superintendent of Grand Teton, opposing demands by local businessmen to enlarge the airport. "When the firing started and I looked around for help, I found I was standing alone."

Some solace was received a few months later from the *Times-Independence* in Moab, Utah, which usually has its own bone to pick with the Park Service over matters in nearby Canyonlands National Park.

> A few months ago, Congressional delegates from the west were nearly unanimous in their criticism of the National Park Service for attempting to kick a poor private concessioner out of Zion. The proposed "kick-out" was one which had been targeted for a number of years, and one which the concession operator was aware of when he took the contract.
>
> The pressure from congressional quarters was enough to convince the Director of the National Park Service that the proposed action ought to be postponed for a few years and the termination was cancelled, at least for the present.
>
> Now Congress is hopping on the other foot. The National Park Service is being accused by a Congressional Committee of being run by the big business interests that control monopoly concessions in a number of the larger parks. Those interests are dictating policy to the NPS, the solons say. I'm wondering if those fellows back there ever talk to each other (or more important, listen to each other). The NPS can't win for losing. . . .

"Parks Are for People"

Although it was not originally intended to signal any great change in policy, in the 1960s the Park Service informally adopted a phrase "Parks are for people," which perhaps understandably provoked suspicion among those who believed there were already too many people in the parks. "Scratch a well-trained employee of the Department of the Interior and instead of saying 'Ouch!,' he will most likely chant 'Parks are for the people'!" reported the Sierra Club *Bulletin* in one of its more fevered indictments. The expression almost bordered on the platitudinous, but there seemed to be hidden subtleties that caused people to choose up sides.

Edward Abbey, whose *Desert Solitaire* is a wry and rebellious—and classic—account of his life as a park ranger at Arches National Monument, viewed the maxim as a public relations gimmick, designed for "the indolent millions born on wheels and suckled on gas." Decoded, parks are for people "means that parks are for people-in-automobiles," said Abbey, who offered some "constructive, practical, sensible proposals" for the salvation of both parks and people. Make everyone walk into the parks, "or ride horses, bicycles, mules, wild pigs—anything—but keep the automobiles and the motorcycles and all their motorized relatives out."

The slogan did, nevertheless, reflect the prevailing sentiment of the Johnson administration whose Great Society programs were directed to improving the quality of life of all citizens, with a special focus on the economically disadvantaged. Lyndon Johnson articulated a new philosophy about the role and purpose of national parks. Historically, parks were created because of their intrinsic values, and almost all were in the remote West. It was time for the nation to take a different view, the president declared when he signed legislation authorizing the Fire Island and Assateague national seashores near the population centers of New York and Baltimore-Washington. Parks must be more readily accessible; sites should be chosen which would bring nature closer to people.

There were other critics of traditional conservation philosophy, some holding that wilderness preservation was so removed from the plight of inner city dwellers that the conservation movement could be accused of pristine elitism. Rather than national parks being endangered by excessive numbers of visitors, too large a segment of the population had been denied any access to the parks. These critics held that wilderness preservationists were ignoring crucial social problems, that they responded more readily to shore birds doomed by oil spills than to poverty and crime in the inner cities.

An article in *Parks and Recreation* magazine entitled "Is the National Parks Movement Anti-Urban?" promoted considerable discussion when it suggested the conservation movement might be accused of being "anti-black, anti-minority, and anti-poor in its actual practice. It is dedicated to a mystic philosophy which has the net effect of trying to preserve a corner of the world for the exclusive preserve of a white upper-middle class for their play and recreation." Saying that problems of race and poverty have never been matters of primary concern to conservation groups, the author advanced an intriguing premise: everyone fortunate enough to have enjoyed the wonders of the natural world would surely agree that all segments of the population have something of value to find there: Logically, then, if conservation organizations are not antiurban, they should play a positive role in facilitating the enjoyment of parks by a great many more people, particularly the economically disadvantaged of the inner cities.

A young black delegate to the Maryland General Assembly, the urban environment director of the Izaak Walton League, put the issue bluntly to a recent conference of national park supintendents. "I do not believe that an American born in the Anacostia area in Washington, D.C., has any less need for a quality outdoor experience than does a boy born in northern Minnesota's lake region or the redwoods country of California." He expressed hope that the Park Service would not espouse the elitism "born of a time when conservationists found it both possible and comfortable to avoid delving into the gut, controversial issues—racial harmony, jobs, etc. I say that day is gone."

An idea that quickly attracted support from both conservationists and those concerned with urban needs was developed by the New York Regional Plan Association. It was a proposal to incorporate several isolated pieces of city and federally owned shorefront into a New York Harbor National Seashore. Few proposed new parks have received such a warm welcome, and, with administration approval, the Park Service assigned a planning team to investigate. As the project picked up momentum, additional sites were identified, including two outdated harbor defense installations and the rundown naval air station at Floyd Bennet field—"picking the bones of the military dinosaurs" as one planner described the process.

When the planning was completed, the blueprint for a park at the entrance to New York harbor included 26,000 acres in two states made up of assorted pieces of holly forest, beaches, and salt marsh along with forts, airports, and landfills. When the legislation for a Gateway National Recreation Area was submitted, it was regarded as a natural, a remarkable opportunity to provide for the people of New York and New Jersey what the western national parks were too far away to do and what the city of New York was incapable of doing.

Conservationists, seeking a way to provide urbanites with a national park experience that did not threaten the wilderness, lined up behind the bill. The Park Service, which had been given a new slogan by the administration, "Bringing parks to people," described the urban park concept as a valid modern outgrowth of the original Yellowstone idea. The New York city government, offered an extensive park system to be bankrolled by the federal government, was understandably enthusiastic. ("It is so good," said an Interior assistant secretary of the Gateway proposal, "that any mayor who didn't say 'that's what I want!' is nuts.")

Even the political winds were blowing from the right direction. In 1972, as Richard Nixon campaigned for reelection, there was a second urban park bill before Congress, a proposed Golden Gate National Recreation Area for San Francisco. Nixon backed both bills as election-year gifts to voters from the two states that happened to have the first and third largest representation in the Electoral College. There was bipartisan support in Congress, and the two "Gateways" were added to the system.

The Park Service was not of one mind about urban parks, and there was a minority opinion that the Park Service was being used to solve social problems. "I'm not against urban parks," said a Service executive, "but what the hell is our policy?" Most people in the organization welcomed the new additions; others, while yearning to be included with the enlightened, had misgivings. If a collection of city parks and excess federal property in New York added up to a national park, what about all the other major cities in the country? No one denied that cities desperately needed attractive, well-run outdoor recreation spaces, but was this the role of the National Park Service? Most portions of Gateway are not served by public transportation: will access to it ever be anything but a dream to the low income families for whom it was presumably established?

As a solution to the recreation problems of a few large cities, urban national parks have been a theoretical success, but the appropriate role of the Park Service has not been well defined. By reason of its traditions, its employee selection, its training, and its agency mission, the Service has had a difficult time adjusting to the city environment. The debate over urban parks—several more having been added since the New York and San Francisco parks—continues, although when the Reagan administration slapped a moratorium on land acquisition for the new urban areas, their development was effectively halted.

Contradictory Conclusions

The evidence presented in the nation's press by presumably well-informed journalists seems to prove conclusively that the national parks, once undefiled, are going to hell. It has also become common knowledge, even the subject of cartoons, that the parks are so heavily congested in the summer that they should be avoided. But anyone who examines these two charges thoroughly is likely to come up with more contradictions than conclusions.

First of all, people who know the history of the parks would dissent from the popular view that in the good old days—presumably before the automobile brought disaster—the parks were totally unspoiled. In 1890 Yosemite National Park was established surrounding Yosemite Valley, with the valley still under state jurisdiction. There were so many complaints about conditions in the valley that in 1891 the Interior Department ordered an investigation. According to the report, the appearance of Yosemite Valley nearly thirty years after it was ceded to California was as follows.

"Great destruction" was evident in all parts of the valley. Much of the land had been cleared of trees and vegetation and the timber fed to a local sawmill. Some of the lumber was used to construct facilities, some for fuel and fenceposts, and the remainder simply removed to provide tillable land. More than half the valley was fenced with barbed wire to protect a large-scale agricultural enterprise—fields plowed and planted with grass and grain to provide revenue for the state. The unenclosed portion of the valley had been converted into pasture where the transportation company grazed its horses and mules to the exclusion of wildlife. The fencing and cultivation confined park visitors to a narrow space between the fences and the walls of the valley. "These acts of spoilation and trespass have been permitted for a number of years," the report concluded, "and seem to have become a part of the settled policy of management." In 1906 California gave the valley back to the federal government as a part of Yosemite National Park.

The photographer Ansel Adams first visited Yosemite in 1916, only three years after automobiles were admitted. The situation then left much to be desired, Adams remembered in a recent interview. Because roads were unpaved, there was a heavy coat of dust over trees and meadows, and people camped wherever they pleased all over the valley. Even with many more people today, "The whole thing is vastly improved," said Adams. Asked to compare present conditions with the Yosemite he had closely observed for more than sixty years, Adams replied, "It's now more beautiful than it's ever been."

The statistics of park use tend to mislead people into believing that parks will shortly be buried under a tide of visitors. In 1960 there were 80 million visits to the national park system; by 1980 the total had passed 300 million. This implies that the number of visits to each park has increased nearly 400 percent. Actually, as has been observed, travel to many of the larger parks has leveled off.

In April 1972, during the Yellowstone Centennial, the *Congressional Record* printed an example of crystal gazing into the future of national parks. The article predicted that in only ten years, by 1982, the parks would be forced to end their traditional policy of welcoming all visitors. By that date the parks would be limited to those who had made advance reservations, and these fortunate people would be required to leave their cars at the park entrances and transfer to some other form of transportation. One of the most experienced writers on the parks, Bob Cahn, won a Pulitzer Prize for his 1968 series, "Will Success Spoil the National Parks?," and one of his essays was a forecast of how people would experience Yellowstone in 1984. Barring a disaster, the predicted revolution will not take place, and a family will see Yellowstone in 1984 just as it did in 1968.

A reporter for the *Washington Post* who had heard about one Yellowstone National Park, the one you are supposed to avoid unless you don't mind crowd scenes, wrote his story about "the other Yellowstone—the ninety percent of the 3,472 square miles (bigger than the state of Delaware) that those thousands of people in cars never see." The writer and his family spent days hiking into peaceful landscapes "that make the heart leap," seldom seeing another human being. "It was like having Yellowstone to yourself—seeing it much as the Indians had seen it. The experience was indeed uplifting."

The "other Yellowstone" that so few people ever see exists in all parks just beyond the roadside. Probably fewer than 5 percent of park visitors head for the backcountry, as remote and untouched as the most determined solitary or the most persistent critic of overuse could hope for. There may be crowds at Old Faithful, but primitive country is not far away. During the summer of 1978 a man was attacked by a grizzly within a few hundred feet of Old Faithful geyser; a few weeks later a woman was mauled by a grizzly on a trail within a mile of the main road.

There is one charge that unfailingly raises the hackles of Park Service people—the mindless assertion that places like Yosemite Valley are veritable "slums." Congestion exists in Yosemite, but it does not equate to squalor. Those who picture Yosemite Valley as a slum forfeit their credentials as responsible observers.

Perhaps it depends upon your point of view. One of the shrewdest and most combative of the conservation writers, Mike Frome, has been scolding the Park Service over a good many years for failing to live up to his stern standards. Frome contributed a commentary to the *Washington Post* in April 1981, "Parks in Peril," which described conditions in Yellowstone: "Congestion, noise, intrusions of man-made structures, pollution from too many automobiles and vandalism all interfere with enjoyment of the natural scene." Frome also authors the Rand McNally annual *National Park Guide,* but in this travel-encouraging publication the parks seem much more attractive, American treasures "that inspire, instruct and stimulate spiritual well being." Yellowstone is said to have unsullied spaciousness that constitutes "a stronghold for people—where city dwellers can stretch their legs beneath a clear sky and parents can show their kids one tremendous unspoiled section reminiscent of what the continent was like."

A few years ago Frome, who has precious little respect for the decision makers in any land-managing agency, publicly washed his hands of everyone in the field, condemning them beyond redemption. "I know of no single federal agency now aggressively committed to protection of the environment or the resources in its trust." In his parks guide, however, Frome speaks with unrestrained approval of "the ever-growing popularity of the national parks." This is, he declares, a tribute to Park Service management practices that pay valuable dividends, "for winning friends wins supporters as well."

PHOTOGRAPHS

When the War Department turned over administration of Yellowstone to the Park Service in 1918, Jim McBride, who had been an army scout in the park since 1900, was appointed chief ranger. In 1921 he exchanged his horse for this motorized contraption. (Courtesy National Park Service)

Carrying a disassembled ski litter, a ranger patrol prepares for a winter rescue mission in Rocky Mountain National Park. (Courtesy National Park Service)

Action on Mt. Rainier's Paradise Glacier in the 1920s. Above, a party of hikers at the edge of a crevasse with an ice bridge spanning the river beyond. (Courtesy National Park Service) Below, intrepid visitors enjoy "Nature Coasting" wearing the breeches furnished by the guide department. According to the original caption, "Usually before the end of the slide is reached the order of starting has been considerably disarranged." (Courtesy National Park Service)

In a bygone era, when guests were treasured by park concessioners, maids, waiters and waitresses, and bellboys would gather to serenade departing guests. Above, a "Sing Away" at the Lodge in Zion National Park. (Courtesy National Park Service) Below, the full staff of Aztec Ruins National Monument in letter-perfect uniforms, ready to greet the first visitors on a sunny morning in June 1940. (Courtesy National Park Service)

A number of women joined the ranger ranks when educational programs were initiated during the 1920s. In 1929, Herma Baggley was serving as a summer naturalist in Yellowstone. She became a permanent naturalist, married a ranger, and coauthored the standard work, *Plants of Yellowstone National Park.* (Courtesy National Park Service)

Seeking to boost passenger traffic, the railroads built the first decent accommodations in the parks. "A great improvement on the tents," Yellowstone's superintendent reported in 1904 when the Northern Pacific completed Old Faithful Inn. It was a model of rustic graciousness with its great balconied and raftered lobby eight stories high. (Courtesy National Park Service)

A horseback party saddles up at Many Glacier Hotel, built by the Great Northern in Glacier National Park. (Courtesy National Park Service)

The charismatic first director, Steve Mather, who delighted in wearing the Park Service uniform and being mistaken for a ranger, formally inaugurated the 1928 travel season in Yellowstone by opening a gate fashioned of elk antlers. (Courtesy National Park Service)

Russ Dickenson, called "a consummate professional" when appointed director in 1980, began his career as a Grand Canyon ranger in 1947. (Courtesy National Park Service)

Left, Horace Albright, while superintendent of Yellowstone, 1919–1929. Albright helped lobby the Park Service bill through Congress in 1916, succeeded Mather as director, and received the Medal of Freedom, the country's highest civilian award, from President Jimmy Carter in 1980. (Courtesy National Park Service) Right, widely esteemed for *Interpreting Our Heritage* and his other books on the parks, as well as for his puckish humor, Freeman Tilden concluded his unique 40-year association with the Park Service as a "literary consultant," just short of his ninetieth birthday, in 1971. (Courtesy National Park Service)

Above, a fetching tableau at Yellowstone's Handkerchief Pool in 1922. A popular place for young ladies to launder their handkerchiefs, the hot spring was destroyed by vandals a few years later. (Courtesy National Park Service) Below, stylish travelers touring the parks in 1925 paused to display their sturdy van, complete with pet dog, window curtains, and tilting windshield. (Courtesy National Park Service)

Although automobiles were not allowed to enter Yosemite until 1913, this Stanley Steamer entered the Valley shortly after 1900; Half Dome is in the background. (Courtesy National Park Service)

In "Auto Stages" furnished by the Mt. Rainier concessioner, guests set out from Paradise Inn for the return journey to Seattle and Tacoma. (Courtesy National Park Service)

Second generation Park Service families are not uncommon. Above, Forest S. "Chief" Townsley, redoubtable chief ranger of Yosemite for nearly thirty years (3rd from right), picnicked with Mrs. Eleanor Roosevelt beneath the giant sequoias in 1940. (Courtesy National Park Service) Below, his son John, who was born in Yosemite and went on to become superintendent of Yellowstone, welcomed President Gerald Ford back to that park in 1976. Ford was a Yellowstone summer ranger (in 1936), as was his son Jack. (Courtesy Gerald R. Ford Library)

During the fall color season, automobile traffic overwhelms Mabry Mill, above, one of the most photogenic attractions along the Blue Ridge Parkway. Many parks have introduced alternate transportation systems to reduce such congestion: In Yosemite National Park, below, shuttle buses and even horse-drawn vehicles help to remove automobiles from popular spots. (Courtesy National Park Service)

SUTLER STORE
200'th PENN
J. BONTZ PROP
LLA
5¢
Bottle
MARSH
WHEELING

The Park Service has emphasized interpretation ever since Steve Mather concluded that education is a primary function of the parks. Left, a living history demonstrator relaxes on the counter of a Civil War store at Fredericksburg, Virginia. Above and below, interpreters at Golden Gate National Recreation Area, San Francisco, illustrate Freeman Tilden's axiom that provocation, not just dry education, is the goal of interpretation. (Courtesy National Park Service)

The national park system contains many kinds of "pleasuring grounds" (a term Congress used in the Yellowstone legislation). Above, rangers deal with a beach incident at the Sandy Hook section of Gateway National Recreation Area, New York City. Below, backpackers head for the Alaska Range in Denali (formerly Mount McKinley) National Park. (Courtesy National Park Service)

6

THREATS TO THE PARKS

National park legislation restricts the jurisdiction of the Park Service to the lands inside park boundaries; appropriated funds, with few exceptions, may not be spent outside the parks. Protection ends at the park boundary. Inside the park everything is planned; beyond the park anything goes, including the development of such flashy gateway towns as Gettysburg or Gatlinburg. Traveling to a national park in the lovely British countryside is a different experience. The parks in Britain are largely designations of sizable areas that include towns and villages and farms. Yet the land-use laws against indiscriminate development are so strict that it is literally impossible to tell where national park boundaries begin or end. British visitors are heard to remark that Americans have an ambivalent attitude toward their countryside; they want everything protected inside the parks, but they want no restrictions elsewhere.

In earlier days, when parks were generally far removed from population centers, there was little concern for outside threats. Rangers focused their efforts on protecting parks from fires, poachers, and souvenir hunters, allowing nature to take its course. This approach worked reasonably well until the world began to shrink and the cities to sprawl into the countryside.

Today it is a different matter. The current search for new energy sources has brought 143 applications to the Forest Service from mining firms for permission to drill into the geothermal lands along the western borders of Yellowstone, within a few miles of the Old Faithful geyser basin. There are other warning signs. The burning of fossil fuels on a prodigious scale is releasing disturbing amounts of sulphur dioxide into the atmosphere. No one can estimate the impact of the resulting acid rain on the forests and waters of the national parks or the effects of dumping toxic wastes into the tributary streams. The consequences of burning coal in the power plants of the Southwest are becoming more evident, as a region that once had some of the clearest skies in America is now being pockmarked by plumes from the generating stacks.

Chaco Canyon

Along an eight-mile section of a broad shallow valley in northern New Mexico stands the imposing and classic ruin of Pueblo Bonito ("beautiful village"), the finest known example of pueblo architecture—800 rooms covering three acres, masonry walls rising forty feet, 2 central plazas holding 32 ceremonial kivas. At the time William the Conqueror invaded England, the civilization in Chaco Canyon was in full flower. Farmers tended a new strain of corn traded north from Mexico; the apartment houses of mortared sandstone grew ever more massive; people from the outlands were lured by the thriving culture until the canyon's population reached 7,000, perhaps the largest concentration of Indians in the prehistoric Southwest.

The remains of a dozen or more of these splendid pueblos, abandoned in the late thirteenth century by the Anasazi, the Ancient Ones, are preserved in Chaco Cultural National Historical Park. A series of expeditions in the 1920s excavated the ruins, and during the past decade a large-scale research project, involving several institutions, has sought to unravel the compelling mysteries of Chaco Canyon. How did such a large population live prosperously in such a barren region? Did the people vanish because of a great drought, raids, soil exhaustion, or disease? Using remote sensing devices archeologists have traced the extensive pattern of flood control dams and mapped the hundreds of miles of arrow-straight roads, some as much as forty feet wide. They lead in all directions out of the canyon, these roads over which abalone shells were brought from the coast of California and live scarlet macaws from Guatemala.

Even in a country noted for its distances and solitude, Chaco Canyon is remote. But it is located in the rich San Juan Basin and almost surrounded by huge coal and uranium reserves, nearly one-fourth of the nation's strippable coal and one-sixth of the world's known supply of uranium. Deposits of uranium have been discovered within a few hundred yards of the monument boundary. A Park Service official described the situation:

> My God, we've got all kinds of uranium smelting plants going up out there. They are going to run the biggest coal strip mines in the country out there. They want to haul uranium on thirty-ton trucks right square through the middle of the monument. Forty companies are looking at sixty uranium mines, several thousand feet deep, in which they'll puncture as

> many as eleven fossil water aquifiers. They're talking about pumping up to 5,000 gallons a minute of radioactive water out to mine the uranium. They'll dump that on the surface and it will run into the monument.

Should the sixty uranium mines now on the drawing boards go in, they would pump out each year as much water as is used by Los Angeles, dropping the water table thousands of feet, with uncontrollable results. Water drainage would likely carry away the canyon's light soil and undermine its ruins. Heavy uranium trucks already are registering on the park's seismograph; a substantial increase in this travel could endanger the walls of Pueblo Bonito. If a projected coal-hauling railroad is built along the edge of the monument, its rumblings could cause more damage than the uranium trucks. Asked to evaluate the seriousness of these threats, the official replied, "They even asked the superintendent how did he want the park when they were through: up on a pedestal or down a hole?"

As these threats pile up on Chaco Canyon, research investigations are revealing that it may have been the most significant prehistoric cultural center in the Southwest, the hub of a vast civilization with thousands of outlying towns. But before the story of Chaco Canyon can be deciphered, energy development may obliterate the record. Chaco Canyon may be a test case; pressure for development in the region is relentless. National parks pay no taxes. Taxes on full-scale uranium development could bring New Mexico upwards of $1 billion a year and thousands of jobs. Counties that receive more than 50 percent of their income from taxes on mining companies are inclined to believe the parks must give way. One New Mexico booster of energy production was quoted as saying, "What is Chaco Canyon—a private playground for a select group of federal employees and special citizens."

"Some people say the Four Corners area might have to become a national sacrifice area," observed the Chaco Canyon superintendent. "Are we so poor that we have to use that kind of rhetoric? Mining need not be exclusive. If we go about it in a cooperative way, there are acceptable compromises." But on a patch of private land inside Lassen Volcanic National Park in California, an oil company bulldozed a site the size of a football field and drilled nearly a mile into the earth, hoping to tap the geothermal reservoir that feeds the park's geysers and hot springs. No prior research was done, although the test well was within a mile and a half of Boiling Springs Lake, believed to be the largest such lake in the world. "It's something you have to live with," said the superintendent of Chaco Canyon. "You're constantly aware that at any time an agency or a county will make an effort to option you out of your land."

The State of the Parks

Unaccountably, the Park Service has no collective record of the extent of these adverse impacts. Scientific research has only gradually achieved standing in the organization, partly because the tradition in the natural areas has been to protect the resources rather than to study them. Congress has taken a generally dim view of Park Service requests for research funds. It seems to be under the assumption that biological investigations of wildlife are interminable and deal with trivialities, seldom possessing any more validity than an attempt to discover why the population of hoary marmots is fractionally lower in odd-numbered years.

Nearly twenty years ago a report prepared by a special committee from the National Academy of Sciences admonished the Service for the poverty of its research emphasis. Unless the organization took immediate steps to better understand the workings of park ecosystems, charged the committee, it was entirely possible that in the near future many, if not all, of the national parks "will be degraded to a state totally different from that for which they were preserved and in which they were to be enjoyed."

Interestingly, two former park rangers now on the staff of the National Parks Subcommittee of the House Interior Committee tactfully drew the attention of the Park Service to the virtues of taking a comprehensive view of the troubling threats to the parks. Through their intervention, the subcommittee officially requested the Park Service to assess existing and potential forces that might be damaging or threatening to the parks. In 1980, after a one-year review, the Service submitted its findings to Congress in a report entitled *State of the Parks.*

"National Parks—An Endangered Species?" and "Parks Under Siege" were typical newspaper headlines when the report was made public, for the findings of the investigation were ominous. No park in the system was immune to internal and external pressures and "these threats are causing significant and demonstrable damage." Unless some mitigating actions could be devised, the report concluded, "this degradation or loss of resources is irreversible."

The scenic landscape was reported impaired in more than 60 percent of the parks. Air quality was endangered in more than 45 percent of the areas. The sixty-three parks greater than 30,000 acres in size (roughly fifty square miles) registered more than double the number of threats than did the smaller units. Immense and unspoiled segments of primitive America such as Yellowstone, Yosemite, Great Smoky Mountains, Everglades, and Glacier "were at one time pristine areas surrounded and protected by vast wilderness regions," the report noted. "Today, with their surrounding buffer zones gradually disappearing, many of those parks are experiencing significant and widespread adverse effects associated with external encroachment."

Not all of the problems attracted headlines, but others were no less serious: poor sanitation in the backcountry; algal growth in caves caused by lights; trails eroded down to bedrock from heavy use; harassment and feeding of wildlife; tamarisk successfully competing for water with native plants in desert areas; establishment of exotics, such as the ice plant and Brazilian pepper tree, that pose extreme management problems ("Others, such as the ubiquitous dandelion are not so pressing"); infestations of pine beetle and gypsy moth, balsam wooly aphids and fire ants; brown trout imported from Europe to improve fishing—and even Dutch Elm disease in the trees on the White House lawn.

The report identified seventy-three different kinds of threats; as the headline indicated, some parks, such as Glacier, did seem to be under siege. There has already been exploratory drilling for oil near the Glacier boundary, and leases are being sought for coal, gas, and oil development. Logging along tributary streams is causing leaching of nitrites and phosphates into park waters; soils and forests are being contaminated by emissions from an aluminum smelter only six miles away; the program to mark the U.S.–Canadian international boundary (which is also the Glacier boundary) by spraying with pesticides is a pervasive threat to plant and animal life.

One of the most dangerous threats to the national parks will come from the inexorable search for energy, principally in the West. The superintendents of almost all the Rocky Mountain parks indicate they are no longer able to assure visitors of clean air and good visibility as a result of pollution from power plants and industrial operations near their parks. Smog from Los Angeles frequently rolls into Death Valley, darkening vistas that were once crystal clear. There are days when you can scarcely see the valley from the Dante's View overlook, a ranger reported. "It's just a sheet of brown."

A massive drive is presently under way to exploit the abundant sources of energy-producing minerals of the Southwest, particularly in a remarkable region of high plateaus and deep canyons in southern Utah. Here, within a rough square no more than 150 miles on a side, lies a country of such wild and varied beauty that some who know it well contend it has no equal on earth. In this relatively small stretch are five national parks—Zion, Bryce Canyon, Capitol Reef, Arches, and Canyonlands—along with Cedar Breaks National Monument and Glen Canyon National Recreation Area on Lake Powell. Grand Canyon National Park is only another fifty miles farther south. Other portions of this area are certifiably worthy of national park status.

The character of the region and its parks could be permanently altered by massive proposals now in the planning stage. One such project, the Allen-Warner Valley Energy System, recently placed upon the Critical Energy Facility list (energy projects that would reduce the nation's dependence upon imported oil), would open a strip mine only five miles from Bryce Canyon. The heavy blasting required would create dust clouds, reduce visibility, and possibly poison the ground water. In addition, there are plans to construct a coal-fired generating plant only seventeen miles from Zion, open a strip mine next to Capitol Reef, and reclaim tar sands that underlie parts of Glen Canyon.

The parks are being caught in the middle of a squeeze as cities reach out for a thousand miles to tap sources of energy. An Environmental Protection Agency monitoring station in Canyonlands has detected smog originating in Los Angeles, 600 miles away. For 100 days a year the view from the rim of Grand Canyon is obscured by haze from nearby power plants and smelters and by pollutants from urban centers. "We thought we were leaving smog in Denver," wrote one visitor in the Arches complaint register. "What's that chemical smell in the air?" asked another.

The Fight For a Grand Teton National Park

According to the *State of the Parks* report, more parks, a total of 153, were threatened by approaching industrial and private land developments than by any other factor. This kind of encroachment has become so prevalent in recent years throughout the country that it is known as the "adjacent lands" problem. Cities expand into the countryside, and people seek relief from the urban overload by building second homes; fast-food stands, motels, and souvenir shops congregate around popular vacation places; the open space around parks, which once seemed secure, begins to disappear. Jackson Hole, in Grand Teton National Park, has been one of the most widely discussed and intensively studied examples of the adjacent lands question.

The story of the establishment of Grand Teton, basic to the Jackson Hole story, is clearly worthy of a digression; some call it the greatest conservation battle of the twentieth century. Dragging on for more than twenty-five years, the park idea was set in motion by Horace Albright when he was superintendent of Yellowstone, bankrolled by John D. Rockefeller, Jr., and attacked by Jackson Hole residents. The controversy pitted the Park Service against the Forest Service, became entangled first in Wyoming and then national politics, and ultimately required the personal intervention of the president of the United States.

In the year the Park Service was established, 1916, Steve Mather and Albright first visited the Tetons on a trip from Yellowstone (Jackson Hole lies only thirty miles south of the Yellowstone boundary). The Teton range—in which sixteen peaks exceed 11,000 feet—rising abruptly and dramatically from the rolling green meadows and sage flats of the Jackson Hole, dominates one of the country's most spectacular landforms. The area must become a national park, Mather and Albright agreed. A Park Service bill to add the Tetons to Yellowstone passed the House in 1919, but expected Senate passage was blocked by Idaho sheep grazers who preferred Forest Service administration. (An inconsequential Teton National Park actually was established in 1929, a "stingy, skimpy, niggardly little park" as one historian called it; it covered only the eastern slope of the mountains and was a Forest Service victory that kept the Park Service out of Jackson Hole.)

After his appointment as superintendent of Yellowstone in 1919, Albright made frequent trips to the Jackson Hole country preaching conservation and trying to convince residents that their future lay with excursionists rather than cattle. Irrigation schemes to dam some of the valley's lakes and streams and the appearance of unsightly tourist facilities eventually led some local people to begin consideration of the most logical way to save Jackson Hole from shoddy commercialism. Out of their concerns came a historic meeting in a Jackson Hole log cabin in 1923, the opening salvo of the Grand Teton National Park campaign. Albright was invited to the meeting by a group of local citizens to discuss plans for a national recreation area under federal administration that would include all of the valley. It was proposed as a "museum on the hoof—native wildlife, cattle, wranglers, all living for a brief time each summer the life of the early West," according to an ambitious but impractical plan that was dependent upon heavy private financing.

Albright persevered. His annual reports for Yellowstone urged preservation of the Teton country, and every congressman or journalist who visited the park received a free trip to Jackson Hole. In 1926 John D. Rockefeller, Jr., spent two weeks in Yellowstone with his sons Laurance and David and received the obligatory tour. Albright stopped at a carefully selected picnic site on a vantage point overlooking the valley, close by the location of the present Jackson Lake Lodge. Moose browsed in the willow flats just below, and across the lake rose the majestic Tetons, sparkling in the sun. The view made an overwhelming impression upon Rockefeller, and he later described the Tetons as "quite the grandest and most spectacular mountains I have ever seen." As Albright expected, he was disturbed by the ugly clutter of cheap tourist cabins, gasoline stations, hot dog stands, and dance halls clustering along the road and the haphazard arrangement of telephone poles that partially obscured the scene as the party motored down the valley.

The fifty-two-year-old millionaire philanthropist listened without comment as the thirty-six-year-old Park Service superintendent spoke of his dream, shared by many in Jackson Hole, to preserve this "sublime valley" as a national park by acquiring the privately owned lands, mostly ranches in Jackson Hole. Quick action was essential, he pointed out, because the Forest Service had recently announced plans to log the shores of Jackson Lake and to open mines elsewhere in the valley.

Albright misread the taciturn Rockefeller, who gave no indication that he favored the park concept, asking only that Albright provide him with a practical proposal. "Mr. Albright, you haven't given me what I want," Rockefeller exclaimed when he studied the map Albright presented to him in New York the following winter. Uncertain of Rockefeller's interest, Albright had prepared a scaled-down version of the ideal project he had sketched for Rockefeller the previous summer—a version that he quickly revised.

To prevent speculation and price escalation, Rockefeller formed a dummy land corporation as a cover. It was a good business move but, as it turned out, a disastrous political strategy. Purchase of large tracts by the Snake River Land Company, organized in 1927, caused excitement and concern in Jackson Hole, and there was no shortage of rumors as to the purpose of the project and the identity of the person behind it. In 1930 Rockefeller's involvement became public knowledge, as did the Park Service connection, for Albright had helped mastermind the arrangements. The revelation outraged a substantial part of the Jackson Hole community and prevented any possibility of a rational reception of the park plan.

Antipark forces organized for battle; Rockefeller was condemned; a banner headline in a local paper proclaimed "FEUDAL LAWS NOW IN FORCE IN JACKSON HOLE: ROCKEFELLER, JR., REQUIRES RENDITION OF FEUDAL SERVICE BEFORE GIVING GRANTS AND PRIVILEGES." Although Rockefeller was charged with cheating landowners out of their heritage, he purchased only from willing sellers at a fair, even generous, price. The state required land to be assessed at true market value; by 1933 Rockefeller had bought 33,000 acres of land, assessed at $520,000, for which he paid $1.4 million.

A bill was introduced to accept the Rockefeller lands and establish a park, but Congress quickly backed away from the bitter hostility in Wyoming. In the western states there has always been deep antagonism to federal ownership of the extensive public domain (witness the recent "Sagebrush Rebellion"), and there is equally strong resentment against plans drawn up "back East" to determine how these lands are to be managed. The Jackson Hole controversy was not lacking in symbolism: poor homesteaders and ranchers pitted against one of America's richest and most influential families; immense wealth being used against the little man; the multiple use philosophy of the Forest Service threatened by the preservation mission of the Park Service; and for Wyoming, states' rights against the power of the federal government.

During the 1930s and 1940s, the Teton park controversy was a factor in every level of Wyoming politics. Several acrimonious hearings were held in Jackson, but the state congressional delegation blocked all efforts at legislation. To the chagrin of the Park Service, some conservationists joined the opposition on the grounds that the inclusion of Jackson Lake, a reclamation reservoir, would violate national park standards. Then, during World War II, Interior Secretary Harold Ickes, who never consciously ducked a fight, presented a solution to President Roosevelt that had been drafted by the Park Service. In 1943, using the authority of the Antiquities Act, Roosevelt signed a proclamation establishing a Jackson Hole National Monument and transferring 400,000 acres of federal land to Park Service control. (Most of the land in Jackson Hole was federally owned; it was the fifty square miles adjacent to Jackson in the southern portion of the valley, purchased by Rockefeller, that was the key to establishing a park free from intrusions.)

Reaction in Wyoming to Roosevelt's coup was explosive anger; a Jackson Hole lady exclaimed indignantly, "We GAVE them the Tetons! What *more* do they want?" Congress criticized the action as a sneak attack on the order of Pearl Harbor, and columnist Westbrook Pegler compared it to the tactics of a Hitler. Jackson Hole then staged its fondly remembered, if melodramatic, act of defiance: essentially a publicity stunt with slapstick overtones, featuring the fading movie actor Wallace Beery and a supporting cast of heavily armed and possibly well-oiled ranchers. They drove 650 yearling Herefords across the Jackson Hole National Monument to show their contempt for federal authority, suffering no casualties and encountering negligible resistance. Ickes ridiculed the "mock heroics" of cowboys in "mail order regalia," but local opposition to the monument was unyielding.

Angry that Roosevelt had established a park in Jackson Hole, which it had refused to do, Congress passed a bill abolishing the monument. Roosevelt vetoed that law, whereupon a rider was attached to every Interior appropriation bill from 1944 to 1948 prohibiting the Park Service from spending a penny on Jackson Hole National Monument. Understandably the Forest Service—which had unwillingly supplied most of the land for the monument—was less than gracious in defeat. It had, after all, been losing a number of its finest scenic areas to the Park Service. Before transferral of the Jackson Hole Ranger Station, a Forest

Service crew not only removed furniture and equipment but every bit of plumbing, the well and its tubing, all doors, drawers, cupboards, and cabinets, and finished by cutting a large square hole in the floor that severed the joists and made the station uninhabitable.

Times do change, however, and after World War II the climate began to improve. Americans in surprising numbers were on the move, Jackson was booming, and property values were doubling and tripling. Just possibly, said more and more residents, Horace Albright was right; the future prosperity of Jackson Hole would be in tourism and a national park might be good for business. A compromise was finally struck, but the Wyoming delegation drove a hard bargain. Local hunters were to be deputized as temporary rangers every year during elk season (the only national park in which this charade is staged); Teton County was to receive an annual appropriation as reimbursement for its property tax loss; and inholders were to receive grazing rights for their cattle. In 1950 the Jackson Hole National Monument was abolished, and President Harry Truman signed the bill creating an enlarged Grand Teton National Park.

Adjacent Lands and Jackson Hole

Park Service employees were quickly made aware they were not a welcome addition to Jackson Hole society. Not uncommonly, rangers changed out of their uniforms before driving into Jackson, and the superintendent chosen for Grand Teton possessed exceptional qualities of patience and forebearance. The old bitterness, however, is mostly, if not entirely, gone these days in Jackson Hole, which has more formidable matters to occupy its attention. The establishment of the park, as it turned out, only temporarily solved the conflict between conservation and commercialism.

Over the years Grand Teton has become one of the most popular of all national parks, drawing more visitors than Yellowstone, upwards of four million annually. Condominium developers and people seeking vacation homes in Jackson Hole are snapping up anything on the market, and the entire area is in the midst of a gigantic real estate boom. Rockefeller decided not to purchase the southernmost section of the valley, near Jackson, and the sprawl that he and Albright had sought to prevent is presently creeping out from the town, home builders preferring sites in full view of the Tetons.

The choice remaining lands are owned by ranchers, many from families that have been in the valley for generations. They prefer to continue ranching and to preserve the character of Jackson Hole rather than selling out to developers, even at astronomical prices, but they are being squeezed by rapidly rising taxes. Should their open fields and meadows be sold and cut up into building lots, the south perimeter of the park would be lined with subdivisions and tourist attractions.

In 1976 a majority of the private landowners signed a policy statement that noted, "It was only a quarter of a century ago that most of us who now favor an expanded role for the National Park Service were in complete opposition to the expansion of Grand Teton National Park." The landowners believed the only way of preserving the scenic and historic values and the quality of life in Jackson Hole was by expanding the boundary of Grand Teton to include their private lands. "Whether we like it or not, we have come to the realization that either we share the pastoral beauty of the valley or we lose it."

The policy statement was preceded by lengthy studies and master plans and frequently acrimonious public meetings as the residents of Jackson Hole, representing a wide range of conservation and development interests, searched for a practical way to achieve the common goal of preserving the valley while allowing some regulated growth. Much more was involved than the disposition of several thousand acres of land or a national park boundary change. Jackson Hole has become a classic example of the adjacent lands quandary being faced throughout the national park system. At Antietam National Battlefield, the superintendent, who is fighting subdivisions with Washington and Baltimore only two hours away, recently commented, "It's coming. It's coming farther and farther out. These developments are just leapfrogging down the road."

In June 1978, almost fifty-five years to the day since Horace Albright met with Jackson Hole residents in the log cabin to discuss their national recreation area plan, a joint congressional committee held a public hearing in Jackson on a bill to establish a Jackson Hole Scenic Area. Drafted by local residents, the bill asked the federal government to assume the major responsibility for preserving Jackson Hole. Just as in the 1923 proposal, the land would remain in private ownership, but this time the federal government would purchase scenic easements and development rights from the property owners.

Most of the eighty persons who testitifed favored the bill, urging quick passage because of the critical pressures on open space. They cited statistics on growth as an argument: Between 1911 and 1972 only 1,800 acres had been developed in the county; from 1973 to 1977 the figure was 2,300 acres, in the first three months of 1978 applications for subdivisions totaling 1,500 acres were submitted or approved. Under the bill's easement plan ranchers would be receiving an estimated 65 percent, or more, of the value of their land in return for agreeing never to develop or subdivide. Nevertheless, ranching being a world of strongly independent people who prefer minding their own interests and resent any interference, ranchers who testified had strong reservations about giving up this much of their authority and had some unkind things to say about perceived imperfections of the federal bureaucracy.

Still, as members of the congressional committee pointed out, the price of scenery certainly comes high in Jackson Hole. The cost to the federal government of buying easements, while allowing ranchers to retain ownership, was estimated at $200 million. A prestigious National Citizens Committee for Jackson Hole had been formed to support the bill, and its local representative, Margaret E. (Mardy) Murie, gave testimony. One of the most respected conservationists on the national scene and a longtime and much beloved resident of Jackson Hole, Mardy Murie was the only witness who spoke sternly to the ranchers:

> I say here very frankly that if I were a rancher in this valley on some of the now remaining private acres, and had the right to sell my development rights at a reasonable price and at the same time keep my ranch and my ranching and my kind of life and hand it on to my children and grandchildren, I should feel that life had dealt kindly with me.

When the senator from Wyoming introduced the Jackson Hole Scenic Area legislation in Congress, he predicted "The use of scenic conservation or open space easements and development rights may prove the single preservation concept which can be applied successfully in other areas." The bill did attract widespread attention as a possible solution to the adjacent lands problem and received considerable support. However, the degree to which the taxpayers of America will subsidize private landowners to insure protection of the national heritage is still to be resolved, for in the case of Jackson Hole, the $200 million price tag was too high.

Modern Poachers

There were old threats as well as new ones listed in the *State of the Parks* report. Game poachers are still working some of the parks, although hardly on the scale of a century ago when the hide hunters threatened to exterminate the wildlife of Yellowstone.

An 1875 army expedition reported that while only a few years earlier the Yellowstone country was "unsurpassed on the continent for big game," the great herds of deer, bighorn sheep, and elk had all but vanished, slaughtered for their hides, the meat left to rot. A principal reason for bringing the U.S. cavalry into Yellowstone in 1886 was to protect wildlife from the poachers. By this time the once great herds of buffalo (more correctly, bison), which once may have numbered 60 million, were gone, and a scientific party surveying the West could find only 540 animals, mostly in Yellowstone. The army did an excellent job, but the park was vast and the poachers were bold. Buffalo heads, increasingly rare, were bringing several hundred dollars, and anyone who could evade the troopers was assured a good living selling hides and heads to taxidermists in Livingstone and Billings.

During the winter of 1894 a notorious poacher set up camp in the park with the intention of methodically killing the entire herd of buffalo that wintered in the surrounding meadows, hanging the "scalps" in the trees, and taking out his trophies by packhorse in the spring. By chance a civilian scout, a tough veteran of the Indian wars, and an army sergeant encountered snowshoe tracks that led them to the poacher as he was skinning out the day's kill of five buffalo. Six more heads were suspended from nearby tree limbs.

By an even greater piece of luck, as the two men were escorting their prisoner back to the guardhouse, they encountered members of the Yellowstone National Game Expedition, in the park to report on the status of Yellowstone's wildlife. One of the party, sponsored by the New York weekly magazine *Forest and Stream,* was Emerson Hough, well-known outdoor writer and author of *The Covered Wagon.* Hough wrote a dispatch on the spot that was carried back to park headquarters by the men and immediately telegraphed to New York.

Field and Stream was the leading outdoor journal of its time. Its crusading editor, George Bird Grinnell, who had been with Custer in the Black Hills in 1874 and on the 1875 army expedition to Yellowstone that reported upon the depredations of the poachers, was a founder of the conservation movement. Grinnell gathered some influential friends and headed for Washington. Hough's article, which dramatically joined the eagle and the buffalo as the twin symbols of the American heritage, caused a sensation. The public, it seemed, had developed a striking sentimental attachment for the buffalo now that it was on the verge of extinction. Thirteen days after the poacher was tracked down, a bill "To Protect the Birds and Animals in Yellowstone National Park" was introduced in Congress and passed the House and Senate, by public demand, in only six weeks. For the first time a national park was given legal authority to arrest and prosecute poachers; previously the only penalty was eviction from the park. With some merit the poacher whose activities provoked the legislation (who later was hired by the army because he "knew all the bad men and poachers" around the park) was heard to remark proudly, "If they have got laws to protect the game in the park, they can thank *me* for it."

Some poaching continues in Yellowstone to this day. Deer, elk, and moose are occasionally taken, but the real prize is the bighorn sheep. Sportsmen from throughout the United States and from foreign countries hunt the national forest lands bordering Yellowstone seeking the trophy bighorn. Probably most of the record size Rocky Mountain bighorns left in the Lower Forty-eight are in Yellowstone, and as prices go up, the poaching pressure increases. A head with full curl horns and cape can bring $10,000 on the black market. One international poaching ring was recently under prosecution on forty suspected violations scattered through Mexico and the United States.

The old time Yellowstone hide hunters have been replaced by modern "horn hunters" who supply what appears to be an insatiable market for aphrodisiacs in the Orient. Although it is illegal to bring elk horns out of the park, Korean buyers are frequently seen on the streets of Gardiner, at the north entrance. At $6 a pound, an average elk rack brings close to $100, and on one trip a poacher can cut up and smuggle out five or six racks. At the National Elk Refuge near Jackson, the annual crop of antlers is auctioned off, mostly to the ubiquitous Koreans. Proceeds from this harvest, oddly enough, provide the main source of funds for the Jackson Boy Scouts, who receive permits to collect the antlers from the refuge.

The poaching of deer in Shenandoah National Park is so wide spread that during the hunting season the Skyline Drive is often closed at dusk, when deer can be spotted with flashlights. Poaching in the parks is not limited to animals. The life-giving ginseng plant is taken from the Fort Donelson battlefield. Cactus is so much in demand for the home-landscaping market in the Southwest that "cactus rustlers" are systematically removing rare cactus plants from Organ Pipe Cactus National Monument and Big Bend National Park, both located along remote stretches of the Mexican border. An estimated 24,000 pounds of petrified wood is taken each year from Petrified Forest National Park by souvenir hunters. Parks are also the victims of modern day piracy. Specimens of coral reef are being taken from Fort Jefferson and Biscayne, and artifacts are looted from shipwrecks by scuba divers. People also prey on people. When hikers park their cars at a trailhead for several days, leaving their gear and valuables stored in the trunk, thieves are attracted.

Even political protest activities are an occasional threat. The most famous of the nation's symbolic structures, such as Independence Hall, the Washington Monument, and the Lincoln Memorial, are the scene of frequent demonstrations. The Statue of Liberty, a favorite target, was most recently "captured" in May 1980 when two men protesting the murder conviction of a Black Panther in California scaled the 300-foot statue with climbing gear. The familiar green patina of the statue is formed by the weathering of a thin layer of copper, which shields the underlying metal from deterioration. Believing the protesters had punched holes in the protective skin during their climb, the Park Service sent a team of specialists to assess the damage. Instead of holes from climbing spikes, they found the statue was a victim of air pollution. The surface was heavily pitted by acid rain and other corrosives, an accumulation of forty years of exposure since the statue had last been overhauled.

A couple of weeks later, a bomb exploded in the museum at the base of the statue, destroying several exhibits but causing no structural damage. Letters to the press and television stations announced the purpose of the bombing was to publicize the cause of "Croatian Freedom Fighters."

Exotic Intruders: The Grand Canyon Burros

Picture this, said a disbelieving newspaper reporter in a story filed from Grand Canyon National Park in 1979. A squad of armed rangers floating down the Colorado River spots a herd of floppy-eared burros; they scramble ashore and fire a volley of tranquilizer darts. Several of the animals are hit, stagger about, and collapse. One stops breathing, is given mouth-to-mouth resuscitation by a ranger, but dies. A helicopter takes position above the action; the burros are trussed with ropes, loaded into the dangling cargo net, and flown out of the canyon. The rangers climb back into their raft and disappear around a bend of the river, their guns at the ready. It's not something out of a comedy of the absurd, explained the reporter, merely another scene in a protracted dispute that has split the environmental movement and provoked a ferocious reaction from animal lovers all over the country.

Nonnative animals that have found their way into the national parks—a part of man's constant "reshuffling of the fauna," as one scientist termed it—obviously represent a conflict with the basic Park Service mission of maintaining the parks in their natural state. Nevertheless most parks contain some exotic plants; pack animals brought into the parks leave behind, in their droppings, seeds that can bear alien fruits. And in 1949, in Hawaii Volcanoes National Park, rangers attempting to rid the area of exotic animals killed 3,000 goats, 261 pigs, 44 mongooses, and 4 house cats.

Soon after Grand Canyon National Park was established in 1919, the burro problem was identified, and sporadically the rangers attempted removal by herding or hunting. The burro's exceptional ability to forage off the "thin of the land" had made it an invaluable draft animal for early settlers and single-blanket prospectors, but with the cessation of mining soon after 1900, many of the beasts escaped or were turned loose and multiplied. In 1932 Grand Canyon's chief ranger stated: "Overgrazed conditions existed on all areas ranged over by burros. In many places, herbage growth was cropped to the roots and some species of shrubbery were totally destroyed." That year rangers using rifles reduced the burro population to a few dozen, then believed to be a tolerable number, but within a few years the process had to be repeated. In fifty years, from the establishment of the park to 1969, 2,888 burros were destroyed.

As the herds once again increased in the 1970s, the park staff conducted an intensive study of the burros' impact on the environment, which included surveys of habitat damage and autopsies of selected animals. Scientists concluded that the burros themselves were healthy and prospering, but they were having a devastating effect on the park. Other animals were being crowded out, including the rare desert bighorn sheep. Believing its evidence conclusive, the Park Service announced the only practical solution was to put an end to the burros of Grand Canyon, then believed to number more than 400 (there are more than 10,000 of the critters elsewhere on the public lands of the West).

In retrospect, the Park Service may not have been guilty of playing its hand clumsily—the conservation community and the press were largely in favor of its position—but it certainly underestimated the wrath of animal lovers, particularly when they learned that the proposed "reduction" program meant the burros were to be shot by the rangers.

Railing against what it called an impending "massacre," the American Horse Protection Association predicted that Grand Canyon would be turned into a "giant bloody butcher shop, leaving the canyon littered with the carcasses of those once free, wild burros." People seemed to have a simplistic idea of the difficulty of the problem and the terrain, remarked one ranger. They suggested, "Why don't you just move the animals? Marlin Perkins does it all the time."

Answering more than 14,000 letters (many containing nickels, dimes, and dollars) gave the Park Service ample opportunity to consider the enormity of its contemplated action. The pleas of young children were especially harrowing, many of the youngsters having read Marguerite Henry's engaging best-seller about the adventures of a donkey, *Brighty of the Grand Canyon.* Park officials hastily transferred a statue of Brighty from its commanding location in the visitor center to a dim corner, replacing it with a display showing burro damage.

While the Humane Society unlimbered its formidable legal and public relations resources, hundreds of concerned citizens volunteered solutions: send the burros back to Africa, where they supposedly originated before being brought to the New World by the Spanish;

import mountain lions to eat them; grow grass in the canyon to feed them; give them to prison inmates to improve rehabilitation; sterilize them with "chemosterilants administered orally or by injection, mechanical castration, irradiation and ultrasonics"; give them to Mexico. (To the latter, the Mexican government politely declined, saying "but we appreciate your offer.") A less sentimental southwesterner observed that the shooting of an animal that "tramples, urinates and defecates in and around" precious water sources would be "good riddance."

Facing law suits and a new children's crusade, Secretary Andrus privately commented, "There must be a better way." He ordered the Park Service to delay action until accurate statistics and more convicing proof of burro damage could be gathered. The full scale Environmental Impact Statement took three years and more than $100,000; it proved once again that the wildly breeding but appealing burros are highly destructive animals that contaminate water holes, accelerate erosion, eat any and all vegetation, drive away numberless small creatures from their natural habitat, and have no natural enemies.

As a part of its search for an alternative to killing the burros, the park carried out two experiments. First, two professional horse wranglers, four horses, and three dogs spent nine days in one of the easiest sections of the canyon. They managed to bring out twelve burros and kill one horse at an average cost of $442 for each burro herded out (at an auction in Phoenix the animals brought $11 a head). Next, twelve rangers armed with tranquilizer guns (including the group described by the reporter) and backed up by helicopters to supply food and haul out the burros, immobilized thirty-two animals. Of those, two died from overdoses and three from falling into the canyon while drugged. The experiment cost $1,400 per burro.

That exercise, coupled with the incredibly tortuous topography of the inner canyon, convinced the Park Service that the cost of evacuating the animals, employing helicopters, might be upwards of $400,000. That would be "a ludicrous waste of taxpayers' dollars," declared an embattled Grand Canyon spokesman. "The park is hurting in too many ways to spend that kind of money on burros." Accordingly, having exhausted all possible options, the park gave notice that it would, regretfully, begin shooting the burros.

At the eleventh hour, amid a flurry of legal and emotional protests, author Cleveland Amory intervened. Amory, head of the New York–based Fund for Animals, whose board of directors includes luminaries of such magnitude as Princess Grace of Monaco, Katherine Hepburn, and Andrew Wyeth, was brought to Grand Canyon by his field representative Richard Negus, a bearded transplanted Englishman. Negus asked whether Amory would be willing "to spend $280,000 or so to rescue 400 donkeys from a bloody great hole in the ground." Accepting the challenge, Amory immediately opened a drive to save the Grand Canyon burros as pets for the children of America and collected $225,000. Dubious of Amory's ability to finance his removal plan, but not wishing to invite the charge that it foreclosed on a mission of mercy, the Park Service agreed to a moratorium. It specified, however, that in order not to be faced with the same problem again in a few years, every burro must be removed. Any that remained would be shot by the rangers.

To the surprise of everyone, not excluding the Park Service, Amory's strike force of eight cowboys, forty horses, seventeen dogs, and two helicopters began to bring out the burros in grand style. It took nearly a year and $500,000, but 580 burros were airlifted from Grand Canyon, the last two named "Over" and "Out." The animals were trucked to Texas to a Fund for Animals ranch for "abused and unwanted" creatures, then offered to children for adoption. At his well-earned victory celebration, Cleveland Amory announced the canyon was free of burros, but a few days later hikers came upon a pair grazing along a trail in the inner canyon. "I don't think we've seen the last of the burros quite yet," predicted a Grand Canyon ranger.

7

WILDERNESS MANAGEMENT

An interesting thing about the term "wilderness" is that Park Service people seldom use the word. Rangers, who shy away from literary pretense, stick with "backcountry" as their workday designation. It would be totally out of character for a ranger back from a few days patrol to remark that he had been spending some time "in the wilderness." It's likely his colleagues would either wince at his feeble attempt at humor or regard him, with suspicion, as a possible "heavy breather," a label often attached to naturalists who tend to get choked up when speaking of the sublime splendors of the parks.

For rangers, who serve in many parks, some wilderness is more equal than others. "I can't regard anything in Yosemite as wilderness after being in Yellowstone," the chief ranger of Yellowstone remarked soon after he transferred from Yosemite. Unaware of the chief ranger's comment, a member of the Yellowstone research staff who had done his doctoral studies in the Canadian Arctic was heard to say, "After spending time in the North Country I have a hard time thinking of anything in Yellowstone as wilderness."

It can be argued that the term "wilderness" has no real meaning. Roderick Nash, whose book *Wilderness and the American Mind* is the accepted text on the subject, would go even further. In a recent speech he declared, "Wilderness does not exist. It never has." Because it has achieved a legal definition in the Wilderness Act and lines have been drawn on maps, "We act as if wilderness were real—rocks, trees, canyons, mountains—but it is actually a state of mind evoked by a state of nature, a quality associated by some people with some places."

Perhaps so, but the finite wilderness has been regarded as the corrective for the maladies of civilization ever since Henry David Thoreau and the transcendentalists came to accept the presence of divinity in nature. Thoreau made history in 1851, when he told the audience at the Concord Lyceum that more and more he was leaving the city and withdrawing into the natural world where he could find the freedom and solitude that was essential for one to come to grips with reason and faith. In the course of that address he spoke the immortal phrase: "In Wildness is the preservation of the World."

Like the enigmatic pronouncements of Apollo's oracle of Delphi, which required translation by the priests of the temple, Thoreau's "murky line" has been variously interpreted. Europeans, with achievements in art, music, literature, and architecture that Americans have not matched, might disagree that civilization cannot exist without wild country. On the other hand, it has been observed that as the forests of Britain declined, so did the fortunes of that nation; by the 1920s only 5 percent of the original forest cover remained, and the end of the Empire was in sight. Leaving aside for a moment the importance of wilderness in God's scheme of things, one is struck by the considerable disagreement that has always existed over the question of where wilderness can be found.

Thoreau, after all, was not especially deep in the wilds during his sojourn at Walden, although he believed himself to be "as solitary as on the prairies." His cabin was only a mile and a half from the center of Concord, to which he walked almost daily, often to have dinner with the revered spokesman of the transcendentalists, Ralph Waldo Emerson, who once declared "the whole of nature is a metaphor of the mind." The cabin in the dunes where Henry Beston lived for a year, only fifty feet from high tide, was in much the same circumstance. While producing one of the classics of American nature writing, *The Outermost House,* Beston could see the houses of Eastham across the marsh. A couple of times a week a friend would drive him into the village to do his shopping. Neither Walden Pond nor the Great Beach of Cape Cod would fit the conventional definition of wilderness, yet Thoreau and Beston proved to their own satisfaction that it is not necessary to repair to primitive country to achieve a feeling of solitude and isolation.

In 1960 Wallace Stegner, the Pulitzer Prize–winning novelist and biographer, sent a letter to the Outdoor Recreation Resources Review Commission as his contribution to that body's nationwide examination of recreational needs. There are some who feel that no one has ever produced a more lasting commentary on the meaning and importance of wilderness than did Stegner, a longtime friend of the Park Service and member of its Advisory Board, when he wrote, not of the uses of wilderness lands, but of "the wilderness idea as something that has helped form our character and that has certainly shaped our history as a people."

> Something will have gone out of us as a people if we ever let the remaining wilderness be destroyed; if we permit the last virgin forests to be turned into comic books and plastic cigarette cases; if we drive the few remaining members of the wild species into zoos or extinction; if we pollute the last clear air and dirty the last clean streams and push our paved roads through the last of the silence. . . .
>
> The American experience has been the confrontation by old peoples and cultures of a world as new as if it had just risen from the sea. That gave us our hope and our excitement, and the hope and excitement can be passed on to newer Americans, Americans who never saw any phase of the frontier. But only so long as we keep the remainder of our wild as a reserve and a promise—a sort of wilderness bank. . . .
>
> We simply need that wild country available to us, even if we never do more than drive to its edge and look in. For it can be a means of reassuring ourselves of our sanity as creatures, a part of the geography of hope.

The Wilderness Act

Yellowstone, initially, was established not to preserve wilderness, but to protect remarkable thermal and geologic wonders; even so, Congress surrounded the relatively small area occupied by these features with a huge 3,500-square-mile preserve. A few years later it was found that extensive gold and silver deposits along the northeast border of the park could not be worked profitably without a railroad connection, for which the only feasible right-of-way was through the park. Despite a powerful lobbying effort mounted by mining and railroad interests, Congress refused to grant them a charter to construct the line. It was a notable victory in which those seeking to protect the park pointed out that although a railroad would not harm thermal features, it would destroy the wilderness that the park also protected.

Congress, however, did not explicitly recognize wilderness in its national park legislation until 1934. In the act establishing Everglades National Park, it specified that the park should be "permanently preserved as wilderness." Because the Forest Service administratively designated nearly 600,000 acres of Gila National Forest in New Mexico as a wilderness recreation reserve in 1934, the argument has been advanced, by some, that wilderness preservation began in the national forests.

In 1929, when the Forest Service spelled out a set of regulations for designating wilderness areas—not as a matter of law, but as agency policy—the term "wilderness" was rejected and replaced with "primitive." One reason was, to the credit of the Forest Service, that it did not believe that wilderness was an appropriate title for areas in which commercial activities such as logging and grazing would be continued. A commentary on the times, the Forest Service also felt that the public might be repelled, rather than attracted, by the connotation of the name wilderness.

By some astonishing stroke of fortune, the Forest Service had in its employment at the time three outstanding figures of the early wilderness preservation movement: Arthur Carhart, Robert Marshall, and Aldo Leopold. They argued for wilderness designation of forest lands to preserve a unique kind of recreation experience and were able to nudge the organization into taking its first steps. *Wilderness Management,* the first comprehensive text on the subject in all of its aspects, published in 1978 under Forest Service sponsorship and written by three of its scientists, suggests there was some modest support for the concept Leopold had proposed in 1921: setting aside "a continuous stretch of country preserved in its natural state, open to lawful hunting and fishing, big enough to absorb a 2-week pack trip, and kept devoid of roads, artificial trails, cottages or other works of man."

Apparently the head of the Forest Service was prompted by other considerations. "He was enthusiastic about creating wilderness reserves on the National Forests largely, to be frank, because he feared that the aggressive leadership Stephen T. Mather was giving the National Parks threatened his own empire," reflected the authors of *Wilderness Management.* "If the Forest Service did not move to protect its spectacular scenery and develop its recreational resources, there was a good chance that some of its land might be turned over to the National Park Service."

A case could be made that the dam builders deserve much of the credit for the creation of a wilderness preservation system. From the time John Muir and his allies failed to prevent construction of a dam in Yosemite, Hetch Hetchy became a rallying cry for conservationists: never again would a dam be built in a national park, they vowed. During the 1940s Interior's Bureau of Reclamation began designing a gigantic ten-dam Colorado River Storage Project, sometimes referred to as the world's largest plumbing system. In 1950 the Interior secretary approved the dam planned for Echo Park in Dinosaur National Monument. Conservationists quickly rallied to defeat the proposal. They recognized that the issue was pivotal, that if the Echo Park dam were built, no park would be safe—particularly when there were known to be nearly thirty other potential dam sites within national parks on the dockets of Reclamation and the Corps of Engineers.

Despite the solid support for the dam by western interests—congressmen, governors, utility companies, civic clubs, chambers of commerce—this time the sides in the conflict were more evenly matched. The conservationists had been able to mobilize only 7 national and 2 state organizations for the Hetch Hetchy battle; 78 national and 236 state conservation groups pooled their resources for Echo Park. They generated a massive public protest, produced pamphlets, books and films, and showed considerable muscle. By 1956, realizing that Echo Park was endangering the entire Colorado River Storage Project, the dam builders capitulated. Not only was Echo Park excluded, but the sanctity of the parks was guaranteed by a new clause in the legislation stating it was the intent of Congress "that no dam or reservoir constructed under the authorization of the Act shall be within any National Park or Monument."

Echo Park demonstrated that for the first time there existed broadly based popular support for wilderness. "Let's try to be done with a wilderness preservation program made up of a sequence of overlapping emergencies, threats, and defense campaigns," declared Howard Zahniser, executive director of the Wilderness Society and a mighty warrior in the dam fight. Now was the time, he felt, for conservationists to take the offensive.

Capitalizing on the momentum from the Echo Park victory, the jubilant Zahniser immediately drafted a bold plan for a national wilderness preservation system, to be authorized by Congress, that would give permanent protection to federal lands designated as wilderness. Primarily written by Zahniser, the Wilderness Act was introduced by Senator Hubert Humphrey in 1956. The Act set forth an ambitious scheme enumerating some 160 areas in the national parks, national forests, national wildlife refuges, and Indian reservations that would constitute the national wilderness preservation system. Congress reviewed and debated sixty-five different versions of the bill and congressional committees held eighteen separate hearings: more attention than Congress had given any other conservation measure.

The reason for the prolonged debate was the opposition of those who feared that a wilderness preservation system would seriously curtail the traditional philosophy of multiple use under which most of the public lands had been available for commercial activities. David Brower, executive director of the Sierra Club, who with Zahniser devised the tactics and directed the conservationists' efforts, maintained at an early hearing that "no man who reads Leopold with an open mind will ever again, with a clear conscience, be able to step up and testify against the wilderness bill." But the oil, mining, cattle, and lumber interests organized forceful resistance to what they contended was an attempt to "lock up" millions of acres of the public domain for the pleasure of a tiny minority of backpackers.

The Wilderness Act was finally signed into law in 1964, a magnificent, even surprising, triumph for wilderness preservation. It was, however, a cautious bill. A considerable price was paid to obtain congressional support, but wilderness legislation could not have passed without the compromises exacted by opponents. Only 9 million acres of Forest Service wild and wilderness lands were placed in the wilderness preservation system. Each additional area proposed for inclusion by the Forest Service, the Park Service, the Fish and Wildlife Service—and later the Bureau of Land Management—was to be separately reviewed and approved by Congress, which has proved a cumbersome and often controversial procedure.

Some of the activities permitted by the legislation were clearly inconsistent with the ideals of the original wilderness bill. To placate ranchers, established grazing was to continue in the wilderness; so were established uses of aircraft and motorboats. As a concession to the wood industry, actions could be taken to control fire, forest diseases, and insects. The opposition of the power interests was defused by the stipulation that, when the president deemed it necessary, dams and reservoirs could be constructed. The most paradoxical section of the Wilderness Act, suggesting the strength of the mining lobby, permitted mining companies to continue their mining activities and to explore and stake new claims until December 31, 1983; after that date production can continue on all claims filed before the cutoff date. The secretary of Agriculture was empowered to issue "reasonable" regulations governing the construction of power lines, roads, and buildings necessary for mining operations in the wilderness.

While thoroughly endorsing the objectives of the Wilderness Act, the Park Service had mixed feelings about inclusion of the national parklands in the national wilderness preservation system. Even the statement of purpose in the act was borrowed, almost word for word, from the language of the Yellowstone and Park Service enabling acts. By any measure, wilderness was being preserved in the parks at a considerably higher standard than that required by the Wilderness Act, so much so that the act stipulated that inclusion of a national park in the wilderness system "shall in no manner lower the standards evolved for the use and preservation of such park, monument, or other unit of the national park system in accordance with the Act of August 25, 1916."

The conservationists, as always, perceived things differently. Perhaps remembering one or two incidents of the past—the Tioga Road in Yosemite comes to mind—conservationists have developed a certain apprehension about Park Service stewardship of the wilderness. They seem to be always fearful, despite firm assurances to the contrary, of secret Park Service plans to build new roads into the backcountry.

The Accessible Wilderness

Notwithstanding 6,000 pages of testimony and countless attempts to define the wilderness concept, the working definition chosen for the

Wilderness Act finally came down to a single descriptive adjective that some people assumed was a typographical error. For Howard Zahniser, "untrammeled" seemed to suggest the essence of wilderness, defined in the act "as an area where the earth and its community of life are untrammeled by man, where man himself is a visitor who does not remain."

As it turned out, mine shafts and roads were not the only threats to the sanctity of the wilderness, nor was it possible, as many thought, to "draw a line around it and leave it alone." Popular support for wilderness had carried the day for the Wilderness Act, but the enthusiasm that was generated for the wilderness experience proved perhaps the greatest threat of all. Muir and a group of Californians had founded the Sierra Club in 1892 for the purpose of "exploring, enjoying, and rendering accessible" the mountains of the Far West. His modern followers are facing problems because so much of the once distant wilderness is now readily accessible.

At 14,495 feet, Mt. Whitney is the tallest peak in the United States outside Alaska; Muir made a solo ascent in 1873, the first year it was climbed. As recently as 1949 a man and his son climbed the California mountain on August 4, taking pride in the fact that they were the sixth and seventh persons to sign the summit register *that year.* On August 22, 1972, they made the climb again and, leafing through the register, learned to their dismay they were the 259th and 260th persons to ascend Mt. Whitney *that day.*

The Wilderness Act specified that wilderness should have "outstanding opportunities for solitude," but the more wilderness was publicized and written about, the more it was photographed and mapped, the less wild it seemed. Improvements in camping technology were another factor. Bulky bedrolls, heavy canvas tents, and canned goods had limited wilderness trips to those using pack animals or to the few capable of toting heavy loads over rough terrain. The introduction of featherweight equipment—pack frames, sleeping bags, and freeze-dried foods—opened the wilderness to anyone of average physical strength. At the same time synthetic rubber rafts, aluminum canoes, and fiberglass kayaks made floating wild rivers a considerably less formidable undertaking.

Perhaps Congress and the conservationists were not of one mind as to the purpose of the Wilderness Act. Conservationists stressed preservation and the retention of the natural character of the wild lands. According to the record, those who voted for the legislation did so with the understanding that wilderness would be open to extensive use. Frank Church, floor manager of the bill when it passed the Senate, later explained: ". . . it was *not* the intent of Congress that wilderness be administered in so pure a fashion as to needlessly restrict their customary public use and enjoyment. Quite to the contrary, Congress fully intended that wilderness should be managed to allow its use by a wide spectrum of Americans."

Zahniser had carefully chosen the word "untrammeled" because it means "not subject to human controls and manipulations," but paradoxically wilderness that receives substantial use can survive only if protected by means of orderly regulations. One of the first people to ponder this dilemma was a Park Service wildlife specialist, Lowell Sumner. After studying the Sequoia, Kings Canyon, and Yosemite parks, he suggested in 1936 that wilderness "cannot hope to accommodate unlimited numbers of people," without its essential qualities being destroyed. Witnessing the impact of pack stock overgrazing the mountain meadows and of fishermen wearing trails around mountain lakes, in 1942 Sumner urged the Park Service to restrict wilderness use "within the carrying capacity or recreational saturation point."

"Carrying capacity" was originally a stockman's term describing the number of cows a stretch of country could sustain without exceeding the capacity of the range; Sumner was the first to apply the concept to people and to recognize that the wilderness could not accommodate unlimited numbers. He postulated that it was the function of wilderness mangers to "determine in advance the probable maximum permissible use, short of impairment, of all wilderness areas." Sumner's premise was eventually accepted, but no one has ever presented a park superintendent with a practical means of determining, on the basis of measurable and supportable calculations, the "saturation point" of his area. How could scientific investigations produce objective conclusions on the basis of subjective evaluations?

Biological carrying capacity, in terms of the impact of human and pack-stock use upon wildlife and vegetation, is a matter of degree; any level of use causes some change in the condition of the resource. Psychological carrying capacity, a term used to describe the level of tolerance one person has for the presence of other people in the wilderness, varies with the individual, for people come to the wilderness with differing and often conflicting attitudes.

In a study of backcountry users in Yosemite, researchers found the key factors contributing to user satisfaction were: the good physical condition of the trail; the absence of horse parties (and horse manure); a limited number of individual hikers traveling in the opposite direction; the pleasant demeanor of people encountered; and the extent to which those people shared similar environmental values. Surprisingly, crowding on the trail seemed less critical to user satisfaction than the perception of "alikeness" in fellow users of the wilderness.

Other people have other criteria. In a recent letter to a conservation journal, a resident of Alaska argued "The wilderness feeling must be earned, the experience is not in the place but in the effort and self-sufficiency needed to get there." In his view, a fly-in trip to one of the new national parks in Alaska would not qualify as a wilderness experience. Better, he declared, to set aside a much smaller wilderness preserve, from which all airplanes would be barred, than to establish the Gates of the Arctic National Park. The reduced area might be visited by more people, "but fifteen people who walk in 30 miles can feel more alone and more in tune with the earth than two people who fly in. The *spirit* of a wilderness is defiled more by an airplane than by a foot path."

Robert Marshall, who was a major force in the formation of Forest Service wilderness, first explored and named the Gates of the Arctic region in 1929, and he too opposed the use of airplanes in wilderness travel. But in offering this opinion, Marshall, a founder of the Wilderness Society, displayed a detachment and a broad-mindedness that sets him apart from so many wilderness devotees today. "In holding this view, I do not feel the least bitterness or animosity toward those who do not."

In 1972 the Park Service initiated a program of restricting use of the backcountry that was soon extended to most wilderness parks. Hikers intending to camp overnight must now obtain a campsite reservation from the ranger station. Campsites are spaced along trails, with the number and the location designed to spread the impact and to maintain backcountry use at an acceptable level. If the camping location preferred by the hiker is "full," another campsite or another trail must be selected.

The whole scheme of wilderness quotas, while necessary, is highly regrettable. Somehow an intensively managed wilderness becomes less attractive, even though with present controls the permit holder is guaranteed a measure of solitude, and the resource is protected from damaging use. It is, however, infinitely better to regulate human activities, in order to preserve the character of the wilderness, than to manipulate resources for the purpose of expanding use. A humorously chilling forecast of what life will be like in the wilderness a hundred years hence, that seems worthy of the science fiction genre, appeared in the Sierra Club *Bulletin* in 1978. The wilderness conservation system will be a global, computerized affair in 2078, according to author William C. Leitch's scenario. A hypothetical applicant attempting to make reservations for a wilderness vacation is told by the computer that there will be an opening in three years for an eleven-day outing—not bad considering the applicant's last trip was only four years before. His movements are plotted on the Big Board in ranger headquarters from data supplied by a radio transmitter attached to his pack; a small chip embedded in his heel would activate a distress signal to guide rescuers should he be overtaken by misfortune, an improbable occurrence as all potentially dangerous animals, such as grizzlies, are also outfitted with transmitters enabling ranger-controllers to maintain safe distances between animals and humans.

The elimination of backcountry fires is one of the more recent protective measures adopted. To keep some areas from being picked clean of down wood and spar trees, the camp fire—ancient symbol of pioneering—is being selectively banned; cooking must be done with chemical stoves. Some park superintendents argue that regulations could be relaxed if it were possible to educate the public to use the wilderness on its own terms. That would involve spartan measures such as a substantial reduction, or even elimination, of trail and bridge maintenance and the removal of trail signs.

Roderick Nash strongly advocates this approach and would go even farther (superintendents respect Nash, an accomplished guide, backpacker, and white water boatman, and consider it deplorable that they must inform the keeper of the wilderness flame that he can't build a campfire in the backcountry). Don't even provide search and rescue assistance, he urges. A person who enters the wilderness should do so knowing his fate is entirely in his own hands, whatever happens. "What this means is that the element of risk, the presence of danger and mystery, should be cherished and protected." At stake is a basic wilderness value, the opportunity to encounter danger depending on one's own resources and with no one around to pick up the pieces.

Superintendents who have the sad task of informing parents when a young hiker is badly injured or a climber killed are unlikely to accept Nash's recommendation that ranger search and rescue teams be abolished and that the lost or injured be left to fend for themselves. But they would likely agree, albeit reluctantly, with the assessment of a seasonal ranger: "I like to think that it isn't really wilderness when you have to find your assigned campsite along well-marked trails. It may not be wilderness but it's the best we have."

Who Runs the Grand Canyon?

It occasionally happens that in an attempt to please everyone, the Park Service irresolutely settles for a compromise that pleases no one and produces a stalemate; the years pass as the opposing parties exhaust their legal remedies; and finally Congress intervenes, usually on the side of those who are pushing for more use and less preservation. This script was followed to the letter in the dispute that followed the Park

Service effort to limit the number of people floating the Colorado River in Grand Canyon National Park.

The one-armed Civil War veteran, Major John Wesley Powell, made the first passage of the Great Unknown in 1869 with a crew of nine men and four boats. There was no retreat once they entered the steep-walled canyon, a hazard that had discouraged other explorers. A geologist, Powell did not credit reports of high waterfalls (which would have been terminal), reasoning that a river so loaded with silt and abrasive rocks would long since have scoured the streambed down to a navigable grade. He found the river, however, wild enough. One boat was smashed beyond repair; the crew swore they spent more time in the water than in the boats; three men gave up the struggle and laboriously made their way out of the canyon, only to be killed by Indians. After sixty-six days, the party emerged into the Grand Wash, and Powell wrote in his journal, "The river rolls by us in silent majesty; the quiet of the camp is sweet; our joy is almost ecstasy."

Probably no set of statistics illustrates the explosive growth of wilderness use more vividly than the year-by-year count of raft traffic on the Colorado River since Powell's journey. Because of severely limited access and the considerable preparation and equipment required for a trip, which attracts attention, an accurate record is available. In the seventy-one years from Powell's initial expedition until 1940, only forty-four people made the passage. In 1950 seven people floated the river, in 1960 there were 205, and in 1970 just under 10,000. In two more years, by 1972, the figure was well over 16,000.

The awesome risks faced by pioneer boatmen—Lava Falls is one of the fastest navigable rapids in the world—had become a piece of cake for modern equipment, the huge inflatable rubber rafts, extremely sturdy and stable, adapted from military models. Babies, the elderly, and the physically handicapped could make the voyage with little danger. On a single day as many as 500 people might gather at Lee's Ferry for the departure. More than twenty tons of fecal matter were being deposited on sand bars by river passengers every year. Linblad tours offered shrimp dinners with ice cream for dessert. *Playboy* magazine posed its bunnies before Vulcan's Throne.

Alarmed by the rapidly worsening conditions along the inner canyon, the Park Service reviewed its options, well aware of the storm of controversy that would greet a limitation on use. In 1972 the decision was reached; the Park Service would hold the line at that year's level. Acknowledging that it could not determine a justifiable carrying-capacity figure without better scientific knowledge of the impact of human use, the Service announced it would not establish a permanent ceiling figure until extensive research studies were carried out and analyzed.

A source of immediate contention was the further decision to peg the ratio between commercial and private use at the 1972 level. In that year the twenty-one concessioners, licensed by the Park Service, consumed 89,000 user-days (a user-day being one person on the river for one day), while private river runners, who organize their own expeditions, clocked 7,600 user-days. Accordingly, the ratio for the interim period was set at 92 percent for concessioners and 8 percent for private groups.

The private river runners, who were just beginning to establish themselves, were enraged by the disparity and by the yearly lottery system installed to award the private permits. In one year there were more than 500 applications for the thirty-seven permits, the lucky names being drawn at random. The arguments of the private river runners were persuasive: their rates were lower than commercial prices; their rafts carried fewer people and their trips lasted longer and allowed more time for leisurely exploring of side attractions; using oars rather than motors, the experience was much more in keeping with the character of the canyon. The concessioners retaliated that over many years they had introduced the activity and developed the techniques; their customers were more representative of the public generally and their safe, regularly scheduled trips were more convenient for vacationists; the private operators catered to the small group of unrepresentative elitists, the same people who wanted to lock up the wilderness.

The Park Service advanced a preliminary plan to gradually, but significantly, reduce the total level of use and to phase out motors. However, it was shortly withdrawn. For six years the process of putting together a workable and acceptable plan dragged on. Public hearings were marked by discord, squabbling, and intense feelings. Researchers looked into the attitudes of river runners toward motorized trips versus oar-powered trips, examined the effects of overcrowding, and studied group dynamics, but the results were somewhat lacking in specifics. Then, in 1978, the Park Service issued its long-awaited Colorado River Management Plan and Environmental Impact Statement. It proposed that, following further public hearings and comment, the number of user-days be doubled, the ratio of commercial to private permits be changed from 92:8 to 70:30, and motorized trips be phased out.

No one was satisfied. Concessioners objected to their reduced allotment and the phaseout of motors. Environmentalists were shocked by the 100 percent increase in river use. Private boatmen, fighting any arbitrary allocation, hired lawyers. A warning of things to come appeared when the Mountain States Legal Foundation filed suit against the Park Service for "unilaterally creating a wilderness area without Congressional approval" by proposing the motorboat ban. "This is an attempt by NPS to arbitrarily limit use of a national park by increasing the time, money and physical stamina required of river runners," the Foundation's director, James Watt, declared in 1979 (only a year before he was chosen as secretary of the Interior). "The end result of this policy will be to render such trips inaccessible to all but a privileged and elite few."

The Park Service proposal was inevitably a bureaucratic compromise, disappointing to environmentalists, yet its recommendation to end the use of motors on the Colorado River was a rather valiant and effective stratagem for moving the "baloney boat" commercial operation in the direction of a more traditional and primitive white-water experience. There was, however, considerable dissatisfaction in Congress with the Park Service plan.

"The concessioners are organized," Fred B. Wiseman pointed out in his article for *Natural History,* aptly entitled "Who Runs the Grand Canyon?" "Their passenger lists can produce thousands of identical messages to senators and representatives, singing the praises of commercial services." The private boaters, of whom Wiseman is one, are a proudly independent lot, he noted, "who really don't care much for organizations, dues, and legislation" and would prefer to meet nature on its own terms rather than by presenting a credit card to a travel agency.

As it turned out, Congress runs Grand Canyon. It attached a rider to the 1981 appropriation bill for the Interior Department killing the Park Service plan to ban motor boats on the Colorado River.

8

THE PROBLEM OF CONCESSIONS

When Nat Reed served, with considerable flair, as assistant secretary of the Interior during the Nixon-Ford administration, he spent considerable time reviewing and arbitrating concession matters. "There has always been a certain amount of tension between the Park Service and the concessioners," Reed observed in a recent speech, "but it's a healthy tension." Everyone familiar with the parks would agree with Reed's assertion; certainly no other aspect of park operations has stimulated more public dissatisfaction or political attention. Queen Mary I of England declared that when she died her subjects would find "Calais," her longtime nemesis, engraved on her heart. For directors of the National Park Service the inscription would probably read "Concessions Management."

A *New York Times* story in 1980, entitled "Park Service Conflict: Concessions vs. Conservation," suggested that the real issue in the long-simmering dispute was the future of the parks: will they be subjected to increased developments in order to serve more and more visitors, as the concessioners urge, or will they, as the conservationists argue, be kept in a more natural state? "The Park Service is cutting back the concessioner methodically so that we have less and less security," declared Don Hummel, then president of the Glacier Park Company, who logged nearly fifty years as a concessioner before his recent retirement. "It's all because of intense pressure from the environmentalists who want to keep the parks pristine and only allow young people who can backpack to use them."

Responding for the organized conservationists, Destry Jarvis of the National Parks and Conservation Association noted that concessioners were too loosely controlled by the Park Service, creating "a highly undesirable situation in which concessionaires' profits appear to be more important than protection of park resources or services to visitors." A longtime student of park policy, Jarvis charged that the business people "cut corners, resist change and stand as a road block to park service efforts to manage park resources properly." The chairman of the Conference of National Park Concessioners expressed the frustrations of his group: "Every time we turned around, the park service was trying to change the contracts on us. We had to protect our rights. They were making it impossible for us to build new facilities or upgrade our old ones. They were making it difficult for us to exist."

Such discord may or may not be healthy, but it is inevitable. The Park Service and its concessioners do not have identical missions. Their purposes are sometimes parallel, sometimes in conflict. The relationship is not a partnership, an arrangement implying equal authority and responsibility. Instead, the Park Service supposedly calls the shots. It invites bids, selects the best-qualified firm to perform the needed services, and issues a contract spelling out the terms under which the concessioner must operate. All rates, whether for a hotel room or a hamburger sandwich, are approved by the Park Service. If the concessioner obtains permission to build a new facility, the location and design must pass Park Service inspection. The opening and closing dates of the season are set by the Park Service; if the concessioner's performance is deemed unsatisfactory, his contract can be terminated.

On paper this authority seems absolute, but in practice the sides are much more even. The concessioner's contract grants him "Preferential Rights," meaning that he is given preference over other competing firms when his contract is up for renewal. This almost impregnable position is strengthened even more by the long-term duration of the contract, thirty years for the larger operators. A concessioner is dealing from strength when he has fifteen years left on his contract, knowing he will be given preference over the bids of any other companies seeking the contract. Beyond these guarantees, the concessioner receives what amounts to an almost free hand to refuse certain Park Service requests: he cannot be forced to take any action that he determines will threaten the profitability of his business. It is an argument that gives the concessioner formidable leverage. Tough-minded concession decisions are difficult when a superintendent stands on such uncertain ground.

For example, should a superintendent propose that a concessioner consider establishing a quick-service snack bar as an alternative to the more expensive and time-consuming restaurant lunch, his request may get a cold reception: there's less profit in a hot dog than in trout amandine. More likely, the concessioner will counter with a promise to give the idea serious study *if* the superintendent will act favorably on his pending request for an increase in hotel rates. Glumly, the superintendent trades his bargaining chips.

There is, however, no bartering on some issues. Should the superintendent draw up a new master plan that calls for a reduction in the level of park use, he does so knowing that the concessioner will be adamantly opposed and that he had best be prepared for a bare knuckles brawl. Wisely, the concessioner does not plead loss of business or reduced profit as the reason for his resistance. Instead, he argues that the concessioner, rather than the Park Service, has a true concern for the preferences of the traveling public. He challenges any restriction on park use as a wrong-headed surrender by the Park Service to the impractical demands of environmentalists who, to repeat a favorite concessioner theme, want to exclude all but the adventuresome young from the national parks.

It should not come as a revelation that concessioners are in the parks for the primary purpose of making profits. A good many people believe there is something intrinsically wrong about bringing big business into the parks to make money from Old Faithful, the Giant Sequoias, or Grand Canyon. Others, who depend on lodges and restaurants, regard them as essential. Congress has decreed that private enterprise should provide these services, but the larger companies are admittedly difficult to control. They may be operating in the wilderness rather than Florida's Gold Coast, but like any corporation whose policies may be dictated by clever tax lawyers, they seem careless of the results of their decisions if the profits improve.

Granted, it is not all easy sailing for the concessioner. Dealing with the federal bureaucracy can be infuriating. A request to initiate an operational change that needs a quick decision may proceed on its inexorable journey from one in-box to another no more expeditiously than if it were consigned to the Pony Express. There have been recent improvements, but in the past park people assigned to monitor concession operations have not had enough experience to competently review the actions of professional food, beverage, and hotel managers, much less comprehend the wizardry of corporate bookkeeping.

When a concession management specialist in a major national park was asked whether the concessioner in his park had a real concern for environmental values, he replied: "He does, if in no possible way will it deduct from his gross." Incensed by this general attitude, Don Hummel once retaliated at a meeting of park superintendents, asking them "Why do Park Service employees who receive their paychecks from Uncle Sam every two weeks without fail feel superior to the concessioner who has to show a profit before he can get paid?"

Concession Origins

Steve Mather was a practical man who once explained the basic reason for having concessions: "Scenery is a hollow enjoyment to a tourist who sets out in the morning after an indigestible breakfast and fitful sleep on an impossible bed." Soon after becoming director, he learned that in the previous forty-three years of national park history no one had puzzled out how to develop a system to control the concessioners who had proliferated in many of the parks and were engaged in chaotic and often cutthroat competition.

When Congress established Yellowstone, it harbored the pleasant thought that the park could be operated at no cost to the national treasury, reasoning that necessary tourist services would be supplied by entrepreneurs who would pay the government for the privilege of doing business. The legislation specified "the Secretary may, at his discretion, grant leases for building purposes, for terms not exceeding ten years, of small parcels of ground, at such places in said park as shall require the erection of buildings for the accommodation of visitors." This vaguely worded sentence, which constituted the only legal instruction for many years, contributed to the confusion that followed. Whether the concessioner was to be closely regulated, whether his profits were to be unlimited, or whether competition would determine price levels, were matters the legislation ignored.

It is a tribute to the zeal of private enterprise that even before Yellowstone was established, primitive hospitality existed in the form of an earth-roofed log "hotel." It was "the last outpost of civilization," according to one guest, "that is, the last place where whiskey is sold." Within a few years, saddle stock could be rented at Mammoth Hot Springs. When business was slow (surprisingly there were an estimated 500 visitors a year through most of the 1870s), the wranglers soaked small objects such as horseshoe nails in the hot springs. After a couple of days' immersion they took on the appearance of alabaster, sold briskly to the tourist, and were probably the first Yellowstone souvenirs.

By the time the Park Service was established in 1916, concession operations in the parks were disruptive and uneconomical; many were of the dog-eat-dog variety that tried to snare tourists from one another with tactics borrowed from a carnival midway. In Yellowstone, one company operated a hotel and restaurant at each of the five major features. It had considerable competition from three permanent camp companies, all providing a camp (canvas sleeping quarters on wooden frames) and lunch station at each of the five centers. In addition, there were three competing stagecoach lines. The situation was similar in

Yosemite where more than two dozen concessioners provided accommodations, meals, and transportation.

Taking over in 1919 as the first civilian superintendent following the army era in Yellowstone, Horace Albright reported upon the freebooting tactics of the hotel concessioner. Although he had neglected to obtain a permit or to make payment to the government, he was cutting away large sections of the forests surrounding his hotels to fuel their fireplaces (Albright forced him to utilize only dead-and-down timber). In like manner, employees were assigned "market fishing" duty, which supplied free trout for the dining tables from the Yellowstone lakes and rivers (a practice Albright promptly prohibited). Even though all facilities were badly overcrowded and in need of extensive repairs, this concessioner established a precedent much favored by his successors. He put as little money as possible into the operation, while extracting the maximum profit. A "soulless corporation," Albright noted. Making an unannounced inspection of a camp kitchen, he concluded it would have turned the stomach of a black ant. That day the camp reported twenty cases of ptomaine poisoning.

Albright was the right man for Yellowstone during the 1920s, for he had two essential qualities of a good superintendent. He loved his park and he genuinely liked people. He traveled constantly, stopping whenever he encountered a crowd of tourists, telling them where to hike or fish, asking whether they were receiving courteous treatment from the rangers and decent service from the concessioner. A favorite practice in the evening was to drop by a campground, build up a fire, and entertain the campers for hours. It was unabashed boosterism, but the novelist Kenneth Roberts wrote a highly complimentary sketch of Albright for the *Saturday Evening Post* entitled "Grand Duke Horace of Yellowstone."

As director, Mather's strategy was to expand use of the parks, a sure method of increasing congressional appropriations. Some of the concession facilities were comfortable, particularly those built by the railroads; others were marginal at best. New facilities would require capital, but banks were not eager to invest in the parks where the customary hazards of doing business were compounded by short seasons, high construction costs, and the unpredictability of government regulations (Mather personally advanced one concessioner $200,000, a typically generous, if indiscreet, act of a man who frequently pulled out his checkbook when the parks needed help).

From Mather's point of view the traditional free enterprise approach had proved itself ill-suited to the parks. There were too many small enterprises and too much squabbling. It would be better, he decided, to license a single company as a "regulated monopoly" not unlike a public utility. Each park would have a single, closely supervised franchise holder to handle everything—hotels, camps, restaurants, transportation. Mather forced the necessary mergers; the leases of the worst offenders were terminated; and, although he was almost blasted out of his job by unwilling concessioners who took the political route, the new policy was in effect by the mid-1920s. The Park Service protected the concessioner against competition while requiring good service at a reasonable price.

The larger concessions in the pre-World War II era were often family-owned companies that catered to the relatively few wealthy tourists able to travel during the doldrums of the Depression. Many arrived by rail, received personal attention in the hotels, and were guided through the park in company touring cars. The pace was leisurely. Beginning in 1946, however, as the wartime rationing of tires and gasoline ended and the economy boomed, the parks were inundated. Massive investments were required to construct new facilities. The companies reorganized; among the casualties of modernization were the old-style methods and tempo.

The new management was uneasy with the somewhat informal concession guidelines laid down by Mather. Periodically, there were complaints against concession operations, occasionally followed by congressional investigations; the concessioners feared that a hostile administration in Washington might change the rules under which they had been operating. At the insistence of the concessioners, Congress put an end to the bickering by passing the Concession Policy Act in 1965, thus making the relationship between the concessioners and the Park Service a matter of law.

Tenaciously involving themselves in the drafting of the legislation, the concessioners were able to gain most of their demands, including preferential rights, long-term contracts, and a proviso placing them in an almost invulnerable position. "Possessory interest" gives the concessioner de facto ownership of all of his holdings; to cancel his contract, the Park Service must pay the appreciated current market value of the facilities. The concessioners argued that without this legal assurance, they would be unable to obtain capital from lending institutions. A "buy out," in today's inflated market, is almost beyond Park Service budget capability. The concessioners were justifiably pleased with the 1965 bill, which generally endorsed their track record. As one conservationist ungraciously observed, the bill's message was clear: the parks couldn't exist without the concessioners. Those people who have been grateful for the chance to explore the parks while retaining a decent respect for the comforts of life might well agree.

Enter the Conglomerates

For many years the Yosemite Park and Curry Company, prime contractor in Yosemite National Park, was warmly regarded by its customers and by the Park Service. Its founders, David and "Mother" Curry, school teachers from Indiana, began their association with the parks in 1894 by leading summer tours from Ogden, Utah, to Yellowstone in prairie schooners. In 1898 they moved their operation to Yosemite and established a permanent camp consisting of a half dozen tents, a cook, and a few college-student helpers. Although it has been greatly expanded and modernized, the site of Camp Curry in Yosemite Valley has never changed, a somewhat rustic retreat in the trees much appreciated by families who return summer after summer.

In 1925, when Mather instituted his policy of amalgamations, the Curry company was consolidated with its competitors to form the Yosemite Park and Curry Company. It became one of the largest of national park concessions, operating the extensive Yosemite Lodge complex and the stately Ahwahnee Hotel, along with a variety of other hotels, cabins, camps, and a ski slope. The company became a respected institution, and it prospered, largely because of the enlightened management of the Curry family. After "Mother" Curry's death in 1948, control passed to her daughter Mary, whose husband was the president of Stanford University. Mary Tressider had style and an enduring love for Yosemite that often took the form of generous bequests for projects the Park Service was unable to fund.

Yosemite Valley, only 7 miles long and 1 mile wide, is the heart of the 1,200-square-mile park. Teddy Roosevelt called it "the most beautiful place in the world," and a great many persons have echoed that assessment upon their first view of the plunging waterfalls and the granite wall of El Capitan rising vertically 3,500 feet. Into this valley come 2.5 million visitors every year. Here live most of the 1,700 Park Service and concession employees and their families, and here are located most of Yosemite's 1,350 buildings. In the early 1970s the Park Service was in the process of preparing a master plan intended somehow to ease the impact of so many people and so much development on the valley.

Then, in 1973, the giant entertainment conglomerate, the Music Corporation of America (MCA), bought the Curry Company. It promptly gave notice that things were going to be different in Yosemite. "We want it to be something a lot more people can enjoy," an MCA executive declared. A new advertising brochure was headed, "Yosemite—Nature's eloquent answer to Convention City." The dignified old Ahwahnee would henceforth provide for all "worldly needs," from bars to barbers to beauty shops. Advertisements proclaimed, "This isn't no-man's-land. Or primitive wilderness. This is civilization." MCA immediately presented the Park Service with a series of proposals, including construction of additional lodge units in the valley, replacement of rustic cabins with modern motel units, a campaign to attract convention business, and an aerial tramway from the valley floor to the Glacier Point overlook.

That kind of hustle brought an immediate response. Newspaper editorials asked whether the corporate giant, geared to making the highest possible profit, would inevitably strive to make a national park more like a resort. Conservation journals asked whether MCA thought it had bought the concession company or the entire park. Critics noted that the MCA takeover was part of a disturbing trend in the recreation business. Large corporations were recognizing that it made more sense to invest in an established popular attraction than to build a new entertainment park, and they were buying concession contracts in a number of parks: AMFAC, the Hawaii-based agribusiness conglomerate and one of the largest sugar producers, in Grand Canyon; the Trans World Corporation in Bryce, Zion, and Death Valley; General Host in Yellowstone.

It may have been an omen that the year MCA came to Yosemite, the Park Service received a new director, Ronald Walker. He was the personal choice of Richard Nixon, who had just fired the previous director, George Hartzog. (This aberration and its aftermath are discussed in Chapter 10.) Walker's only known qualification was his personal association with Nixon. Walker named as his chief of concession management a person equally unfamiliar with parks, who had served with Walker as a White House advance man before joining the Committee to Reelect the President. The Nixon administration had close ties to MCA; henceforth, the concessioners were assured that their concerns would receive a warm and friendly reception from the new leadership of the Park Service.

MCA quickly accepted the invitation, transmitting its dissatisfaction with the direction being taken by the Park Service master planners who proposed to reduce the level of services and overnight accommodations in Yosemite Valley and to remove a substantial amount of Park Service and concessioner administrative activities and employee housing to a location outside the park. By anyone's standards the MCA counterattack on the master plan was well coordinated and aggressive.

Critics of MCA tactics in Yosemite were further outraged when its subsidiary, Universal Studios, moved a large filming crew into the park to produce a network television series. The short-lived series, "Sierra," involved a group of park rangers in a succession of wildly farcical adventures. Under the circumstances, it did not seem farfetched that one of the anticipated spin-offs from "Sierra" was publicizing Yosemite, thus attracting more customers for the Yosemite Park and Curry Company. The series quickly bombed, but not before a widely reported incident in which the film director decided to improve the appearance of Yosemite by painting the rocks.

In December 1974, things came to a head. There had been accusations by conservationists, reported in the press, that the original Park Service planning objectives for Yosemite had been subverted by the high-pressure tactics of MCA. The draft plan "appeared to be written by MCA," Assistant Secretary Reed observed, whereupon the Park Service decided to scrap the plan and start over. In December also, after several months of investigating the Yosemite situation, Representatives Henry Reuss and John Dingell chaired a joint hearing of the House Committee on Conservation and Natural Resources and the Committee on Government Operations. The hearing turned up irregularities in the planning process that were difficult for the Park Service to explain. The degree to which the Park Service "buckled," as Dingell charged, is arguable, but the hearing did make it clear that a corporate concessioner like MCA is motivated by a different set of values than the Park Service. The committee obtained a memorandum written by the able and unflappable regional director, Howard Chapman, as a precaution after a meeting with MCA. In it Chapman described the performance of the MCA representative as a blunt attempt "to take control and give direction to the objectives for the Yosemite Master Plan." Chapman's assessment of big business methods was perhaps understated:

> I feel that MCA came into this meeting taking the hard-line in the presentation of their objectives largely expressed in economic terms and with minimum sensitivity to some basic concepts of preservation and use that have been a part of the history of NPS. We have found them to be demanding of flexibility on the part of the NPS and staunchly adamant on the positions that they have taken with respect to their operations. I do not feel that they are entering the spirit of planning for Yosemite in a manner conducive to objective input and evaluation.

Representative Dingell's much-quoted rebuke, "Our investigation thus far suggests that the concessioners, not the National Park Service, are running the parks," is the kind of rhetorical excess much favored by politicians. (Most recently, Interior Secretary Watt has rebuked the Park Service for *not* giving concessioners greater responsibilities in park operations.) The Yosemite incident confirmed public perception that the conglomerates would, if given the opportunity, manipulate policy. Investigations of concessions in a number of parks followed immediately, conducted by the General Accounting Office and the Department of the Interior. Their conclusions echoed the verdict that the Park Service was not effectively monitoring its concessioners. The Service was sternly admonished for not granting the public the same free access to planning discussions that MCA had received; it was also directed in the future to conduct all planning in full view of the public and with its active participation.

Unquestionably, the Yosemite affair damaged the credibility of the Park Service, and the allegation that it had not played square with the public was by far the most troubling reproach. But a lesson was learned. Starting a new master plan for Yosemite, the Park Service involved the public to an extent that bordered on overkill. Forty-eight public hearings were held in California and across the country, with participants receiving a workbook that took them four or five hours to complete, recording their opinions on every conceivable detail. The workbooks required computerized tabulation. One newsman reported, "The process was so satisfying that it drew 62,000 participants. At hearings in 1978 the audience applauded the final draft plan."

After his well-publicized hearings, Representative Dingell introduced a bill to amend the 1965 Concessions Policy Act by eliminating some of the entrenched privileges and strengthening the authority of the Park Service to control its concessioners. The bill, predictably, attracted little support and soon died, its demise no doubt hastened by the well-organized cavalry charge of the concessions lobby. "We have those oversight hearings every few years," an Interior Committee staff member explained, "but nothing ever comes of it. The political climate is just not right."

The End of the Yellowstone Park Company

In April 1977, shortly before the opening of the travel season, the *New York Times* exploded a bombshell after one of its reporters came into possession of an unreleased Park Service evaluation of the operations of the Yellowstone Park (YP) Company. The front-page story was devastating. According to the official report, food service bordered on the outrageous; hotel rooms were dirty; the employees were underpaid, inadequately trained, and often rude or indifferent to guests; and the general atmosphere was one of tawdry exploitation and decay. Yellowstone, the flagship national park, was a disgrace, its facilities "decrepit, unpleasant and potentially unhealthy." A report of this severity, indicting the performance of one of the largest park concessioners, was without precedent in Park Service history.

People were appalled by the findings of the report, which soon appeared in other newspapers, but the general reaction in the Park Service was that anyone who had ever been to Yellowstone would not be surprised. The YP Company had been an embarrassment for more years than anyone cared to remember. Family-owned since before 1900, the company had been swamped by the post–World War II travel boom and plagued by feeble management. As public complaints rose, the Park Service met the problem head-on, for a change; it cancelled the company's contract, despite murmurs in Congress, something of a landmark action against a concessioner.

The YP Company had been purchased in 1966 by the General Host Corporation, a conglomerate whose diversified holdings included baking companies and mines. General Host proclaimed a new era for Yellowstone, now that its commercial activities were being directed by men of large affairs. Customers, however, could detect little, if any, improvement in the quality of service provided by the new owners. In fact, the letters of complaint were as numerous as ever, prompting the Interior secretary to issue a press release one spring promising that conditions would improve: "We fully intend that the Yellowstone Park visitor this summer will see improved service and accommodations." Despite such promises, easily promulgated in Washington, the operations and facilities of the company continued to deteriorate unchecked.

The eye-opening 1977 report had its origins in the failure of General Host to carry out a key provision in its contract that required the expenditure of $10 million for repair and replacement of substandard facilities. When the deadline for the investment passed, General Host informed the Park Service that it did not intend to spend the required amount because there was no assurance it would receive an adequate return on the venture. General Host regarded its position as invulnerable; the only option open to the Park Service was to buy out the company, and the chances of obtaining funds from Congress for that purpose, as General Host well understood, were extremely remote.

Biding its time, the Park Service gave General Host a two-year extension on its contract obligation, time enough for a team of carefully selected concession experts to carry out an in-depth investigation. One could speculate that it was the intention of the Park Service from the beginning to make the deplorable practices of the company a matter of public knowledge. Upon completion of the investigation, the report on it was subjected to interminable reviews in various offices of the Department of the Interior. It seemed destined for bureaucratic oblivion, the fate of so many government reports that are likely to create controversy. Then, in some fashion never satisfactorily explained, a copy of the report fell into the hands of the *Times.* A few excerpts on various topics contained in the 535-page document indicated that the comment to a newspaper reporter a century earlier by Commodore Vanderbilt, "The public be damned," described the attitude of the General Host management:

- Company philosophy: "The management cannot respond to visitor needs because the company is not oriented to service to the public, but only to the generation of profit dollars."
- Management efficiency: Bonuses were being paid to company executives because they were able to extract a surplus from the operations but it was a profitable enterprise "not because of good service or quality facilities, but because of the thousands of visitors who enter Yellowstone National Park and have no other place to eat or sleep. Without a captive audience, and in a competitive situation outside of the park environment, the company could not survive as it is presently constituted."
- Food service (The company served 1.3 million meals every summer in sixteen separate facilities): Sanitation did not meet accepted public health standards and "the service varies from adequate to unbearable, often at the same time in the same facility." Hastily trained, unsupervised college students assigned to cooking duties displayed slam-bang work habits for study-team observers. In one instance, a cook casually dumped a ten-pound package of frozen chicken parts into a deep fry kettle, which had the obvious effect of dramatically lowering the temperature of the cooking oil. This practice, the report noted, substantially increases the amount of oil absorbed by the chicken, thereby insuring "a greasy, unsatisfactory product to the customer."
- Lodging (In their hotels, lodges, motels, and cabins the company provided overnight accommodations for more than 8,600 guests): "The furnishings in most rooms are mismatched and shabby. There are no apparent standards for maid service. Generally, the lodging facilities are poorly decorated, poorly furnished and equipped, poorly lighted, poorly cleaned, poorly heated and insulated, and merely tolerated by the typical visitor." In short, the rooms lacked charm, perhaps proving the contention of Robert Lewis Stevenson who said it is better to travel in hope than to arrive.
- Employee turnover (About 1,500 employees were recruited every year, mostly from college campuses): Company records showed that employees left the park in droves, with no replacements available. The reported turnover rate for 1973 was 50 percent; in 1974, 57 percent; in 1975, 65 percent; and in 1976, a horrendous 80 percent. "From mid-July through August, large blocks of rooms were taken out of service because of the lack of maids to service them. This situation results in huge revenue losses to the company, and inconveniences thousands of potential guests daily."

- Employee attitude: It was observed that employees displayed little respect for the company and were not hesitant to complain to the visitors they served. Their major complaints were the six-day work week, poor housing, low pay, unsatisfactory food and eating conditions, and lack of supervision, with the result that they deeply distrusted the company. "Of all the complaints and comments from employees that are reflective of their attitude, the most succinct is 'If the company is going to rip us off, we are going to do our best to rip them off.' Many consciously set out to do just that."
- Company attitude: "The company attitude toward most employees is that they are necessary evils to accomplish an end."

Considerably strengthened by the public's reaction to the Yellowstone report, the Park Service submitted to Congress a plan for the government to purchase the Yellowstone Park Company lock, stock, and barrel, upgrade the facilities, and then lease them back to a private firm on a short-term contract. The proposal marked a significant change, reversing the long-standing policy of private ownership of concession facilities. The YP Company was in part the victim of a self-inflicted wound. Upset with the lamentable performance of General Host, Congress in 1979 appropriated funds for the buy out.

But concession issues tend to prove the political axiom that all solutions create new problems. When the Park Service conducted an engineering survey of hundreds of structures scattered around the park, it found them in an alarming state of disrepair. The company obviously had not diminished its profits by spending money on maintenance. The purchase price for the Yellowstone Park Company was $20 million; the engineers estimated repair and replacement costs at $45 million. When presented with the $45 million bill, Congress quickly lost interest in Yellowstone concession matters. The Park Service was only partway down the road. The new operating company, chosen to manage the facilities on a trial basis for two years, has tried to improve things, but with only modest success. In 1982 a new arrangement will be made for leasing the facilities, perhaps with income being used to systematically upgrade the physical plant. A permanent resolution of the Yellowstone concession problem does not yet appear in sight.

Small Is Better

In almost all accounts of national park concessions (including this one), there is a regrettable tendency to focus on the handful of large parks where most of the problems occur and to imply that they are typical. They aren't. Probably more than 50 percent of all concession complaints involve Yellowstone. But altogether there are nearly 300 individual concessions, grossing about $200 million a year; most are of modest size, some handling such noncontroversial activities as boat rentals, firewood sales, and instruction in mountain climbing. All but seven concessions, in fact, meet the qualifications for Small Business designation, an annual gross of less than $2 million.

Small firms continued even after Mather's enforced mergers, either because a monopoly was not practical or because an exemption was advantageous to the park. There are many of the "Mom and Pop" variety, run by people who love the parks and have no urge to profit excessively from them. The fact that they have spent a good portion of their careers living in a park has had no less impact upon them than upon park employees. It most generally happens that Park Service people, who transfer every few years, are the transients in the park community, and the concessioners are the ones who provide continuity. The reason they choose to stay in a business whose returns are modest is little different from the reason Park Service people stay: both enjoy a life that has many compensations. Former director Gary Everhardt commented on concessioners he has worked with: "You look around and see some great people who have given their lives to the parks just as much as Park Service people have."

Inevitably, the field of photography has drawn a number of remarkable individuals to the concessioner ranks. Emory Kolb, who led one of the first expeditions down the Colorado River after Major Powell's, opened his photographic shop before Grand Canyon became a national park in 1919. For more than sixty years Kolb operated his studio in a cottage perched on the rim of the canyon at the entrance to the Bright Angel Trail. Every mule party paused there to have its picture taken through a window of the studio before descending into the canyon. As a tribute to Kolb, the Park Service has made his studio into an historical museum.

The master photographer Ansel Adams and his wife, Virginia, have operated a photography and book store in Yosemite Valley for nearly forty years. On the board of directors of the Sierra Club, and almost as highly regarded for his conservation work as for his incomparable photographs of the American landscape, Adams has been an adviser to many Park Service directors.

Following the Frontier is the title of Freeman Tilden's biography of F. Jay Haynes, photographer of the early West. As the official photographer of the Northern Pacific Railroad, Haynes documented the building of the western railroads and recorded soldiers at frontier forts, Indians in their tepee village, and the cowboys of the open-range era. Haynes was awarded the first Yellowstone concession in 1884, and his splendid pictures did much to publicize the park. A man of exceptional talents with an engaging personality, Haynes became a Yellowstone legend; he made a 330-mile ski tour through Yellowstone in midwinter taking the wildlife pictures that helped obtain passage of the 1894 Lacey Act to protect Yellowstone from the poachers. At the suggestion of Horace Albright, a mountain peak was named for Haynes, a rare tribute.

The Mesa Verde Company, prime concessioner in Mesa Verde National Park, is one of a number of concession companies with a rich history worthy of a narrative. It was founded by the first chief naturalist of Yosemite, Ansel Hall. He was a forestry graduate of the University of California who joined the Yosemite staff as an information ranger in 1919 after army duty in France. A born collector, Hall set out to develop a museum at Yosemite, gathering Indian artifacts, building display cases and scale models of the valley, and mounting wildlife specimens with the help of chief ranger Forest Townsley (father of the present superintendent of Yellowstone). Hall's activities, which included writing and lecturing, attracted the attention of the American Association of Museums; the association sent him on a year's field study of museums in the United States and Europe. After serving for many years as the chief naturalist of the Park Service, strongly influencing the early development of interpretive programs, Hall retired in 1937 to launch the Mesa Verde concession.

Bill Winkler, who now heads the company, is in the tradition of Ansel Hall. Winkler worked summers for the Park Service as a back-country horse ranger in Yosemite, while attending Colorado State University (the "ranger factory" in Park Service terminology). Directly upon receiving his natural science degree in 1953, he went to work for Ansel Hall and moved steadily upward until he was appointed company president following Hall's death. Active in Colorado civic affairs, Winkler is no less familiar with the story of Mesa Verde than the succession of rangers, archeologists, and superintendents who have come and gone during his nearly thirty years in Mesa Verde. "We think our visitors should have an opportunity to see the landscape in the evening, to listen to the coyotes talk to each other, to see the deer browse, and to see the constellations at night." Winkler has said, when asked about the role of a park concessioner. "We feel that we're interpreters. That's where our greatest satisfaction and services lie."

9

THE ALASKAN PARK SYSTEM

To do the state justice, it should always be written ALASKA! The name is from an Aleut word meaning the Great Land, but in fact Alaska is many lands. Even for this brief discussion of the disposition of its federal lands, some familiarity with the awesome geography of the state might be helpful. To repeat a well-known comparison, Alaska is more than twice the size of Texas. A better way to suggest its extent is to place a map of Alaska over a map of the continental United States: if the tip of the southeast panhandle is placed on Savannah, Georgia, the Aleutian Island chain will extend to the south coast of California at Los Angeles and the northern edge will rest on the Canadian boundary.

Alaska is a peninsula, the largest in the Western Hemisphere. Its coastline, measuring 35,000 miles, is in view of Russian Siberia and reaches to within 1,000 miles of Japan. Along the Gulf of Alaska tall mountains rise directly from the sea, with peaks above 19,000 feet. Portions of the range are covered by permanent ice fields, the source of massive glaciers, one of them larger than the state of Rhode Island. The Alaska Range, snow covered year round, stretches across central Alaska. Its dominant peak, Mt. McKinley, at 20,320 feet is the highest point in North America. The entire 600-mile length of the Brooks Range, extending across northern Alaska above the Arctic Circle, is the finest remaining American wilderness. Perhaps a few hundred people inhabit an area the size of Italy. When Robert Marshall explored this inaccessible region from 1929 to 1939, he encountered little evidence of man except for a few tree stumps, hacked by Stone Age axes, along the Eskimo overland routes.

Between the Brooks and the Alaska ranges is the Yukon River Basin, referred to as interior Alaska, an immense expanse of low relief containing large bands of permafrost, tundra, and numberless lakes, a splendid nesting ground for waterfowl.

Precipitation is heavy along the southern panhandle where mountains catch most of the moisture; the climate resembles that of Washington and Oregon, and there is a 16-million-acre strip of national forest lands, a northern extension of the rain forests of the coastal Northwest. The capital city of Juneau gets sixty inches of precipitation yearly, and its winters are milder than those of Chicago. Fairbanks, in the interior, receives only twelve inches of precipitation (much of Alaska is arid country); summer temperatures reach 100°F, and in winter the temperature drops to 75°F below zero. At Point Barrow, on the north coast, the precipitation averages five inches a year, and the highest summer temperature ever recorded was 78°F.

Equally important, Alaska contains a native population. The ancient rights of the aboriginal people to ownership of land precipitated a long legal and propaganda battle and produced two landmark congressional measures—the Alaska Native Claims Settlement Act of 1971 and the Alaska Lands Bill of 1980. Numbering about 60,000 (compared to some 30,000 in 1867), the native Alaskans live in small villages scattered thinly through the interior and along the coast. The Aleuts, almost wiped out by the brutal subjugation of Russian fur traders, number a few thousand and occupy the Aleutian Islands. Indians live mostly in the interior; the Haida and Tlingits in the southeast. Eskimos live along the western and northern coasts and inland along several of the northern rivers.

Although they receive small and irregular incomes from infrequent jobs and from welfare, the native villagers are largely self-sufficient, depending upon the luck of the hunt and the harvesting of animals, fish, birds, eggs, berries, and various edible plants. Native Alaskans are in transition. The older people hold on to the traditional life-style against the influx of modern ways. In a sense, the young Eskimos are stranded; they have been educated at Bureau of Indian Affairs schools, but there are no steady jobs in the villages and few opportunities beyond.

The Park Service will be closely associated with the Eskimos in the administration of several new parks. One of these, the Bering Land Bridge National Reserve, preserves a portion of the route believed to have been used by animals and Early Man in their migrations from Asia to the Americas. The land bridge, which disappeared about 10,000 years ago, was nearly 1,000 miles wide. It emerged during the glacial era when so much ice formed in the northern regions that the oceans fell 300 feet below their present level.

Archeologists have not yet uncovered unarguable evidence that would prove when the first humans arrived in Alaska. Some scholars believe the date for first occupancy is as recent as 12,000 years ago, but there is more general acceptance of the evidence of the Old Crow site on the Yukon River in Canada. Carbon tests of implements there (about which there is some question) date them to 27,000 years ago. A few skeptics of the land bridge route theorize that Early Man might have crossed the Bering Sea by boat or on the pack ice, a distance of but fifty miles at the only place where the Alaskan mainland can be seen from Asia.

Because this section of Alaska received little moisture, the land bridge and much of Alaska escaped the ice, permitting animals to cross the rolling treeless plain. Mastodons, bison, mammoths, musk-oxen, and deer were followed by their predators—lions, cheetahs, sabre-tooth tigers, and wolves. Coming out of Asia in pursuit were the Stone Age hunters who unknowingly entered the New World and who followed the sun southward, occupying North and South America. Commenting on this feat, a scientist remarked that only when space age man settles another planet will he again explore and occupy so vast a frontier.

The Eskimos, about whom more needs to be known, cannot be classified as belonging to either the Indian or the Asiatic-Mongoloid race. They arrived perhaps 6,000 years ago and chose not to journey toward a warmer climate. Instead, these hardy people remained in the Arctic, sweeping through Canada and Greenland so rapidly that their language remains today little changed. The only people who live in the Arctic year round, they make their homes in one of the earth's harshest environments where there is barely two months between spring and fall frosts. Some subsist on the caribou herds and fish of the interior; others have become the hunters of the sea, taking seal, walrus, polar bear, and the bowhead whale, until recently with primitive weapons.

Alaska Versus the Feds

Before the Prudhoe Bay oil strike in 1968, few people in the Lower Forty-eight had ever heard of the Brooks Range or the North Slope, and most Americans knew little and probably cared less about political or economic conditions in Alaska. From the purchase in 1867 to statehood in 1958, the policy of the federal government toward Alaska could only be described as one of ignorance and indifference. This "unique neglect," as it has been termed, is largely responsible for the long-standing resentment of Alaskans toward Washington and toward "Outsiders" with no real knowledge about matters in Alaska who have never been hesitant in making decisions affecting the state. Alaska, it should be emphasized, did not receive remotely the same treatment that other states enjoyed prior to joining the Union.

It began in 1867 as a military district. For convenience it was governed by army and navy officers, who presumed their role was temporary and would soon be replaced with a territorial government and the protection of the general laws of the United States. But for seventeen years Congress ignored the petitions of businessmen seeking to get a head start, frontiersmen from the West, and aspirants for public office. Without civil government, no prospective settler could acquire title to land, no pioneer homesteader could clear the trees and build a cabin with assurance of ownership, no prospector would stake a mining claim, no will was valid, nor could any marriage be performed.

Unfortunately, the original image of Alaska as essentially worthless and inhospitable was difficult to change. In 1880, when the nonnative population was only 430 persons, mostly military personnel, nicknames like "Iceburgia," "Polaria," and "Walrussia" were still being used by the press. The rush to the Klondike in 1898 brought thousands of gold seekers to Alaska, but the famous photograph of a solid column of men carrying heavy packs as they struggled up the treacherous snow and ice of the Chilkoot Pass—to say nothing of the poems of Robert W. Service—reinforced the popular impression expressed by one member of Congress that such a barren, unproductive country perpetually covered by ice and snow "will never be populated by an enterprising people."

In 1884 Congress finally made Alaska a civil district, with the general land laws of the state of Oregon to be the law of the district. All officials, including the governor, were appointed by the president. After forty-five years, in 1912, Congress authorized territorial status and an elected legislature, but gave it restricted powers, noting the bill "provides more than usual safeguards against unwise or vicious legislation."

In his first State of the Union message, in 1913, President Woodrow Wilson declared that Alaska should receive free and full territorial government—which never happened—and that as a rich storehouse it "should be unlocked." Alaskans would argue that the reverse took place, that the federal government locked up the entire state.

In western states the government began to withdraw land only after many of the most productive public lands had been claimed by private and commercial interests. In Alaska the process was reversed. Congress, the president, and the federal agencies withdrew large tracts of land for military reservations, for national forests and wildlife refuges, for potential hydroelectric sites, and for national parks and monuments. The remainder was placed under the jurisdiction of the Bureau of Land Management.

These large federal reservations further angered Alaskans. They denounced the land-managing agencies for empire building, holding incredibly vast expanses of land for some undetermined future use. Alaskans were no better than "tenants upon the estate of the national landlord," Alaska's delegate complained to the House of Representatives.

Addressing the Alaska Constitutional Convention in 1955, the governor—still a presidential appointee—entitled his remarks, "Let Us End American Colonialism." At statehood, 99.8 percent of Alaska was still owned by the federal government.

Before World War II, Alaska's economy depended upon salmon, furs, and gold. Alaska was not eligible to become a state, many people felt, because its nonnative population was under 40,000 and because its business and industry could not support the basic government services a state must provide—schools, police, roads, and hospitals. Abruptly, after Pearl Harbor, the strategic importance of Alaska was recognized. Billions of dollars were spent on airfields, army bases, and naval stations. More than 300,000 military personnel were stationed in Alaska. Some 7,000 lend-lease bombers were ferried from Alaska to Russia. For a time, when the Japanese invaded the Aleutians, a campaign that cost 2,500 American lives, Alaska was on center stage.

Realizing that a sound Alaskan economy could only be achieved by development of its lands and resources, Congress stipulated in the Statehood Act of 1958 that the state could select for its own use 103 million acres, an area the size of California. This grant exceeded the total of all federal lands awarded to the seventeen western states. A further benefit that has enriched Alaska, and one not enjoyed by other states, was the provision that 90 percent of the royalties and net profits from oil, gas, and mineral leases on the public domain would go to Alaska. Congress, however, was unable to resolve the thorny issue of native land claims during the statehood deliberations and side-stepped the issue, promising to make it the subject of future legislation.

Native Alaskans believed their claim to hunting lands was legitimized by thousands of years of use, although these rights were not formalized by land titles. Never able to unite their scattered constituency, the natives had no power in Alaska's politics. When the new state proceeded to select lands with mineral and oil promise that the natives considered to be theirs by right of long use, the reaction was a movement toward native unity for the first time and an assertion of native rights. In 1966 they formed the Alaska Federation of Natives and laid claim to more than half the state of Alaska. Sympathetic to the plight of all native people, Interior Secretary Stewart Udall the same year confounded and outraged nonnative Alaskans when he suspended all further land transfers to the state until the matter of native claims was resolved by Congress.

Little progress was made in preparing the necessary legislation until the oil companies determined that a pipeline would be the most effective method of transporting North Slope oil and then discovered that the most feasible route for the pipeline was covered by a checkerboard of native claims. In one of the more unlikely political coalitions of American history, the oil companies joined hands with the Alaska Federation of Natives, and in 1971 Congress enacted the Alaska Native Claims Settlement Act.

A monumental piece of legislation, the Settlement Act was as generous as political realities permitted. Not all of the natives were satisfied; while oil had made the settlement possible, they received no known oil lands in the transaction. To strengthen their political clout, Eskimos formed the North Slope Borough. It encompasses nearly all of northern Alaska and is larger in area than forty of the fifty states.

By the terms of the Settlement Act all previous claims were extinguished in return for a grant of a billion dollars and 44 million acres of land, an area the size of Pennsylvania. As one native remarked, the timing was probably ideal. If the Settlement Act had come earlier, they wouldn't have received the money; if it had come later, they couldn't have gotten the land. Beyond these tangible assets, the bill gave the natives political recognition and contributed strongly to their growing sense of self-worth and pride in their identity. In a rather remarkable change of status, the natives were also transformed into capitalists, for administration of the land and funds was placed with twelve native-owned, profit-making regional corporations. Soon the natives were owners of a new Sheraton Hotel in Anchorage, a reindeer ranch in Kotzebue, and oil-drilling rigs on the North Slope. One of the corporations is included in *Fortune* magazine's list of the nation's 1,000 largest companies. Professional jobs with these corporations have given young natives attractive goals to train for.

The d-2 Lands

The statehood and settlement acts had dealt with the land interests of the state and the natives. Conservationists and many others believed there were federal lands in Alaska that were of vital concern to all U.S. citizens. The now-famous Section 17(d)(2) was inserted into the Settlement Act late in the legislative deliberations. Called the "Bible amendment," after Senator Alan Bible of Nevada, it was concerned with these "national interest" lands. The secretary of the Interior was given two years, until 1973, to carry out studies of 80 million acres of the "d-2" lands and to recommend their establishment as national forests, parks, wildlife refuges, and wild and scenic rivers. He could also make further withdrawals under Section 17(d)(1). Congress was given an additional five years, until 1978, to act on the proposals.

National parks can be created only by an act of Congress, and they have been intermittently set aside, one by one, mostly after interminable deliberation. Now it seemed possible the national park system might be doubled in one stroke, with the inclusion of parks so enormous that entire ecosystems could be preserved and so undisturbed that a person could hike or paddle a canoe for hundreds of miles and never encounter another human being.

Nevertheless, there were many critics of the d-2 lands. Some questioned whether the public, in any significant numbers, would ever be able to enjoy parks that would be so costly to reach. The Park Service countered that precisely the same argument had been advanced a century earlier when the wonders of Yellowstone were even more remote from civilization and when it seemed also that the available wilderness was almost endless. Replying to those who were against locking up so much land, conservationists granted that fifteen Yellowstones worth of Alaska was conservation on a grand scale but contended that it was the last such opportunity the country would ever have.

Those Alaskans who traditionally regarded national parks as just one more example of federal interference, which should be restricted to the Lower Forty-eight, heatedly opposed the d-2 provision. According to them, not content to have given a large piece of Alaska back to the natives, the federal government was now proposing to give an even larger chunk to the bears. The future of Alaska's lands, they insisted, should be decided by Alaskans.

Looking at ample evidence of past mistakes in states where developers looted the land of its resources, there were many who took the view that Alaska must not be a replay of the Old West. Incredibly, the country was being given a second chance and the consensus seemed to be: this time let's do it right.

Alaska and the nation were fortunate that Jay Hammond was elected governor in the critical year of 1974, on a platform of controlled growth, and returned to office in 1978. Bush pilot, big game hunting guide, fisherman, and sometime poet from the native village of Naknek on Bristol Bay, Hammond had impressive credentials as a pragmatic conservationist—no other kind is tolerated in Alaskan politics. However, he expressed the sentiment of a majority of his constituency, united in their love of the wild country and their distrust of Washington, when he said that if the d-2 lands were established, "it would be a de facto repeal of statehood." Hammond was invariably guided by reason, except perhaps when he praised the level of environmental concern among his fellow Alaskans.

During the two-year planning period for the d-2 lands, extensive studies were carried out by Interior's Fish and Wildlife Service, Bureau of Outdoor Recreation, and National Park Service with the results and recommendations being coordinated by an Alaska Planning Group under the direction of a Park Service veteran of Alaska strategies, Theodor Swem. Alaska was not unfamiliar territory for the Park Service. Katmai and Glacier Bay National Monuments and Mt. McKinley National Park dated back fifty years, and the Service had been carrying out planning surveys for more than twenty years. In 1969 Secretary Udall and the Park Service had placed before President Lyndon Johnson national monument proclamations covering 7 million acres in Alaska, which required only his signature. Initially determined to sign the proclamations, Johnson reluctantly changed his mind when Congress strongly opposed the action as a bold attempt to bypass congressional authority (which of course it was).

In 1973, at the end of the planning period, Secretary Rogers Morton converted the planning results into legislation, which he submitted to Congress. The bill was partly the result of painstaking agency studies and partly political horse trading by Morton. Boundaries for all parks, forests, refuges, and wild river proposals, amounting to 83.5 million acres, were carefully drawn to exclude all known mineral or oil deposits. The national park portion contained 32.2 million acres involving nine new parks and substantial additions to Katmai and Mt. McKinley. At that point, after 101 years, the 285 units in the national park system contained just under 30 million acres.

As the self-imposed deadline for action on the lands bill was not until 1978, Congress made little progress the first several years, nor was there much sympathy for conservation generally in the Nixon-Ford administration. In 1977 Cecil Andrus was named Interior secretary by Jimmy Carter; the Morton legislation was replaced by a new and considerably expanded package in which the national park portion was increased to 41.8 million acres. Carter called the bill the most important conservation measure of the century and committed his administration to its support. In an unprecedented example of cooperation, fifty-two national conservation organizations formed the Alaska Coalition. It became a strong factor in deciding the outcome.

Morris Udall, chairman of the Interior Committee, led the fight in the House, and it passed a bill even more conservation-oriented than the administration's proposal. Then, just a few days before final adjournment of Congress in 1978, a Senate compromise bill that had been laboriously worked out and had seemed to have the support of all parties was unexpectedly torpedoed by Senator Mike Gravel, another in a string of irrational acts by the junior senator from Alaska. With the protection given the d-2 lands about to expire, Carter countered by placing them under various federal protective authorities, including 50 million acres proclaimed as national monuments. In making the announcement, Andrus pulled no punches: "We have no intention of letting Alaska become a private preserve for a handful of rape, ruin and run developers."

The Carter withdrawals, bitterly opposed in Alaska, opened the final chapter of the "Great Alaska Lands Dispute." The action was temporary, contingent upon congressional passage of a lands bill, but it effectively checkmated both the state, which could not proceed with its withdrawals, and the development interests, which could not undertake oil and mineral surveys. A lands bill was now in the best interests of all parties. Ironically, the goal Carter and his administration worked so hard to achieve was accomplished after—and in part because of—the Carter defeat in the 1980 presidential election.

Again the House had passed a strong conservation bill by an overwhelming vote of 360 to 65. Just before the November election, the Senate passed a somewhat leaner bill. Under the circumstances and considering the parliamentary maneuverings of the Alaska delegation, it was a most commendable performance. This bill, too, passed by a large majority: 78 to 14. The question of how or whether to seek a compromise—the Alaska Coalition favored waiting another year to pass a stronger Senate bill—was made moot by the Ronald Reagan landslide and by the surprising Republican victory in the Senate.

Recognizing this to be in all likelihood the last chance for conservation in Alaska, the House accepted the Senate version of the bill. In one of his final official acts, and certainly as one of the crowning achievements of his administration, President Carter signed the Alaska Lands Bill in December 1980, ending the nine long years of conflict. For those strategists in Congress, members of the Alaska Coalition, and key figures in the agencies who were invited by the president to the signing ceremony, it was the greatest conservation victory ever achieved.

Considering the top-heavy votes in the House and Senate in the face of the heaviest and most unrelenting pressure ever from the well-financed industry lobby, Carter was undoubtedly speaking for most Americans when he said, while signing the bill (officially the Alaska National Interest Lands Conservation Act), that it "strikes a balance between protecting areas of great beauty and value and allowing development of Alaska's vital oil, gas, mineral and timber resources."

Appropriately enough the *Wall Street Journal* was one of the few dissenting voices. Long disgruntled that "romantic notions of tundra and caribou," rather than hard-headed business philosophy, were motivating Congress, the *Journal* declared that the lands bill bore the unmistakable imprint of the Sierra Club. The reason, it said, was that "there are more votes to be had from cocktail party environmentalists in places like Cambridge and Sausalito," with the deplorable result that "a vast area of the United States with undoubted riches in fuel and minerals cannot be developed." Understandably the *Journal* did not go into specifics on the latter charge, frequently advanced, as the legislation in fact guaranteed that of Alaska's potentially productive oil and mineral lands, 100 percent of the offshore areas and 95 percent of the mainland would be open to exploration and drilling.

A Second National Park System

The Alaska Lands Bill more than doubled the size of both the national park system and the national wildlife refuge system, more than tripled the size of the national wilderness preservation system, and established twenty-six new wild and scenic rivers. The 43.6 million acres of national parklands created the equivalent of a second—and even larger—park system. Five new national parks were set aside: Kenai Fords, Kobuk Valley, Lake Clark, Gates of the Arctic, and Wrangell-St. Elias. Katmai and Glacier Bay National Monuments were enlarged and designated national parks. Mt. McKinley National Park was more than doubled in size and given the traditional native name for its dominant peak, Denali. Of these eight national parks, six are larger than Yellowstone.

Alaskan hunters, apparently most of the male population of the state, opposed national park expansion, and they were accommodated in the lands act. Ten national preserves were established, totaling 19 million acres, in which hunting and trapping are to be permitted. Six of these are immediately adjacent to national parks. As an example of the popularity of hunting in Alaska, in the period from 1965 to 1975 the number of resident hunting licenses issued jumped from 93,000 to 170,000—this with a population of 400,000 people. Reflecting this hunting pressure, in the area around Anchorage the moose harvest dropped significantly during the period, from 500 in 1965 to 46 in 1975.

The horizon-to-horizon parks in Alaska are in keeping with the prodigious scale of a country whose vastness is deceptive. Alaska, both awesome and vulnerable, has fragile resources whose remoteness has, thus far, provided protection. The caribou must move over hundreds of miles of tundra to find food; a single grizzly needs a hundred square miles of undisturbed habitat. The lands bill gave the Park Service five years to prepare master plans for the new areas, and director Russ Dickenson has told the planners "to make sure that the *abundance* of resources there is not subjected in any way to abuse that would preempt choices for future generations." Many parks will contain no developments or accommodations, will have minimal services, if any, and will be accessible only by foot or floatplane.

Not all of the Alaskan parks were established to preserve scenery and wildlife. For archeologists, Cape Krusenstern National Monument on the Chukchi Sea, north of the Seward Peninsula, provides a unique record of Eskimo life in the Arctic. It is unlike most archeological sites, in which evidence of successive cultures exists in horizontal layers, the most recent closest to the surface. Beginning thousands of years ago, winds and currents formed successive ridges of beach gravel at Cape Krusenstern, one in front of another. Settling as near to the coast as possible, in order to hunt the sea mammals, the Eskimos continued to move to each newly formed beach ridge. They left behind their pit houses with discarded weapons and implements. Today, the 114 lateral ridges contain the evidence of ten prehistoric cultures dating back more than 5,000 years. The record is still being written, for Eskimos continue to live at Cape Krusenstern.

Some of the new parks, like the Yukon-Charley National Preserve, contain both historic and natural values. Winding down through low mountains to its junction with the Yukon, the Charley River is considered to have the cleanest and clearest water in Alaska, an ideal stream for a float trip. This is gold rush country, not far from Canada's Klondike, where the cabins abandoned by prospectors and fur trappers still stand empty in the woods. One of the largest known concentrations of the rare peregrine falcon occurs in this stretch of the Yukon, a breeding ground for eighteen kinds of raptors.

Almost inaccessible, persistently hidden by clouds, the spectacular Aniakchak Caldera was not discovered until 1922. Only a handful of people have ever walked the floor of this six-mile-wide volcanic crater along which one can view lava flows, cinder cones, and warm springs and encounter grizzly bear, caribou, and eagles. The waters of Surprise Lake rush through a 2,000-foot vent in the caldera wall, emerge as the Aniakchak River, and flow through ash fields to the Pacific Ocean. In spawning season sockeye salmon fight their way up the Aniakchak, now designated a wild and scenic river.

In 1929, during the first of Robert Marshall's several explorations of northern Alaska, he came upon a valley in the central Brooks Range that narrowed as it passed between two facing mountain peaks; he named the formation "Gates of the Arctic." Traveling by snowshoe and dogsled, on foot and horseback, Marshall mapped unknown territory and provided more than 150 new place names. He found every stunning landscape surpassed by an even more splendid vista, a "revelation of fresh grandeur."

Marshall's description of the hidden valley suggests the origin of the key word of the Wilderness Act; he found it "just as fresh and untrammeled as at the dawn of geological eras hundreds of millions of years ago." He likened the valley to Yosemite. It was flanked by mountains that rose like escarpments with rock domes more spectacular than Half Dome, but he confessed an inability to convey "the sense of the continuous, exulting feeling of immensity."

The opportunity for discovery and for solitude still exists in the Gates of the Artic National Park, a complete Arctic wilderness. Except for the small village at Anaktuvuk Pass, the central Brooks Range is virtually uninhabited. Marshall reported that perfect as the Yosemite-like valley seemed when first sighted, into it debouched even more magnificent gorges, each unforgettably distinctive in character. "In the continental United States every one would be considered worthy of preservation as a national monument."

Assigned to the Gates of the Arctic at the beginning of the Park Service survey, John Kauffmann became almost as familiar with its geography as Robert Marshall had been. In his fine account of Alaska and Alaskans, *Coming Into the Country,* John McPhee describes a float trip down the Kobuk River in the company of Kauffmann, a companion on a number of similar adventures. A writer himself, Kauffmann has pondered the ticklish question of how to plan for public use of a park like Gates of the Arctic without endangering what Marshall called "the elation of the days spent in the little-explored, uninhabited world of the arctic wilderness." Most importantly, Kauffmann advises those who would explore the Gates of the Arctic, "You take this wilderness on its own terms, not yours."

> If the quality of the experience which the region can provide is to survive, use will have to be carefully and strictly regulated. This is not country for the many, for the many would destroy its character and mood. And it is no country for the casual. But it is readily usable and enjoyable for men and women of all ages who are willing to accept its challenges, who cherish solitude and adventure. They will never forget the beauty through which they walk and climb and canoe.

Subsistence on the Kobuk

A 1974 study by the Federal-State Land Use Planning Commission confirmed that Alaska's natives are among the few populations for whom subsistence—hunting, fishing, and gathering—is still the prevailing life-style. In a group of villages in northwestern Alaska that had a population of fewer than 4,000 people, the survey team reported the following take in a single year: 2,900,000 pounds of game, 1,436,000 pounds of fish, and 47,000 pounds of birds and waterfowl (the hard-to-believe average of nearly 1,100 pounds for each man, woman, and child is substantially reduced by the unrecorded amount of meat fed to the sled dogs or traded for other products). Almost all of the protein of these people and about half of their carbohydrates come from subsistence. Native ways have been extensively modified by civilization, the study noted, yet "hunting and fishing are still cornerstones of these people's cultural experience."

For nearly ten years the Park Service in Alaska has been discussing subsistence matters with the natives as well as inviting their participation in the planning of the parks. Hunting, prohibited in all national parks prior to passage of the Alaska Lands Bill, is foreign to Park Service philosophy, yet subsistence hunting, where established by previous use, will continue in the Alaskan parks. There are certainly some difficult problems involved, including the determination of how hunting activities can continue, through good years and bad, at a level that will meet native food needs without seriously depleting a park's wildlife resources.

And there are subtleties. Subsistence goes far beyond merely providing meat for the table, skins for garments, firewood for the long winters. Subsistence involves an emotional commitment to a life-style and requires an extraordinary knowledge and understanding of the land. "They opt for a subsistence livelihood, not just because it gives them the food they most desire or allows them to live where they most prefer, but because it permits them to be what they value most as human beings" is the assessment of an authority on Eskimo life. "Their sense of identity as Eskimos is fundamentally dependent upon living as hunter-gatherers. If they lose their subsistence life style, they are no longer 'real Eskimos'."

The native Alaskans did surrender all of their claims in return for the considerable benefits they received in land and money. Still, Park Service planners could not do better than turn frequently to the reproving words of an Eskimo elder.

> I tell the people here, Eskimos should make laws for those people Outside. That would be just the same as what they try to do to us. We know nothing about how they live, and they know nothing about how we live. It should be up to us to decide things for ourselves. You see the land out there? We never have spoiled it.

Preparing for its task of administering the proposed Alaskan parks, the Service commissioned a number of scientific studies during the 1970s. One was a comprehensive investigation of the role of subsistence in the lives of the Eskimo people living in the five small villages of the Kobuk River valley, a population totaling no more than a thousand persons (the Kobuk Valley National Park covers one small section of the valley). The survey was carried out by a group of anthropologists

Life was hard for our elders, "but they had their identity and sense of usefulness that we young people are losing our grips on," said Louie Commack (Aquppak) to the survey team. "The looks on their faces when talking about the past life proves how much life had meant to them."

> Yes, we have the stores to ease the starvation, movies to keep us from boredom, alcohol to take us away from our problems, running water to save us from many trips to the river, and schools to help us teach one another about the American heritage which sometimes does us no good in the village. But most of all we still have those people to show us how to fish and hunt, and tell us about our culture if we are only willing to listen.

The Park Service Turned Upside Down

In the 1980s the Park Service will be on trial in Alaska, even more than it was at Jackson Hole during the 1950s, at Redwood and Cape Cod in the 1960s, and at Gateway National Recreation Area in the 1970s. It begins its responsibility at a time when many Alaskans have a strong bias against the new national parks and against the National Park Service. But these generally negative attitudes may be changing, for opinions about Alaska's future are divided. Considerable disillusionment followed the get-rich-quick euphoria of the North Slope oil strike. "North to the Future" was the optimistic slogan on license plates after statehood, but during the pipeline construction boom the favorite bumper sticker in Fairbanks announced "Happiness is 10,000 Oakies going south with a Texan under each arm."

The Alaskan parklands are unlike any others. One planner has said the Park Service will succeed only if it recognizes that in Alaska the traditional values of the organization are "turned upside down." In some ways the situation can be compared to that faced by Steve Mather and Horace Albright in the founding days of the Park Service. As was the case in 1916, there are not many people to help carry the load. The Park Service received only twenty-four additional positions to administer the new areas, roughly the equivalent of one ranger for each section of parkland the size of Yellowstone.

When the protection of the Settlement Act expired in 1978 and President Carter gave security to the proposed parklands by designating them national monuments, his move—part holding action and part political counterstroke—placed the Park Service in an awkward position. Because the monuments were officially a part of the park system, the Service was obligated to enforce standing park regulations. Assuming immediate control over more territory than it was already administering in the Lower Forty-eight was a sizable task, complicated by the president's oversight in failing to provide additional staff for the purpose. A contingent of twenty-one hand-picked rangers was assembled from the other parks and dispatched to Alaska to patrol thirteen national monuments covering 41 million acres. It was a spunky effort to show the Park Service flag with a corporal's guard of rangers, but Alaskans vowed open defiance of the monument regulations, especially the prohibition against hunting. "We don't want anybody telling us we can't use this country the way we always have," was a frequently heard comment.

"We were on the front pages almost daily in the Anchorage papers," one ranger said later, noting that the local congressman had publicly declared the rangers to be members of the Park Service gestapo. "We were refused service in many areas. Three members of our team were evicted from their quarters in one town. Arsonists destroyed one of our airplanes." The climate improved somewhat when two of the rangers, experts in mountain rescue work, responded to an emergency call from Mt. McKinley National Park and completed a grueling recovery operation, bringing down the body of a Japanese climber who had fallen to his death at the 14,000-foot level.

Now that the parks are a reality, the consensus in the Anchorage office of the Park Service is that attitudes are beginning to improve, although the press, reflecting hard-edged sentiment in Juneau, Anchorage, and Fairbanks, is still generous with its criticism. The future of the Park Service in Alaska will be determined, largely, by the people selected for duty in the new parks. It takes considerable sensitivity, and toughness, to deal with extremes both in climate and in the environmental persuasions of Alaskans. Employees seeking transfers will be carefully screened, director Russ Dickenson has said, "because significant psychological and sociological differences exist in Alaska. The whole pattern of human activity there produces stress that may not be experienced by those of us who are used to the rhythm of life in the Lower Forty-Eight."

Most travel to parks is by chartered plane, and flying with bush pilots in uncertain weather is one of the hazards of duty in Alaska. In September 1975, a routine flight was scheduled to the proposed Lake Clark National Park. The planner making the trip decided to charter a larger plane to bring along the office secretaries who had typed and filed many reports on the new park areas, but never had the chance to see one of them. Coming through a mountain pass on the return leg of the 350-mile trip, the DeHaviland Beaver crashed. Six secretaries, the planner, and the pilot were killed, the worst such tragedy in Park Service history.

The lands bill gave the Park Service five years, until 1985, to prepare master plans for the new parks. Much of this work is being accomplished by a gifted group of Park Service professionals, many of whom have been on the scene since the early 1970s. They possess a variety of talents and an unshakable enthusiasm. They spend considerable time in the bush, absorbing the geography of the park to which they have been assigned, getting to know the local residents, and receiving and testing ideas. Keyman for the Yukon-Charley park and a vintage Park Service historian and savant, Bill Brown suggests that in the outlying sections of Alaska you encounter people who are the end product of a frontier tradition that began at places like Cumberland Gap. Admiring their spirit of independence—and something of an insurgent himself—Brown and a colleague chose to join the local community: "getting the anger part over with" and seeing if the park proposal might not offer a more livable future for the region than a lot of other futures being advanced by the locals.

> We rented a cabin, we cut our own wood, and we spent time up there when it's cold and dark. We knew that we could not gain understanding or respect if we were simply fair-weather bureaucrats. We suspected, too, that we had to have time, in this cultural milieu, to get past public-meetings posing and sit down with individuals around an oil-drum wood stove and talk and argue and lay our *shared* values on the line with these people . . . then coming back for more and being accountable this time for what we said last time.

In the course of building an invaluable photographic record of the Eskimo subsistence life style, Bob Belous has made friends in about every native village in northern Alaska. A dramatic, double-page Belous picture of an Eskimo seal hunt, appearing in the June 1975, *National Geographic,* is described as a scene "as old as man in America." It showed two hunters dragging homeward the carcass of a 500-pound oogruk, or bearded seal, which leaves a trail of blood across an endless expanse of pack ice. Whoever lands with Belous in the most remote village is assured of a friendly reception, particularly from the children who crowd around the plane and greet him with shouts of "Hi, Bob!"

Regional director John Cook, a third-generation Park Service hand and erstwhile rodeo rider, was the in-house optimist who spoke only of *when* the Alaska Lands Bill would pass, never granting that the final outcome might be in doubt. Cook, however, is a pragmatist. While grateful that the Park Service image seems to be on the upswing, he is not yet ready to replace a window in his office that looks as though it could be a souvenir from Londonderry or Belfast. "When the time comes," Cook says, thinking of earlier, nastier times, "I'm going to take out that glass with five bullet holes in it, frame it, and it's going to be part of a montage of keepsakes."

10

THE POLITICIZING OF THE PARK SERVICE

Joseph Califano remarked in his book *Governing America,* an account of his brief and stormy career as Jimmy Carter's secretary of Health, Education and Welfare, that when he took on the tobacco industry with his antismoking campaign, the action generated 10,000 letters, considerably more than he received on any other issue he faced as secretary. Having received some 14,000 letters of protest over its burro-removal program in Grand Canyon, the Park Service is well aware that its activities are likely to make headlines somewhere in the country every day of the year. An agency with that kind of visibility is acknowledged to be "political."

Since the days of Stewart Udall, the secretary of the Interior has been regarded as the guardian of the environment. With the passage of the National Environmental Policy Act (NEPA) in 1970, conservationists for the first time had legal redress against proposals they regarded as destructive to the environment, particularly those for activities on federal lands. They made widespread use of NEPA provisions to block large-scale projects, resulting in a near logjam in the courts. Because there is no established national policy to balance environmental protection and resource development, the issue of resource development has become a factor in most political campaigns. Administering lands that contain 80 percent of the country's oil shale and 40 percent of its coal reserves along with extensive deposits of minerals, oil, and gas, Interior has become one of the more sensitive—and political—departments in government.

The Stewardship of James Watt

When he was appointed head of the Mountain States Legal Foundation in 1977, James Watt represented the interests of miners, timber cutters, and oil drillers who, he charged, were being oppressed by "those bureaucrats and no-growth advocates who create a challenge to individual liberty and economic freedoms." Considering that Watt had taken dead aim on the Interior department, demanding that it must "unleash" private industry by opening federal lands to development, his appointment as secretary of the Interior by President Ronald Reagan was received by many Americans with something more than disinterested amazement. He quickly became the most controversial member of the Reagan administration.

The statutes that govern utilization of federal holdings are often quite general, giving an Interior secretary wide discretionary authority. There is no law against building additional facilities in the parks, making features more accessible, or turning over entrance stations to the concessioners—a Watt suggestion. An ideologue with a drop-forge hostility toward conservationists and a zest for belligerent confrontation, Watt was given to thoughtless witticisms in his early pronouncements. "I don't like to paddle and I don't like to walk," he observed after a float trip through the Grand Canyon, admitting he experienced a certain degree of boredom after the first day. To his credit, he has made his position perfectly clear. "We have a bias for private enterprise," he told a meeting of national park concessioners, promising them that if any member of the Park Service gave them a problem, "We're going to get rid of the problem or the personality, whichever is faster." He labeled wilderness protection "a greedy land grab by the preservationists." In his policy decisions on parks, he declared, "I will err on the side of public use versus preservation." Told that Ansel Adams had criticized such statements, he replied, "Ansel Adams never took a picture with a human being in it." According to Watt, when he outlined his environmental battle plan to Reagan, the president replied, "Sic 'em."

The Watt appointment came barely a month after passage of the Alaska Lands Bill, a measure for which organized conservationists, through their ad hoc lobbying arm, the Alaska Coalition, could take great credit. Formed of representatives from all major conservation groups, the coalition worked tirelessly for more than five years, consulting agency specialists, attending hearings, dogging congressional offices. With the victory in Alaska the coalition was disbanded, and there was no issue sufficiently compelling to unite the conservationists—until the arrival in Washington of James Watt.

The Alaska experience was a turning point for the old-line conservation groups, most of which had never been known for their political activism. Restrained from politicking by vagrant misgivings, they were more comfortable speaking to their own membership through their own journals. They had no mechanism for meshing their respective strengths and had seldom joined hands except when confronted by such key issues as the Wilderness bill or the Echo Park dam. In the 1970s they began to broaden their focus, filing law suits that brought projects on the scale of the Alaska pipeline to a halt. Support from the general public gave them cause to feel for the first time that conservationists were not voices crying in the wilderness but were a part of mainstream America. The country was developing an environmental tilt, and the conservationists had supplied much of the push.

The Reagan administration signaled its intention to change environmental controls on the grounds that they have stifled economic growth and energy development. Conservationists, who argue that polls have shown the public is not willing to turn the clock back on environmental gains, are gearing up to do battle: building grass-roots support through state and regional affiliates, improving staff professionalism by hiring experts with government and political experience, and taking strong positions on such issues as offshore drilling and strip mining as well as national park policy.

The Wilderness Society hired two members of Congress with impressive environmental records, who were defeated in the 1980 elections. Former senator Gaylord Nelson of Wisconsin, one of the recognized founders of the environmental movement and the author of many resource protection laws, was appointed chairman. He advises on political strategy. Former representative Joseph L. Fisher, a recognized economist who previously served as president of Resources for the Future, for a time headed an economic study group that enabled conservationists to employ the results of economic analysis in their debate with development interests over resource utilization.

James Watt can take considerable personal credit for the sharp rise in the membership rolls and the increased contributions to conservation organizations, which now seem well on their way to becoming a strong and permanent force in environmental politics. "A gang of modern day buffalo hunters has been appointed to protect the nation's air, land, water and wildlife," said Russell W. Peterson, president of the National Audubon Society, in a message to members explaining that the accelerated political activity of Audubon was a direct reaction to Reagan administration actions. "It's a sorry spectacle—but from it comes new hope. Thanks to Interior Secretary James Watt and other resource exploiters now in high public office the environmental movement is really moving again."

"The Politicians Will Choose"

In the late summer of 1976 President Jerry Ford's reelection bid was in trouble. According to the polls, he was losing ground steadily to candidate Jimmy Carter. On a day in early August, Assistant Secretary of the Interior Nat Reed paid a visit to the White House campaign staff. One of the few administration officials with credibility to the conservation community, Reed suggested that the president was overlooking the political attractiveness of the national parks. Just about everyone, Reed pointed out, was lamenting the state of the parks during the Bicentennial year. Much of the criticism was being leveled at the Nixon-Ford administration for failing to provide adequate support. In June the House Government Operations Committee had issued a report, *The Degradation of Our National Parks,* that had received widespread publicity.

Reed offered a proposal: pick an appropriate time and place for the president to make a dramatic announcement of a program to rehabilitate the entire national park system as a Bicentennial gift to the nation. There was a flaw, Reed granted. This would constitute a rather abrupt reversal of the Nixon-Ford policy of cutting back on park funding; in both budgets Ford had submitted to Congress, he had asked for substantially less money than the Park Service had requested. And with the election only a few months off, the Democrats would assuredly accuse the president of playing politics with the parks. Still, the White House campaign experts judged, the program sounded like a surefire vote getter; Reed was asked to have the Park Service put the package together.

On August 29 Jerry Ford "returned home" to Yellowstone, where he had served as a park ranger during the summer of 1936. From a platform erected in front of Old Faithful (which performed on schedule at the climax of his speech), he called upon Congress to appropriate $2.5 billion for land acquisition, maintenance and rehabilitation of facilities, and increased staffing for the national parks and wildlife refuges. As Nat Reed had predicted, the Democrats fired back. An "election year flip-flop," charged Jimmy Carter. After being subjected to embarrassing questioning by the Senate Interior Committee, Interior Secretary Thomas Kleppe argued, with little effect, "The time frame makes it look like political hypocrisy, but I deny that."

While grateful for Ford's election-time conversion, Park Service people figured he did well to get through his speech with a straight face, considering that on several recent occasions he had refused to allow the Service to use the funds or fill the positions already provided by Congress. To hear him tell it, Ford had never forgotten that glorious season he had spent in Yellowstone forty years before, but in the memory of the oldest Park Service graybeard he had never turned a hand to help the parks during his entire career in the House of Representatives. Ford's ploy failed to turn his campaign around, but the parks profited despite his defeat: President Jimmy Carter endorsed the additional funding and Congress cooperated.

The parks were in financial trouble in 1976—and are today—partly because there are so many of them. The considerable number of parks added in recent years has inflicted enormous strains on the organization. Many of the additions have been parks of the traditional type, historical or scenic areas in which all or nearly all of the land is acquired, making its administration fairly straightforward. But more recently parks have been created in which ownership of the land is divided among federal, municipal, and private holders, with administrative authority shared among several governmental entities. Where once the cost of a new park was measured in the millions of dollars, now the price can be in the hundreds of millions.

A change has also taken place in the criteria by which proposed parks are evaluated. In the past, national significance was the irreducible requirement: the uniqueness of the terrain or the influence of the historical event must be of national consequence. Recently a new test has been advanced: if the *need* for recreation is deemed sufficiently great—which is the situation in most cities—and if a proposed site or group of sites can accommodate this need, then the area is deserving of national park designation even though its resources are admittedly substandard and will likely serve only local residents. This new guideline, that parks should be established where people have easy access to them, was proposed by Representative John Seiberling of Ohio during floor debate over the Cuyahoga Valley National Recreation Area bill. Extremely controversial, the proposed park was made up of parcels of state, city, and private green space—including municipal parks, scout camps, ski areas, a golf course, and the home of the Cleveland symphony—located in the pleasant but scarcely spectacular twenty-mile-long Cuyahoga Valley extending from Cleveland to Akron. Subjected to heavy industrial use, the Cuyahoga River achieved a fame of sorts when a heavily polluted section near its junction with Lake Erie once caught fire.

There was considerable public opposition to the Cuyahoga project from those who felt that the federal government, already operating municipal recreation areas in New York and San Francisco, should not go any further into the city park business, particularly when the resources were substandard. Sieberling, who represented the Cuyahoga district, is a staunch park advocate (he chaired a special House subcommittee on the Alaskan lands), but he argued that cities are entitled to federal recreation areas. "Ninety-five percent of your constituents and mine, unless they happen to live in California, or Wyoming, or Arizona, will never see Yosemite or Yellowstone or the Grand Canyon," Seiberling told the House. Every year the members of the Ohio delegation voted appropriations for those distant parks, Seiberling reminded his associates, "and yet our constituents are beginning to say, 'Are not we who put up a lot of taxes and pay for those parks entitled to some return on our investment?' "

The Seiberling message was explicit and was not just a matter of equal treatment of taxpayers, but of practical politics. If the Park Service wants Congress to continue to support the established parks, he warned, it needs to begin putting parks closer to the people, even if the quality of the lands set aside fails to meet the traditional test of national significance. Seiberling's philosophy prevailed. Although the Interior Department testified against the legislation, recommending that Cuyahoga not be authorized, Congress accepted the Seiberling argument. Cuyahoga Valley became the third urban national park, soon followed by number four, Chatahoochie National Recreation Area at Atlanta, and number five, Santa Monica Mountains National Recreation Area near Los Angeles.

Should there be any doubt that parks are increasingly influenced by political considerations, it was later revealed by a high Interior official that Cuyahoga was also involved in Jerry Ford's 1976 reelection campaign. "We sent a blistering veto over to the president," said the official. Otherwise, Ford was told, "the floodgates will open" as other cities demand federally funded national recreation areas. The Interior recommendation put Ford in a bind, as it is axiomatic that a president never vetoes a national park bill. Debating what to do, Ford asked the advice of Senator Robert Taft of Ohio, who told him, "Mr. President, if you veto that bill, you'll almost be sure to lose Ohio in the election." Ford then turned to Interior Secretary Morton, who had hand carried the veto message to the White House. Morton said, "Mr. President, Bob's right," whereupon Ford "scribbled his name on that bill faster than you can blink your eye." The moral of the story, according to the Interior informant, is that "the politicians, not Park Service experts, are going to decide" which parks will be added to the system.

The "Park Barrel" Bills

It was Representative Phil Burton of California who demonstrated the political rewards that can be gained from park legislation. A leading House liberal, noted for his legislative savvy, Burton was favored to become Democratic Majority Leader of the House in 1977, but lost the post to Jim Wright of Texas by a single vote. Determined to win the party leadership job the next time around, Burton cast about for a committee assignment from which he could attract national attention, and, equally important, dispense favors to fellow House members. He surprised his colleagues by passing up the available Education and Labor subcommittee chairmanships, choosing instead to take control of the Interior subcommittee on national parks and territories. From this seemingly insubstantial post he proceeded to build a power base.

Burton discovered his vehicle in a routine measure called an omnibus bill. Because any boundary change or increase in the ceiling for land-acquisition costs requires a separate act of Congress, the Park Service has routinely packaged a dozen or two of these minor changes into a single piece of legislation. In the first session of Congress after taking over the parks subcommittee, Burton introduced an omnibus bill that was the largest piece of legislation affecting the parks ever drafted, carrying a price tag of $1.2 billion.

It took only five minutes for the Burton bill to clear the ponderous House Rules Committee. "Notice how quiet we are," said a committee member. "We all have something in there," which was only a slight exaggeration. The bill contained provisions affecting 200 members, nearly half the House, in forty-four states. So many projects were included for so many congressional districts that the press labeled it the "Park Barrel" bill and suggested that park funding might become as popular in Congress as the old politics of passing out the pork for the civil works projects of the Army Corps of Engineers. The bill easily passed the House and Senate in the closing days before Congress adjourned in 1978. The conservationists were ecstatic: "Representative Phillip Burton has almost singlehandedly pulled off the biggest legislative feat for park and wilderness protection since the park system was created," declared the National Park and Conservation Association's magazine.

Burton's feat was unprecedented. Eighteen new parks were created, there were additions to twenty-nine existing parks, and studies were commissioned for nine proposed parks. Conservationists were especially delighted with Burton's solution to the long debate over the planned Disney development of the Mineral King valley in California: the disputed area was removed from Forest Service jurisdiction and made part of Sequoia National Park. New developments as well as maintenance and rehabilitation projects were funded for thirty-four parks. Eight rivers were added to the wild and scenic rivers system, with seventeen rivers designated for study. The national trails system was tripled (under a separate Burton bill) to include the Continental Divide National Scenic Trail from Montana to Mexico, the Oregon Trail, the Louis and Clark Trail, and the Mormon Pioneer Trail from Nauvoo, Illinois to Salt Lake City.

Two years later, in 1980, once again in the hectic days just before Congress adjourned, Burton engineered passage of another "Park Barrel" bill. Somewhat more modest in scope—the price tag was only $130 million for twenty-two projects in fourteen states—this omnibus bill began as an attempt to correct the names of several national parks and "just grew," according to Burton. It traveled through Congress so quickly that Interior pleaded with the Speaker of the House for a short delay so that the Park Service could at least read the measure and comment on the provisions, but the request was ignored. "It seems to me that parks authorizations are one of those activities that the Congress regards as peculiarly its own," said a disgruntled Interior spokesman.

The bill was a skillfully crafted document that no one could oppose without antagonizing powerful constituencies, including women, blacks, and labor. Burton even provided something nice in the package to disarm the Republicans: There was a monument for the late Interior Secretary Rogers Morton, a historic site for former president Jerry Ford, and a lake named for Keith Sebelius, a well-liked Republican retiring from the House Interior Committee. Labor leader George Meany received a historic site; there were historical parks for civil rights leaders Mary McLeod Bethune and Dr. Martin Luther King, Jr.; the Womens' Rights National Historical Park was created at Seneca Falls, New York, site of the first American feminist convention in 1848. The overwhelming coalition that easily passed the omnibus bill "could have passed a test ban treaty," observed one congressman.

The Park Service was grateful for the omnibus legislation, certainly, but not without a few reservations. Burton seemed willing to make any compromise or add any politically attractive proposal so long as he could inveigle votes, at the expense of the once high standards of the national park system.

On the credit side, the system, whose historical holdings at one time seemed limited to birthplaces and battlefields, was enhanced by a number of richly varied parks more reflective of the nation's cultural achievements. Other areas established fit no known category. The Park Service had considerable difficulty locating the site of the Palo Alto battlefield in Texas, included in the 1978 bill. "We had to do all kinds of fancy archeological work to find the thing," a Park Service official remarked. A provision added to a parks bill designated the David Burger statue outside the Jewish Community Center in Cleveland Heights, Ohio, as a national memorial. It is a testimonial to an American citizen who was one of the eleven athletes representing Israel who were murdered by terrorists at the 1972 Olympics in Munich. The tragic event deserves to be memorialized, but Congress should not automatically turn to the park system as a mechanism for commemoration.

While omnibus bills authorize establishment of new parks, they do not provide the additional funds and positions needed to open the areas for public use—and the local communities clamor for immediate action. The year after passage of the 1978 omnibus bill, which added eighteen new parks, Congress actually reduced the number of full-time Service employees and cut the operating budget by $40 million. The Park Service has only one recourse, to staff the new parks by taking positions away from the old. Yellowstone has lost nearly seventy-five seasonal positions in the last several years.

Congress hastens to create new parks because it shares with the public the belief that places of history and beauty should be protected. Local pressure groups and determined individuals advocate pet projects, perhaps a piece of urban green space that should be preserved, and they come to Congress seeking a sponsor. On his first day as a member of the Interior Committee, newly elected Senator Daniel P. Moynihan proposed federal intercession to save New York's Central Park, saying that it was badly in need of maintenance funds that the city was unable to provide. "Something irreplaceable is being lost," he told the committee, meanwhile introducing a bill to include Central Park in the national park system.

Because the Park Service is about the only federal agency that preserves things, people who want to save something large like Lake Tahoe (Burton promised to include it in a future bill) or something small like the old toll collector's cottage by the local canal say "Let's make it a park!" Not all the recent authorizations are ones the Park Service would have chosen. The 1980 omnibus bill was drafted without any meaningful Park Service participation. In the 1981 budget its appropriation for studying proposed new parks was reduced by 90 percent. Making thorough field studies of areas under consideration for addition to the system has always been an important Park Service function, but Congress apparently no longer desires that advice.

"The national park system shouldn't be toyed with this way," the *Washington Post* commented editorially on the 1980 bill, noting that members of Congress could hardly have been acquainted with the legislation, as the committee reports describing its contents had not yet been printed when the bill was debated on the floor. Don't diminish the integrity of the park system by minor additions designed to spread federal preservation support politically or geographically, the *Post* cautioned. "Its good parks are so exceptional that the public expects near perfection wherever the Park Service sign hangs."

There is even a proposal before Congress to establish a Legionville park near Pittsburgh because the site gave its name to the American Legion, although it is reportedly now a used car lot. "It has no historic integrity," a Park Service information officer has commented. "There should be some recognition granted to the Legionvilles of the world, but whether it deserves to be a national park. . . ."

In the opinion of director Russ Dickenson the tremendous expansion of the system in recent years must be halted and all park proposals judged against strict standards. "We're running out of candidate parks," says Dickenson, who is concerned the park system will be diluted. "It's important that we keep the quality of the areas extraordinarily high. Each area must meet the test of national significance for entry into the system."

Five Directors in Eight Years

After the ceremony of swearing in Steve Mather as first director in 1916, Secretary of the Interior Lane casually remarked, "By the way Steve, I forgot to ask you, what are your politics?" It was Lane's way of saying that the Park Service job would not be subjected to political pressures and that Mather, well known to be a Bull Moose Republican, was welcome in Woodrow Wilson's Democratic administration. Mather served under three presidents and five Interior secretaries, and for more than fifty years no director was ever removed as a political measure.

That tradition was broken, and the decline in the fortunes of the Park Service began, in November 1972, shortly after the reelection of Richard Nixon. Director George Hartzog was summoned to the office of Interior Secretary Rogers Morton and told that his services were no longer required by the department. If it gives you any satisfaction, Morton informed Hartzog, the president himself gave the order to fire you.

Serving from 1964 through 1972, Hartzog might be termed the last director of the "old" Park Service. His departure came only a few weeks after what may have been the agency's finest hour, when it was host to the second World Conference on National Parks, convened in Yellowstone and Grand Teton in September to honor the 100th anniversary of the world's first national park. It was a gathering of nations, with participants arriving from Chad and Chile, from Finland and Fiji, from Iran and Israel and Ireland, and from the Soviet Union—more than 1,200 representatives from eighty-three countries. Most of the speakers were not unmindful that many countries developed their park systems after first observing the American model.

At the time of the conference, Nixon was already preparing to remake the government, following the November election. One of the changes he intended to make, apparently an obsession with him, was the removal of Hartzog. Nixon's dislike of Hartzog originated in an incident remarkable only for its triviality. With a certain wry humor (and under the proper stimulation), Hartzog will relate the story.

When the Park Service was acquiring the land for Biscayne National Monument, not far from Nixon's Florida retreat, it purchased the Biscayne Club. This imposing lodge was formerly owned by a group of wealthy sportsmen, of which Nixon's pal Bebe Rebozo was a shareholder. As was customary, the Park Service continued to employ the resident caretaker, who happened to be Rebozo's brother-in-law. Before the Park Service takeover, the caretaker had been granted exclusive use of the club's boat dock, but after he was placed on the federal payroll this privilege ended and the dock was opened to the public. As it turned out, Nixon and Rebozo had been the actual beneficiaries of the private dock, using it as an occasional stop on their jaunts in the Rebozo pleasure boat. Nixon was furious with Hartzog for not taking the necessary steps to maintain the dock as a presidential enclave. Thenceforth he preferred to anchor out in the bay rather than share the dock with the public.

"I was told the only thing Bebe Rebozo asked of Nixon in 1972 was that I be fired," Hartzog has said. Nixon declined an invitation to appear at the world conference in Yellowstone, sending his wife instead, and Hartzog remembers being told to stay clear of all pictures taken of Pat Nixon. "On her tour of the park, when she walked through the Old Faithful Geyser Basin, I was informed I was not welcome in the party," Hartzog remembers.

Nixon had had good reason to mark Hartzog when he came into office four years earlier. Interior Secretary Walter Hickel ousted all of his bureau chiefs except Hartzog, backing off when it became apparent that Hartzog was highly respected in Congress and that if he were fired, the Nixon programs for Interior would receive a cold reception. In an administration noted for its colorless executives, Hartzog attracted considerable attention as a virtuoso bureaucrat. Boldness was perhaps his best quality, and it could not have gone down well with his less-than-charismatic superiors that he was the subject of a *New Yorker* profile by John McPhee. Among the Hartzog anecdotes that still abound is a testimonial to his awesome energy and capacity for sustained hard work, told by the wife of one of his colleagues: "I could always tell when Myrl came home in the evening whether or not he had been briefing George Hartzog on some proposal, because if he had, even his shoelaces would be wilted."

For Hartzog's successor Nixon picked Ronald Walker, a White House advance man and former Allstate insurance operator. Walker, 35, had no previous experience with parks or environmental concerns and no known credentials for the job of managing a large and complex enterprise.

It was a worst-case choice that shocked and angered the conservation community. The Park Service was placed in the hands of a director whose single qualification was his proved fealty to Richard Nixon.

Sending Walker to the Park Service was part of a deliberate and cynical scheme drawn up by Nixon at the start of his second term. A hairline victor over Hubert Humphrey in 1968, he had not felt sufficiently impregnable in his first term to make the bureaucrats toe the line. This time around he intended to bring the entire federal bureaucracy under tight control by placing White House loyalists in key positions in all of the agencies. In his book, *The Ends of Power,* H. R. Haldeman described how he, John Ehrlichman, and Nixon spent almost two months at Camp David planning the takeover. There were wholesale firings, and positions were filled only by those who met the eligibility test—party affiliation and allegiance to Nixon. "We did it in ruthless fashion," Haldeman acknowledged. He quoted from a tape that revealed Nixon's morbid bitterness, hatred really, toward those he suspected of disloyalty, including perceived miscreants in the National Park Service.

> H.E.W., the whole damn bunch . . . get all those resignations in and say, "Look, you're out, you're out, you're finished." Knock them the hell out of there. . . . Let's remember the V.A., any Goddamn thing. Clean those bastards out. . . . Take that Park Service, they've been screwing us for four years.

Walker implemented Nixon's objective in the Park Service bureaucracy. From the White House, the office of Vice-President Spiro Agnew, and the Committee to Reelect the President, he recruited an unremarkable staff of a half-dozen administrative assistants, executive assistants, and confidential assistants.

Ron Walker lived up to his White House code name, "Roadrunner," by spending an inordinate amount of time on travel status, admiring the skills of the rangers, floating rivers, and driving snowmobiles. His personal advisers, who seemed to be captivated by something called "PR," endeavored to convince the organization that it was being led by a man of undoubted repute. Periodically they released figures proving that Walker had shaken hands with more employees than had any other director in history. He made a pilgrimage to California to consult with Founding Father Horace Albright, hoping perhaps to win some support. "It's impossible not to like the boy," Albright remarked after the visit, "but we simply must return the office to the merit system."

The misadventures of the Walker regime were not without comic relief. In the summer of 1974, he elected to launch a nationwide computerized reservation system covering 10,000 campsites in twenty-one national parks. Despite a nationwide publicity campaign that promised "virtually instantaneous" response to callers, the phone reservation company went into operation with only one toll-free WATS line and one regular line, each capable of handling a predicted twelve to fifteen calls per hour. The system collapsed instantly, with a recorded overload of 38,250 calls the first four days. Newspaper readers were entertained by stories of people who suffered through busy signals for days, some organizing families or office workers in marathon dialing attempts before giving up in disgust.

The situation became less amusing when it was learned that the president of the firm receiving the reservation system contract was a personal friend of Walker. Notwithstanding a bid from Ticketron, Inc., which had the necessary experience and facility outlets, a firm had been selected that had no previous experience and, in fact, had been organized solely to bid on the Park Service contract. Although Walker was grilled by a Senate investigating committee, he was cleared of any wrongdoing. The handling of the whole matter, however, left much to be desired on the part of Walker and an embattled Park Service.

Walker, it should be noted, became a genuine park enthusiast, yet his impetuous approach to complex problems would occasionally resemble a Chinese fire drill. His imprudent actions became a political liability to the administration, and, perhaps by coincidence, shortly after Nixon's resignation in 1974 Walker received a summons from Secretary Morton and was invited to do likewise.

The Walker interregnum was a confused and dispirited time for the Park Service, its policies subjected to political meddling, its director never acquiring more than a superficial understanding of the responsibilities of the job. Employees resorted to gallows humor and adopted a low profile. The Walker experience had one virtue: it was a weighty argument against making another political choice. Morton's decision to select the next director from the career ranks of the Service caused profound relief.

He picked Gary Everhardt, the superintendent of Grand Teton National Park, a deceptively genial administrator who was well known as a shrewd operator with an effortless style that produced consistently good results. A popular choice, Everhardt took charge in January 1975. There was one nagging worry—the next presidential election was less than two years away. If the Democrats won, a likely possibility after Watergate, would they follow the Republican precedent of selecting their own man to be director of the Park Service?

Under Everhardt the Park Service did an outstanding job during the 1976 Bicentennial year, the only federal agency to put together a sustained program of activities. The Carter victory in November, however, was followed by disquieting rumors. A member of the campaign staff, who had worked with Carter in Georgia, announced he had good reason to believe he would be appointed director of the National Park Service. Carter's Interior secretary, Cecil Andrus, probably appointed more people with noteworthy conservation credentials than any other secretary in history, but some of them had little talent for efficient management. Conflicting signals were given about the Park Service job by the assistant secretary, and lists of possible candidates, some from within the Service and some from outside, were drawn up and discussed. After six months Gary Everhardt and his deputy Bill Briggle, the intrepid trouble-shooter, were summarily fired, without explanation.

The dismissals were regarded in the Park Service as a signal that henceforth the directorship would be treated as a political post. The new leaders were chosen from the Park Service, a hopeful sign. Yet it seemed significant that the positions of director and deputy director were filled by superintendents of the two major urban parks, rather than men from the more traditional parks. The administration was making it clear that it wanted its own men in charge of the Park Service.

The new director, Bill Whalen, 36, was generally well regarded. He had shown exceptional skill in dealing with the volatile civic and political factions of the Bay Area when he put together the Golden Gate National Recreation Area. There were raised eyebrows in the organization, nevertheless, for both Whalen and his deptuy, Ira Hutchison, had relatively brief Park Service careers spent almost entirely in urban assignments, in contrast to their predecessors who had served considerably longer apprenticeships in the old-line parks. It was presumed that Hutchison, a black, was expected to help the Park Service improve its subpar record in the area of minority employment.

Three years later, in 1980, Whalen was fired. He had gotten crosswise with House Interior Committee Chairman Mo Udall, a longtime friend of the Park Service, who demanded that Whalen be dismissed after he had made some indelicate remarks at a meeting of the concessioners. Cecil Andrus was known to be concerned about the sinking state of Park Service morale, and there were indications that he was upset by other things that Whalen, who could be feisty, had done. A sensitive man, unswerving in his concern for the parks, Andrus was aware that the rapid turnover in leadership was having a destructive effect on the organization. This time he turned for advice to the Park Service, asking regional directors and field superintendents to come to Washington and help him make the selection. Their choice was Russell Dickenson, regional director of the Pacific Northwest region, and Andrus promptly named him director.

The news of Dickenson's selection had the effect of a spring tonic on an organization suffering from a severe case of frustration and uncertainty. As noted in Chapter 2, Dickenson is esteemed as an old pro, having moved steadily through the ranks in his thirty-three-year career. When he served as Ron Walker's deputy director, he never lost his cool and did much to hold the Park Service together during trying times. A letter to the editor that appeared in the Park Service newsletter shortly after his selection may explain why Russ Dickenson was a popular choice to be director of the Park Service and Ron Walker was not.

The letter was from a retired employee who had been a ranger in Big Bend National Park, along the Rio Grande in west Texas, many years ago. He told of an old, enfeebled horse that had somehow wandered across the Rio Grande into the park. He recognized the animal as the property of a poor Mexican farmer from across the river and called his chief ranger to explain it would take the best part of a day to lead the horse back and to ask permission to make the trip. That's a job for two people, the chief ranger told him; I'll give you a hand. Pushing and pulling a sick horse through desert canyon country would have been tough enough, the ranger recalled, but the horse was apparently suffering from a bowel disorder. They had to clean themselves off as best they could when they crossed the river. Their only reward was sharing the farmer's gratitude and his one bottle of warm beer.

I'm telling this story, the former ranger explained, because that chief ranger was Russ Dickenson, and he really knows what it is to be a ranger. A homely story, perhaps, but it was undoubtedly appreciated by readers of the newsletter, particularly the rangers who are the backbone of the Park Service and who often are called upon to do the grungy work in the parks.

Russ Dickenson brought steadiness and optimism when both were badly needed by an organization that had begun to lose its self-confidence and could no longer depend upon continuity in its leadership. This unsettling outlook can be repaired if future secretaries of the Interior will respect the need for professional leadership of the Park Service and will consistently choose a director on the basis of experience and competence rather than political considerations. The fortunes of an organization regarded as one of the most dedicated in government may rest with this decision.

11

PARKS AROUND THE WORLD

When she addressed a gathering of park superintendents a few years ago, the noted conservationist and writer, Mardy Murie, expressed her belief that the National Park Service has the most idealistic mandate of any federal organization. She also observed that the national park idea was not solely an American concept: "It was the beginning of an idea for the whole world and I wonder if it is not the best idea the U.S.A. ever gave the world." Yellowstone was the first instance in history of a nation setting aside a vast preserve for all people to enjoy; since 1872 more than 2,000 national parks and equivalent reserves have been established in more than 120 countries.

There were a number of reasons why the United States pioneered the national park movement, one of which was an accident of history. A modern culture existed along the eastern seaboard, while wilderness existed in the interior even throughout much of the nineteenth century. People from the East, mostly city dwellers, who traveled through this country developed a strong sentiment for preserving nature, and they began to voice regret over the passing of the wilderness from the American scene.

Another obvious reason for the park movement originating in the United States was the vast extent of the country's natural resources. In the Old Country, where the land had been occupied for thousands of years, there were no surplus acres. During his presidency Theodore Roosevelt set aside 150 million acres of land as national forests, an area larger than France, Belgium, and Switzerland. Few other countries could have afforded to take so much land out of production or to provide facilities and services. Most countries had other priorities to meet.

Important also to the flourishing of the national park idea was the presence of a democratic tradition. The kingly practice of establishing game preserves for the pleasures of the chase had existed for centuries.

(It is the Norman *parc,* the hunting estate of French feudal nobility, that is the source—with its connotation of uncultivated land—of the word "park.") Preserving game in the royal deer parks was an English tradition—the kings razed entire villages to safeguard the wildlife—and the present Gran Paradiso National Park was once the hunting ground of the Italian dukes of Savoy. But all of these noble preserves were created to protect the land from, not for, the people.

It would be a disservice to the world park movement, however, to suggest that other countries simply copied the U.S. experiment. Yellowstone did provide motivation: "the seedling sown in Wyoming was transported to flourish in both islands of New Zealand," reported a park administrator from down under. Other countries shaped the original concept to fit their own resource conditions. Some established larger parks: Kruger National Park in South Africa is more than twice the size of Yellowstone. Great Britain, with a land area of only 94,000 square miles and with 95 percent of its countryside in private ownership, developed a different, but no-less-rewarding, national park system than did Canada, which occupies 3.6 million square miles, much of it uninhabited.

Yellowstone was also the product of an emerging concern in the United States that steps be taken to protect the national heritage. In his book, *The Environmental Revolution,* the British conservationist Max Nicholson suggests that if one is looking for the origin of the world conservation movement, look to the United States before 1900, when an able group of scientific and professional leaders were urging the federal government to assume responsibility for solving resource problems in the national interest. The result of this agitation was the formation of a number of federal conservation agencies, including the present Forest Service, the Fish and Wildlife Service, and the National Park Service. Nicholson concludes, "All these developments in the United States during the three closing decades of the nineteenth century may be said, for the first time in any country, to have put conservation on the map as a serious public issue."

USNPS Assistance Programs

The United States National Park Service, generally referred to in international park circles as the USNPS, has provided assistance to more countries than has the Peace Corps. Each year it supplies training opportunities for more than 300 foreign nationals sent here at the expense of their governments to study the American parks. Some stay for a few weeks, others may spend a year, and those who are taking advanced degrees at American universities use the summer vacation for travel to the parks. The USNPS International Affairs Branch designs an itinerary for the touring park professionals, who arrive at the rate of almost one a day, arranging for them to visit parks where they can observe selected programs and consult with specialists. Some may be detailed for extended periods to a park or regional office. Others are invited to attend courses in the two Park Service training centers. One encounters park visitors from far-off lands almost as a part of the daily office routine.

For more than fifteen years the International Seminar on National Parks and Equivalent Reserves has provided one of the most effective training opportunities for the world park community. Designed for administrators and resource managers who are responsible for park and conservation systems, the Seminar is jointly sponsored by USNPS, The University of Michigan School of Natural Resources, and Parks Canada. A field training experience with academic instruction, the 1981 seminar traveled to national parks and other preserves in western Canada, the Pacific Northwest, the Southwest, and Hawaii. The seminars, which are held every summer and last about a month, have been attended by more than 500 participants from ninety-four countries.

It is physically, as well as financially, impossible for the Park Service to keep pace with requests from overseas for American planning and operational expertise. Every year individuals and teams are sent off on assignments. In 1981 there were technical assistance requests from twenty-six countries, ranging from Argentina (planning a curriculum and teaching an environmental education program at Argentina's National Park Service Training Center) to Venezuela (providing an urban park planner to design facilities for a park in Caracas). There were also requests for people who could design visitor centers in India, plan a marine park for Indonesia, prepare a national park management plan in Portugal, and develop specialized courses on park management for the College of African Wildlife Management in Tanzania.

The kinds of assistance needed by other countries have been changing. In past years many countries were starting from scratch, and the USNPS was asked to plan entire park systems. More recently countries that have established parks and are already knowledgeable want to do things better; a major request is to train their personnel. Still, in 1981 the Secretary of Commerce relayed a request from Gabon: Could the USNPS provide people who could plan a national park system—selecting the areas, developing management plans and policies, and training the rangers and administrators?

A single assistance project may require a long-term commitment. Nearly ten years ago Saudi Arabia decided to establish its first national park at Asir, an impressively varied area in the southern part of the country. It extends from coral reef formations in the Red Sea to a high mountain plateau and contains plentiful wildlife and 4,000-year-old petroglyphs carved by Sabateans from the land of Sheba traveling the ancient spice trail to the Persian Gulf. The first two phases of the project have been completed; the resources were inventoried, a development plan was drawn up, and roads, campgrounds, employee housing, and a visitor center have been constructed. The final phase is now under way, with four Park Service specialists in administration, resource management, maintenance, and interpretation on assignment in the park to train their counterparts.

Other agencies provide park-related assistance to countries that lack funds or experience. The Food and Agricultural Organization (FAO) of the United Nations, through its Conservation and Wildlife Branch, is probably the most generous in providing for a variety of national park projects. The World Wildlife Fund (WWF), established in 1961, gives priority to the saving of habitats and the rescue of endangered species. WWF raised funds to purchase key areas for the establishment of Spain's Doñana National Park in one of the least disturbed sections of western Europe. It is providing an ecologist to collaborate with a USNPS team that is helping the Spanish government develop a management plan for the park, which eventually will combine conservation and scientific research with public access.

The USNPS has formal cooperative agreements with a number of countries; none, however, is of such long standing as the United States–Canada Joint Committee on National Parks. Every year representatives of Parks Canada and their U.S. counterparts meet to exchange ideas and consider problems of mutual interest. The U.S. government has signed protocols with both the Soviet Union and the People's Republic of China for cooperation in the field of natural and cultural resource management, with national parks a specific subject of concern. Several delegations of Soviet specialists have visited U.S. national parks, and USNPS personnel have traveled in Russia, particularly to inspect the massive historic restoration projects carried out after the devastation of World War II. In 1981 the first Chinese delegation toured national parks, refuges, and forests in this country. The friendly relationship between Japanese and U.S. park administrators, which goes back to the founding of the first Japanese national park in 1934, has been formalized by the creation of the Park Panel of the United States–Japan Natural Resources Agreement. In all such exchanges park people have much to learn from each other, for technological advances are being constantly introduced: solar-powered remote radio repeater stations have been developed for Mount Kilimanjaro National Park; methods of immobilizing large animals for research or transportation purposes have been perfected in the wildlife parks of East Africa; and techniques for restoring alpine meadows have been investigated in Switzerland.

Japan has been helpful to the USNPS on several recent projects. The newly established War in the Pacific National Historical Park in Guam and American Memorial Park in Saipan, which commemorate the Pacific campaigns of World War II, are 12,200 miles from Washington, D.C., but only 1,500 miles from Tokyo. By law, the interpretive programs must be given in the Japanese and Chamorro languages, as well as in English, and the majority of park visitors are from Japan. The Japanese government will provide research, artifacts, translations—and a Japanese perspective—for the interpretive programs of these two parks.

Returning from a panel meeting in 1980, a Japanese member visiting Grand Canyon was impressed with the large number of Japanese nationals he encountered (an estimated 500,000 of the park's 2.5 million annual visitors are from foreign countries). He noted that his countrymen could better appreciate the park if their special language needs were accommodated, and in 1981 a Japanese ranger was posted to the United States—duty station Grand Canyon National Park.

National parks in developing countries have been important in attracting tourist dollars, and the economic returns from international tourism was a strong factor in the establishment of many national park systems. The economic factor has become an important one in the United States; in 1980, for the first time, tourists coming into the country outnumbered American tourists vacationing overseas. Of the ten most popular destinations of foreign tourists, nine are national parks. The $10 billion industry is vital to the American trade balance. The return in petrodollars to the United States as payment for federal and private technical services in the planning and construction of Asir National Park in Saudi Arabia far exceeds the total costs incurred by the USNPS for its international assistance programs since Yellowstone was established in 1872.

The World List

A story is told of American ecologist Ray Dasman that helps illustrate how widely national parks differ among the nations of the world. Appointed senior ecologist with the International Union for the Conservation of Nature and Natural Resources (IUCN) in Geneva several years ago, he decided to spend his first free weekend backpacking in the mountains. Consulting a map of Switzerland he located the largest blank space, a high alpine valley, drove to the vicinity, and set forth on foot. Neither the road nor the succession of cultivated fields and pastures ever ended. At about the place he had planned to camp for the night, he found himself in the midst of a well-tended farm. On his return to Geneva Dasman permanently retired his backpack to the closet.

Switzerland has some of the most spectacular scenery in Europe, but it has no undeveloped lands. The Swiss National Park (its only national park) was established in the Swiss Alps in 1914 as a biological sanctuary under the provision that it be "protected from all human influence and interference." Both camping and mountain climbing are forbidden. Access is limited to daylight hours, and visitors must stay on the trails. Animals are free to roam; people are not. The park is also administered as an alpine field laboratory where research can be carried out on a longtime basis under unchanging conditions, as far as human activity is concerned. If Dasman had chosen to hike in the park, he could have stepped off the trail to eat lunch only at the small areas designated for this purpose.

The founder of Swiss National Park was largely responsible for the International Conference for the Protection of Nature, held at Basel in 1913, at which agreement was reached among participating nations from Europe, Asia, and North America to develop an international body devoted to the cause of nature preservation. Efforts to implement the recommendation were not successful until after World War II, when Switzerland again took the initiative. With the support of France and the newly organized Economic and Social Council of the United Nations (UNESCO), a conference was held at Fontainbleau in 1948 at which the International Union for Conservation of Nature and Natural Resources was created.

IUCN, with a membership of 400 government agencies and private conservation organizations, has become the leading voice, and often the instrument, for worldwide action on environmental matters. In 1958 IUCN established an International Commission on National Parks to promote the worldwide park movement. An immediate handicap was the lack of a recognized standard to identify, among the many kinds of parks, preserves, and reservations, those that qualified as national parks. Endorsing the national park concept as a contribution "to the inspiration, culture and welfare of mankind," the United Nations in 1959 requested IUCN to develop criteria and make a world inventory of national parks.

It was a monumental task. The term "national park" was being used loosely in some countries, and as someone observed, the title "equivalent reserve" could convey any meaning from strict permanent protection to temporary nonuse. In 1969 IUCN adopted standards for the World List (actually the United Nation's List of National Parks and Equivalent Reserves). A national park must be established by the national government, which in turn guarantees that three basic requirements will be met: legal protection of the resources against hunting, agriculture, grazing, mining or lumbering; a minimum size of 5,000 acres if the population density of the country is less than fifty people to the square kilometer or 1,250 acres if more than fifty people; and an adequate staff and budget to protect the resources. Additionally the governing authority must provide for public use, deemed to be one of the primary purposes of national parks. Equivalent reserves (some countries prefer this term) must also meet the above three criteria.

Most of the countries of the world subscribe to the national park idea. Where resources might be endangered by public use, countries have modified the concept by developing Strict National Reserves from which the public is excluded. "The ban on visitors to Strict Natural Reserves is in effect waived for naturalists engaged in research," is a typical notation from the World List. Since the greater part of the landscape of Europe has been altered, "natural areas" are often places reclaimed from other uses. With an area only half again the size of Yellowstone and one of the highest population densities in the world, the Netherlands has embarked on an ambitious program to create twenty-two national parks. They will be "predominantly natural" in character; contain lakes, water courses, forests, and animal life; and be at least 2,500 acres in size.

Many parks are the result of private generosity and idealism. Francisco Perito Moreno, an Argentine scientist-explorer, was granted an 18,000-acre tract near Lake Nahuel Huapi in the heart of the Andes as a reward for his efforts in the exploration of the Patagonia Cordillera. Dr. Moreno gave the land back to the government with the hope that it would become a national park, observing that it would contribute to "the greater benefit of present and future generations, thus following the example of the U.S.A. and of other nations who own superb national parks." Enlarged by the government to nearly 1 million acres, Nahuel Huapi National Park was established in 1934 and is now one of a dozen sizable parks in the Argentine system.

The present park system of New Zealand had its origin in the request of a Maori chief, in 1887, that three volcanic mountains in the center of the North Island, sacred to the Maori, be donated to the Crown as a gift from himself "for the purpose of a National Park," rather than opened to settlement. Tongariro National Park, established in 1894, contains the country's most active volcano and the only glaciers on the North Island.

The global network of national parks protects many of the world's most famous natural features: the Great Barrier Reef off the coast of Australia; Mount Fuji in Japan; the Serengeti Plains of Africa; Lake

Baikal in Russia's Siberia; Tierra del Fuego at the tip of South America; the world's highest waterfall, an unbroken drop of 800 feet at Angel Falls in Venezuela; and Mt. Everest on the border of Nepal and Tibet. Included also are some of the most venerated cultural sites: the Cambodian ruins at Angkor; the ancient city of Jericho in Jordan; Greece's Olympia, site of the first Olympian Games; and the largest of the Mayan ruins at Tikal in Guatemala.

A glance at the U.S. entries on the World List reveals the extent of resource preservation in this country by the federal government, as well as by many state and private bodies, on a scale unmatched elsewhere. So many U.S. national parks and equivalent reserves are included that the customary descriptive data for individual sites could not be included. It is also significant that the majority of the entries are not areas administered by the Park Service. About one third are wilderness and primitive areas administered by the Forest Service, along with a number of refuges operated by the Fish and Wildlife Service. Nearly one hundred state parks are included, as well as a sprinkling of natural preserves under the jurisdiction of the National Audubon Society, The Nature Conservancy, and the Smithsonian Institution.

Canada and Latin America

Among all countries Canada, whose geography and frontier history parallel those of her neighbor to the south, comes closest to matching the park system of the United States. Canada was the first country to follow the Yellowstone example, with an almost identical beginning. Construction workers pushing the Canadian Pacific Railroad through the Canadian Rockies in 1885 came upon a cluster of hot mineral springs, as had the 1870 Yellowstone expedition. Although some of the men filed claims and built an access road and primitive accommodations for the expected tourist trade, the Canadian government reserved the land from sale or settlement and established Banff National Park in 1887.

Canada has kept pace quite well and sometimes exceeded the United States, establishing a park service organization in 1911 that was used as an argument when Congress established the American version five years later. Possessing enormous stretches of undeveloped country to the north, Canada's national parks are large in scale; Wood Buffalo on the boundary between Alberta and Northwest Territories at 11 million acres is five times the size of Yellowstone. In 1932 the Canadian Parliament and the U.S. Congress created an International Peace Park, which unites Glacier and Waterton National Parks. The two countries have also joined hands to establish a park at the former summer home of Franklin D. Roosevelt at Campobello Island, New Brunswick, where Roosevelt contracted polio. The Canadian and U.S. park systems share equally the operating costs and management direction of the house and grounds.

Many of the Latin American countries have extensive national park systems, particularly Argentina, Brazil, Chile, and Venezuela. The most difficult and pervasive problem facing Latin American parks is the occupation of reserved areas by *colonos* (settlers or squatters) who are desperate for land to feed their families. "Spontaneous settlement" is a deeply embedded tradition in these countries, and freedom to settle on any unoccupied land is considered a right. A peasant settles his family in a forested area of a national park and clears the land to establish his right of ownership. An estimated 30,000 families are living illegally within the national parks of Venezuela.

La Macarena National Park in Colombia protects a rain forest with such a rich variety of plants and animals that, despite the limited number of scientific surveys, more than 450 species of birds have been identified. Established in 1948, the park initially contained more than 3 million acres. In the past thirty years, so many *colonos* have established farms, using the slash-and-burn method of clearing the forest, that the park has been reduced to less than half its original size, and there is little realistic hope of relocating the peasants. In his Ph.D. dissertation on the management problems of Colombia's national parks, R. A. Megaack recounted an interview with a ranger from La Macarena who explained the difficulties involved in establishing preserves when people need land to grow crops:

> Many of the people poaching and farming in this park are poorer than we and have been our friends for years. Do you really think that we are going to arrest them? We also have been forced to cut the trees and kill some animals in order to supplement our diet out here in the field and are therefore also technically breaking the law.

Costa Rica, which had no reserves on the World List ten years ago, has since created thirteen national parks and six biological reserves. This is a remarkable record by a country only half the size of Virginia, blessed with a diverse geography and twice as many species of trees as the continental United States. Dividing the Caribbean lowlands from the Pacific beaches is a chain of high volcanic mountains covered by lush forests. The highest peak, over 12,500 feet, is no more than fifty miles from either coast.

According to an intriguing story, Costa Rica's Monteverde Cloud Forest Reserve, a virgin forest, is a tribute to a toad. Straddling the continental divide and incorporating six ecological communities, the reserve had attracted scientists from many countries. Some of them came to study the golden toad, a small, brilliantly colored amphibian that exists only in local rain pools at altitudes between 5,000 and 6,000 feet. When developers began to buy nearby land, international conservation groups joined the government in establishing the preserve, which contains 2,000 species of flowering plants, 100 mammals, and 320 birds, including the elusive quetzal, one of the most beautiful birds of the Americas.

Many parks and reserves have been created primarily to revive vanishing species. The Pampa Galeras National Vicuña Reserve was established in the high Andes grasslands of Peru in 1966 to protect the gentle and most graceful relative of the camel. Centuries ago, when vicuñas were abundant, the Incas organized hunts in which thousands of the animals—the population has been estimated at over a million—were captured by a great ring of beaters. The animals were released after being shorn, and the silky fleece was woven into royal cloth, forbidden to commoners on pain of death. After the Spanish conquest the slaughter began, for the wool of the wild vicuñas, one of the world's finest, has brought five times the price of cashmere. The vicuña population has recovered sufficiently to reintroduce herds in other areas, and it is expected that, under careful restrictions, vicuña wool and meat will again be available.

Now protected also are the extraordinary animals and plants living in what Charles Darwin called "this strange Cyclopean scene," the Galapagos Islands, which straddle the equator 600 miles from the coast of South America. An unpaid naturalist on H.M.S. *Beagle,* Darwin explored the Galapagos in 1835, finding there the clues that led to his theory of evolution by natural selection. The 3,000 square miles of islands and rocks in the volcanic archipelago received protection in 1934 when Ecuador established Galapagos National Park.

Centuries of isolation had protected the remote, stark, unearthly islands, until sailors discovered that the giant tortoise, which weighs up to 500 pounds, could provide fresh meat for the long ocean voyages. Captain David Porter, commander of the U.S. frigate *Essex,* described the practice when he stopped at the Galapagos to provision his ship in 1815: "Vessels on whaling voyages among these islands generally take on board from two to three hundred of these animals and stow them in the hold, where strange as it may appear, they have been known to live for a year without food or water." The whalers, men-of-war, sealers, and merchantmen decimated the tortoise population, which at one time must have numbered in the hundreds of thousands. Fewer than 10,000 survive today. Visitors marvel at the strange and abundant wildlife of the Galapagos, but settlers introduced domestic animals—there are an estimated 25,000 goats on one island—that have had much to do with the disappearance of tortoises on some islands and the dwindling numbers of land iguanas. Marauding pigs, dogs, and rats kill the young, while goats and donkeys take the meager food supply. Plants and animals receive legal protection from the park designation, but the destructive activities of the feral animals remain a serious problem.

Europe

The comparatively small, but heavily populated, countries of Europe have of necessity farmed and grazed almost every acre of available land. Natural ecosystems have been converted into parklike settings, and national parks have been shaped by this tradition. Established in recent times, long after the original forests and wildlife disappeared, these preserves display the living landscapes characteristic of large areas of Europe.

The British countryside is one of the most attractive in the world, in part because the nation has been a leader in developing strict planning laws to protect the countryside, leading a prominent conservationist to remark on the curious fact "that with so many parson naturalists in England the national park idea did not originate there." Following the National Parks and Access to the Countryside Act of 1949, ten national parks were created in England and Wales. None was less than 150,000 acres in size and the ten totaled 3 million acres. It is a notably extensive system for a small country, despite the fact that almost all of the land remains in private hands.

British national parks are stretches of countryside so designated because of their unique natural beauty. They contain farms and villages—and have a quarter of a million residents—but are protected against encroachments by strict regulations. Because the English parks do not meet the criterion of total protection, none is included on the World List. It notes, rather condescendingly, that nevertheless these parks "from a social point of view have a considerable importance." They deserve a better summation. In a country occupied for more than 4,000 years, with little public land, the British national park constitutes a magnificent contribution to the protection of the countryside. Widely used and enjoyed, it has been fittingly described as "a thinly inhabited region where the natural scenery is safeguarded for amenity and recreation."

Scotland, a much-less-heavily industrialized region, has more than fifty National Nature Reserves, but it has no national parks. In 1945 an official government survey recommended creation of five Scottish national parks. However, as the Countryside Commission for Scotland has observed, imposing an international concept on a democratically elected local government, with its own planning authority, was not deemed appropriate "in a Scottish context." Recently the Commission has identified forty areas of outstanding scenic value, covering one-eighth of the land area of Scotland and proposed that they be designated as National Scenic Areas. Protection would be achieved by purchase of scenic easements from the landowners. Enabling legislation, apparently, is not assured.

Poland has a dozen national parks, one of which contains the largest virgin forest in central Europe as well as the only remaining herd of European bison. Most of the land is in public ownership, extensive research is carried out, and in all parks, according to the World List, "the fundamental principle of total protection is observed." Tatras National Park in the Carpathian Mountains and Tatra National Park in Czechoslovakia constitute one of the best-known of the international "twin" parks. The two countries began joint scientific efforts there in 1924.

Only the northern portions of Norway, Sweden, and Finland contain wild lands that approach American standards. Sweden was the first European nation to establish national parks, setting aside six in 1909 (it now has ten). The northern parks are inaccessible, and recreational use is light, with only a few thousand visitors counted annually. In Sweden there is a common-law principle, a reaction against feudal restrictions on land use, that allows everyone to wander freely in open country—whether private land or national park—and to camp and gather wild fruits and berries at will. A more difficult problem for several of the northern Scandinavian parks is the presence of the native Lapps, who have traditionally pastured their flocks, hunted, and fished in the park areas. Their continuing right to do so is recognized, although park authorities were less than enthusiastic when the Lapps switched from ski and dog sled travel to snow machines.

One of the best-known examples of the protection of an artificial pastoral scene is Germany's Luneburger Heide Nature Reserve, near Hamburg, one of only three man-caused heath landscapes in Europe. The heather moorland resulted from the elimination of the natural forests by fire, timber cutting, and grazing that took place from prehistoric to medieval times. Heath covered northwestern Germany from the Middle Ages to the eighteenth century, when the decline of grazing and expansion of agriculture effectively destroyed most of the heath. Extensive maintenance methods are necessary to prevent the heath from being replaced by natural forest cover. Sheep graze the area, and mechanical and chemical controls are used. On fall weekends when the heather is in bloom, as many as 200,000 people are attracted to the 50,000 acre preserve.

Asia and the Pacific

In many Asian nations with enormous populations and the resulting need to till every acre of arable soil, there are few places where natural conditions still exist, except in the most remote and inhospitable regions or in high mountain country. After the 1917 revolution, the Soviet Union created a nationwide system of *zapovedniki,* which the USSR delegate to the second World Conference on National Parks described as "research institutions called upon to reveal the laws governing wild nature, develop basic principles for a rational utilization of natural resources, and raise the productivity of land." More than fifty of these areas, whose purpose is primarily scientific research, were included on the World List, although accompanied by the tactful comment that no documentation was submitted on the *zapovedniki*—literally forbidden areas. They were selected "by the authorities in Moscow, who stated that in doing so they have vigorously applied the criteria." Some of the areas are known to contain wild country with virgin forests, wolves, and snow leopards, and occasional hiking and camping permitted.

The Soviet political system, with its absolute control of the land and abrupt changes in policy, makes the creation—or elimination—of protected areas an uncomplicated process. In 1951 most of the reserved areas were disestablished, presumably because the land was needed for economic activities associated with the current Five Year Plan. Since then, for reasons not clearly explained, the system has been partially reconstituted. Plans have been announced to provide recreational opportunities for the Russian people through establishment of national, or "Natural," parks—Lake Baikal already has been so designated—but the program is as yet only in the inventory stage.

Most of the places listed in the World List are natural areas, but Turkey, which contains the remains of ancient civilizations, has established a number of historical parks. Among them is Troy, a name that conjures up the deeds of Achilles and Hector, the compelling beauty of Helen, the ten-year siege—and the priceless treasures of gold that emerged from one of archeology's most dramatic adventures. Heinrich Schliemann, the German merchant who never doubted Troy was real, fulfilled a boyhood dream by excavating the site of Homer's Troy in northwestern Turkey close by the Dardanelles. He found that it stood on the rubble of six earlier cities and was itself buried under two later settlements. The walls are now preserved in Troy National Park. Along the Aegean Sea, in Ephesus National Park, inscriptions eighteen centuries old testify to the grandeur of this Greek and Roman center, a strikingly well-preserved white-marble city of outdoor theaters, temples, and markets. Here the Apostle Paul preached, and to the Christian residents here he directed the epistle to the Ephesians that is included among the books of the New Testament.

In India, the Hindu reverence for all living things helped protect the remarkable variety of wildlife supported by diverse habitats: the Himalayas to the north, mangrove swamps along the east coast, desert regions to the west, forests covering the central plateau, and reed jungles along the great river valleys. During the British raj sportsmen enjoyed fabulous hunting, but the maharajas protected game in their preserves and British civil servants regulated shooting in the forests. Then in 1947, with independence, came disaster. Rejecting hunting prohibitions as a vestige of colonialism, Indians began to kill wildlife everywhere, even on private estates and in sanctuaries. The slaughter reduced once vast herds to mere remnants. "It was our disaster period," recalled an Indian ecologist. "You had the same thing in the American West—in the 1800s everybody started shooting, and the great herds were destroyed." The turning point came in 1969 when IUCN held its triennial meeting in New Delhi. The gathering of so many conservationists and scientists and their review of the plight of India's vanishing wildlife helped generate international concern. The support of Prime Minister Indira Gandhi, who addressed the IUCN convention, was pivotal. The killing of sixty-one endangered species was outlawed, and in 1973, with the help of a million-dollar pledge from the World Wildlife Fund, India launched Project Tiger to preserve a species that had dwindled from 40,000 animals at the turn of the century to fewer than 2,000.

The tiger is now on the increase in Kanha National Park in the sparsely settled region of central India, a preserve started by the British on the edge of one of India's last great forests. Visitors observe the wildlife show there from the backs of elephants. When the reed jungles along the Ganges Valley were converted to croplands, the great Indian one-horned rhinoceros was hunted almost to extinction because of the purported wondrous medicinal properties of its horn. Now protected in Kaziranga National Park in Assam, the rhinoceros population has grown from a few dozen to nearly a thousand. Kanha and Kaziranga are among the few success stories in India, however, and there is a question of whether it is too little and too late. Faced with dwindling forests and the demands of its 600 million people for agricultural production, the Indian Board for Wildlife believes the only possible strategy is to concentrate its efforts on national parks and sanctuaries. There is little hope for preserving wildlife elsewhere in India.

The national parks of Japan—a nation of 115 million people in an area smaller than California—are the most heavily used in the world. On a clear day in Tokyo, an increasingly rare occurrence, the perfect cone of Fuji is in sight, and the easily accessible Fuji-Hakone-Izu National Park receives nearly 80 million visitors annually (the forty-eight U.S. national parks recorded 47 million visits in 1980). Every year a million people climb the final 5,000 feet from the end of the road to the summit of Fuji. Because of heavy snow, the climbing season is limited to the summer months, when as many as 25,000 people *per day* pack the five trails to the rim of the crater. According to an official of the National Parks Association of Japan, "every climbing route is filled with long queues of people so that no one can find space and time to stop and rest."

In a heavily populated and industrialized nation like Japan, where land must be intensely utilized, park authorities cannot reject commercial and residential development in the national parks. National Vacation Villages, actually public resorts, are located in the parks as are some of the best ski areas. The Japanese solution is a zoning system. Land containing the most valuable features, about 10 percent of the total national park territory (although in individual parks the percentage can be much higher), is placed in the Special Protection Area category. Most of this land is federally owned and given traditional national park protection. In the Special Area category, comprising some 60 percent of the land, farming, lumbering, mining, and power dams are deemed compatible, but strong efforts are made to minimize their impact on the landscape. The Ordinary Areas (about 30 percent) are, as might be expected, little more than buffer zones with few restrictions on land use.

Both Australia and New Zealand experienced European settlement in comparatively recent times, and both have extensive national park systems. Australia has more than 240 parks and preserves on the World List, most of them along the populated areas of the south and east coast. Like Canada, Australia has vast, nearly inaccessible regions that are worthy of national park classification. Unfortunately, almost no other country in the world has suffered such devastation from the introduction of exotic species. Rabbit, domestic cat, European fox, rat, mouse, and wild dog (dingo)—their populations have at various times exploded until they have threatened the national economy and the survival of native marsupials.

New Zealand is a visually exciting land. Ten national parks have been established on the two main islands, along with more than a thousand scenic and special preserves, putting under protection 13 percent of the land area. Included are most of the country's unique land forms—active volcanos, snowcapped mountains, waterfalls, and fjords. Mt. Cook National Park has seventeen peaks of over 9,000 feet and a glacier twelve miles long.

Africa

Africa contains significant remnants of the community of plains animals that existed during the Pleistocene era in one version or other throughout the grasslands of the world. East and south of the Sahara are the parks and preserves that have provided a sanctuary for the vast herds of wildlife, easily the most diverse and extensive animal populations left on earth. Although the most spectacular national parks were set aside during the colonial era, many new parks have been created by countries since they received their independence. Still, developing countries desperately need to open more land to feed their people. In the past three decades more than 20 million acres of virgin forest have been cleared by timber companies in the Ivory Coast. In the remaining forests of Africa, the trees are being cut as farmers move in to grow their patches of millet and maize. Shrinking range and poaching are serious long-term threats to African herds as the growing human population moves into wildlife habitat areas.

Some of the African countries—Zimbabwe, Malawi, Senegal, South Africa—strictly enforce their conservation laws, but Uganda, Chad, and Angola are countries where, through political unrest or indifference, wildlife is being decimated. The World Wildlife Fund, the New York Zoological Society, and IUCN sponsored a recent survey of Africa's elephant population and found it to be dangerously reduced. In Uganda's Kabalega National Park (formerly Murchison Falls National Park) in 1966 there were 8,000 elephants. Ten years later, in 1976, poachers had reduced the herds to fewer than 1,700 individuals. In the chaos following Idi Amin's fall, guns fell into the hands of hunters and poachers; by 1980 only 160 elephants remained.

When the price of ivory soared from fifty cents a pound in the 1960s to six dollars a pound in 1975, poachers and traders began to supply the ivory warehouses of the world. Nairobi became one of the principal ivory capitals, exporting nearly a million pounds of elephant tusks in 1976. Then on Kenya Independence Day, in 1977, President Kenyatta announced a total ban on hunting and trading in wildlife trophies, skins, and ivory. Poaching was reduced in Kenya, but there and elsewhere on the continent the ivory drain continues, as smugglers and corrupt officials combine with the poachers to supply the world ivory markets.

Hunters who threatened to exterminate the mountain gorilla in the then Belgian Congo were responsible for the first African national park. Shortly after World War I, King Albert of Belgium visited a number of American parks; while at Yellowstone, he conceived the idea of using the national park concept to protect African wildlife. In 1925 Albert National Park was created in what is now Zaire, the first park anywhere in the world devoted almost entirely to systematic scientific research. Since that time most of the African nations have established parks and preserves; despite population pressures, poachers, and political changes, they are unsurpassed for the variety and extent of their wildlife.

A typical inventory of one park on the World List—Victoria Falls in Zimbabwe—suggests the diversity: "Elephant, hippopotamus, buffalo, giraffe, kudu, bushbuck, waterbuck, roan and sable antelopes (the latter in one of the largest concentrations anywhere in the world); lion and leopard; crocodile; innumerable baboons and vervet monkeys; plentiful birdlife, especially along the Zambesi, including herons of many species and cormorants."

Tanzania is a favorite destination for many international travelers who come to Africa to view the game preserves. Wildlife in Serengeti National Park exists in "astonishing concentrations," according to the World List: more than a million wildebeest take part in the annual migration, the recent subject of a superb television documentary. Serengeti Research Institute carries out extensive studies of geology, soils, vegetation, and animals. Fifty years ago Ernest Hemingway saw stretches of what is now Tanzania as "virgin country, an unhunted pocket in the million miles of bloody Africa." The country has set aside 40,000 square miles of wildlife preserves, 10 percent of its territory, and where Hemingway stalked lion and kudu, his son Patrick has taught conservation to rangers from many African countries in the College of African Wildlife Management.

An Information Exchange

It is axiomatic that all parks are different, yet park people in all countries face similar problems, as nearly all are engaged in protecting resources while making them available for public enjoyment. Because there were few ways for the world park community to exchange ideas, the delegates to the second World Conference on National Parks urged "that an international periodical be published as a medium for exchange on national park operation and management." In 1976 *PARKS* magazine began publication, sponsored by USNPS and Parks Canada with the assistance of a handful of organizations in and out of the United Nations and an editorial staff provided by USNPS. Printed quarterly in English, French, and Spanish editions, the popular magazine now circulates to

167 countries and their dependencies and gets into the hands of the managers of most of the protected areas of the world.

In a recent issue (fall 1981), topics included the first five national parks in Indonesia, an inventory of efforts to protect representative samples of tropical rain forest in the Amazon/Orinoco region of South America, and conversion of industrial refuse dumps to attractive parkland in the British city of Stoke-on-Trent. The "Park Techniques" department included information on building a boardwalk through a mangrove forest (in New Zealand), designing outdoor signs, exhibits, and litter bins (in Scotland), and constructing low-key barriers to restrain visitors in historic buildings (at Fort Necessity, Pennsylvania). An official of IUCN has said *PARKS* "is the most efficient way of providing beleaguered park people in developing countries with technical and moral support."

The World Heritage Convention

"The basic concept of a world heritage trust is disarmingly simple," suggested Russell E. Train in a paper delivered at the Yellowstone conference in 1972. "It is merely an international extension of the concept of national parks." A distinguished American conservationist who was then serving as chairman of the president's Council on Environmental Quality, Train had at several previous international meetings proposed the idea that there are sites of such outstanding universal importance that they belong to the heritage of the world and should be accorded a special status of protection. Their preservation is important to the inspirational and educational welfare of all people, Train declared. "Consequently, these areas should receive recognition as part of the world heritage, and as such they should be eligible to receive necessary assistance in their protection and maintenance from the world community."

Later that year the World Heritage Convention was adopted by the General Conference of UNESCO meeting in Paris, but six more years passed before the first sites were approved by the twenty-one-nation World Heritage Committee. The list now includes more than 100 sites, whose preservation has been deemed essential "for the whole of humanity." Auschwitz Concentration Camp, Poland. Independence Hall, Philadelphia. Katmandu Valley, Nepal. Ancient Thebes with its Necropolis, Egypt. Ngorongoro Conservation Area, Tanzania. Chartres Cathedral, France. Sites are not allotted on the basis of a country's size or wealth. Presently, the United States has seven areas on the list, as do Ethiopia and Yugoslavia. All of the U.S. sites—Everglades, Grand Canyon, Independence Hall, Mesa Verde, Redwood, Yellowstone, Wrangell–St. Elias—are a part of the national park system.

Many places of equal importance are missing from the list—the Great Wall of China, the Hermitage in Leningrad, Stonehenge in England, Greece's Acropolis, and India's Taj Mahal—because only about one-third of UNESCO's member nations have signed the convention (and because some nations who have ratified the convention have not yet nominated sites). In the yearly review of nominated sites (a number have been turned down), political considerations are not totally absent. Independence Hall was more controversial than Auschwitz because some members of the committee believed that accepting the nomination would suggest endorsement of the U.S. Constitution. The nomination by the United States of the site where the Wright brothers' first powered flight took place was withdrawn, following a negative reaction that reflected what one American observer called "the Continental philosophy": that in the absence of any visible remains or evidence a site alone may not be of predominant importance.

More serious political tensions were created in 1980 when Jordan nominated the Old City of Jerusalem and its walls, a part of Jordan before Israel annexed the Arab section in 1967 following the Six Day War. Israel, which has not returned the area to Jordan, is not a party to the convention. The World Heritage Committee "should not be the forum for determining which country has sovereignty," the chairman observed. At a meeting in September 1981, Old Jerusalem was accepted by a vote of fourteen to one, with only the United States voting against it and five nations abstaining.

The function of the World Heritage Committee is not just to prepare a global inventory. Acting as a kind of "international Red Cross for world wonders," the committee expects its greatest service will be in saving endangered sites, particularly in developing countries where there are fewer protective remedies. Once on the list, a threatened site is eligible for technical and financial assistance, although the committee is hampered by a limited budget. The committee cannot guarantee protection; it has no authority to act in a country unless invited to do so. It hopes to be able to mobilize the weight of world opinion when necessary, as was done when UNESCO issued a world appeal for the rescue of the Nubian Temples from the waters of the Aswan Dam.

A companion to the World Heritage program is Man and the Biosphere (MAB), founded by UNESCO in 1972 to study major environmental problems throughout the world. The USNPS is involved in MAB's program to establish a worldwide network of Biophere Reserves. These are areas in which representative, although not necessarily unique, ecosystems, both undisturbed and man-modified, can be studied and the response of those systems to human use and development can be monitored. There are now nearly 200 Biosphere Reserves in fifty countries;

of the thirty-five reserves in the United States, twelve are national parks. When the network of Biosphere Reserves is complete, each biotic province in the world will be represented.

In 1982 the world park community will gather for the third time, in Bali, Indonesia. The previous conferences were in Seattle in 1962 and Yellowstone–Grand Teton in 1972. It is expected that the sessions of the Third International Congress on National Parks and Equivalent Reserves will be devoted less to philosophy and policy than to practical operational and management problems. Still, the world park movement is notable for its idealism and the dedication of its participants. It does not seem likely the people who gather in Bali will hear a more-uplifting message than the one delivered in 1972 when the conference chairman called upon John F. Turner, the local representative of Teton County to the Wyoming legislature, to give the closing address to the departing delegates. Turner said, in part:

> I would like to congratulate you for your vision and deep commitment to an idea which promises much for the lasting well-being of our planet, to thank you for your convictions, energy, and, even, bravery. For I think that there is a requirement for bravery in the task ahead, not because of the grizzlies, lions, tigers, or elephants, but because it will be your responsibility in your work to directly and indirectly challenge some of the world's present value systems. These systems have been distorted in favor of consumption, technology, and materialism, and I, as a common citizen, wish you well in your efforts to preserve some of the Earth's remaining quality areas. Through these efforts, humanity will hopefully attain new heights in relationship to the Earth, to the other life forms with which we share the Earth, and, most important, to each other. I wish you well and a pleasant and safe journey to your homes.

12

A FORECAST

In the final chapter of a book of this kind it is traditional to speculate about the future welfare of the parks, although just about everyone you encounter these days seems convinced that the parks have been irrevocably spoiled by their fame and success. Historians have been unable to agree on the origin of that now-famous lament, "The national parks are being loved to death," but support is developing for the date August 27, 1915. On that day the driver of a Tallyho stage coach in Yellowstone encountered his first automobile, a 1911 Winton with bicycle wheels and tiller steering, and it almost scared the daylights out of his four-horse team. "This park as I have known it and loved it is as dead as a dodo," the usually taciturn driver told his passengers, a party of Shriners, unaccountably in full regalia, who were on their way to a convention in Boise.

People, it should be noted, have always had contradictory expectations about the parks and how they should be used. The largest number of park visitors, who want good roads and ready access to famous features, are generally chagrined to find that so many others had the same idea at the same time. Organized conservationists, who never hesitate to criticize the Park Service for its egalitarian ways, condemn travelers who stay close to their cars, careless of the pleasures that can be found away from the roadside. The only thing likely to cause the conservationists greater dismay than seeing crowds in the parking lots and overlooks would be to meet all of these people on the backcountry trails.

It is hardly a secret that Park Service people and members of the conservation hierarchy are frequently at sixes and sevens. One of the reasons for this prescriptive arrangement is that the two occupations attract people who differ considerably in personality and outlook. The Park Service bureaucracy, which values loyalty immoderately and provides few rewards for risk takers, selects park superintendents who can be trusted to exercise prudence and restraint. For the most part they are pragmatists, rather than romantics—problem solvers who have learned that compromise is to be sought, rather than avoided. While not unmoved by scenic splendor, for this is what originally attracted them to the parks, they are aware that composing a strong budget justification for a new sewage treatment plant is as essential as protecting the high mountain meadows. It is an approach, admittedly, that sometimes can result in a narrow-gauge viewpoint and a willingness to accept small gains. A superintendent, said Mardy Murie, "is right there in the sensitive spots where things are happening, subject to all the pressures from visitors, from concessioners, from the local businessmen, from the conservationists on the one hand, the four-wheel-drive vehicle enthusiasts on the other."

If I can be forgiven for making a generalization, the confirmed conservationists tend to be high-minded idealists, utterly devoted to basic park principles (as they define them)—seekers of perfect solutions who bombard the Park Service with the heady schemes of the unconstrained. They are quick to do battle on behalf of the environment, but are inclined to be guided by their emotions and to personalize attacks on their enemies; even worse, they have been known to suggest they could do a far better job of running the parks than the Park Service seems capable of doing, although management does not seem to be their strong suit. Their motto is Thoreau's nebulous epigram, "In Wildness is the preservation of the World," an example of environmental extremism that almost leads one to ask, what have we come to when people take trees more seriously than Mozart or martinis?

The Park Service will not impose restrictions on the number of people entering the parks.

Perhaps a more precise statement would be that Congress will not permit the Park Service to impose such restrictions, for there are political realities as well as ecological assessments involved.

The credo of the national parks is carved into the Roosevelt Arch at Yellowstone: "For the Benefit and Enjoyment of the People." When he dedicated the monument, President Theodore Roosevelt suggested that the most admirable feature in the management of Yellowstone was its essential democracy. Certainly the parks are cherished for their superlative beauty, but they are widely supported because they are open to all. The appropriation committees of the Congress have been, on the whole, rather generous with the parks, not the least reason being that congressmen vote for programs so long as their constituents are well served.

Economic considerations are also involved. Any action taken by the Park Service that will reduce the level of travel to a particular park is regarded as an attack on the local or regional tourist industry, whose membership immediately turns to Congress for relief. In a famous incident not likely to be repeated, the Park Service responded to a severe budget shortage in the 1960s by closing several parks for one or two days a week, including Carlsbad Caverns National Park in New Mexico. The effect of this action on the state's tourist business was "catastrophic," according to the infuriated governor, and the beleaguered Interior secretary quickly ordered the parks to resume normal schedules.

There are debates within the Park Service about whether some parks are reaching their "carrying capacity," but putting a ceiling on the number of park visits is a touchy subject. "I can't think of a policy that would more quickly alienate the American people from the Park Service than that," an Interior official told a reporter. "People pay their taxes to support these parks and they expect to be able to use them."

Concession facilities will not be removed from the parks.

Moving overnight accommodations, restaurants, and related facilities outside the parks has been the imperious demand of most conservationists, although the intensity of their campaign has lessened in recent years. Quite often the large hotel complexes, built in the early days of the Park Service or even before, were placed in the midst of the most important park features. Canyon Village on the South Rim of Grand Canyon is one of the more distressing examples of this practice. Moving these intrusions is an appealing idea, but, as described in Chapter 5, opponents of the Park Service effort to remove the overnight facilities from Zion went the political route, and Congress ordered that the facilities should remain.

The focus of conservation wrath presently is on the giant business concerns that have purchased a half dozen of the largest park concessions. Conglomerates, which someone aptly termed a hate word for the incredible hulk in the wings, are in the parks for the sole purpose of making money. Because of their size they are difficult to restrain, as was evident in the quarrelsome takeover in Yosemite by the Music Corporation of America.

In its final report to the president in 1972, the National Parks Centennial Commission recommended, surprisingly, that the Park Service initiate a long-term program to acquire concession facilities. It concluded: "The Commission can foresee the eventual demise of the fully private concessioner in the National Park System." Fed up with the ignoble performance of General Host in Yellowstone, the Park Service broke with tradition, canceled the General Host contract, and asked Congress for funds to buy the facilities so they could be leased to a private firm under tight supervision. Then, having acquired the facilities, in a somewhat surprising reversal the Park Service leased them back to another conglomerate.

The Park Service will continue to move in the direction of preservation, but only slowly.

The safest prediction that can be made about the future is that any changes in policy or philosophy are likely to be gradual ones. It is likely that every person who knows anything about the parks has a different opinion of how they should be operated, which may not be a bad thing for it guarantees against revolutionary change.

Management of the parks comes down to carefully weighing the values of preservation and use, then striking a plausible balance between the demands of those who would eliminate all but the most elementary facilities and services and those who favor amenities that permit the parks to be savored with a maximum degree of comfort. An acceptable equilibrium has evolved in which economic, political, historical, and sentimental factors all have played a part. The Park Service moves cautiously in the direction of preservation, castigated by conservationists for its timidity, scolded by Congress for its temerity. The disquieting announcement by Interior Secretary Watt that he intended to err on the side of public use signaled a reversal of the stated policy of recent Park Service directors that the only forgivable errors are those in behalf of preservation. The intensity of public concern for the integrity of the parks suggests Watt will have a difficult time.

There will be a more urgent need for money than for new parks in future years.

Back in the early 1960s, when Stewart Udall emerged as the first environmental prophet of the modern era, he provided a seemingly irrefutable answer to the question that Interior committee chairmen have asked since the days of Steve Mather: "Why do you want more parks when you can't take proper care of the ones you already have?" Land is our most precious resource, Udall would reply, arguing that it was quickly disappearing and all that we would ever be able to save must be set aside in the next few years. Despite this prediction, the establishment of new parks has in fact accelerated over the years. More than 150 have been added since Udall took office. With the passage of the Alaska Lands Bill in 1980, the equivalent of a second national park system was created.

The Park Service has, in a sense, gone broke every twenty years, repeating a familiar cycle: facilities deteriorate and crumble away because of inadequate funding; staffs are reduced rather than expanded; eventually headlines denounce the cheeseparing treatment of the parks and the current administration is convinced that it is time to rescue the parks. Witness, after the creation of the agency in 1916, the conservation-oriented recovery programs of the mid-1930s, Mission 66 in 1956, and the Bicentennial Land Heritage Program in 1976.

In the past it was possible to upgrade the parks with obtainable amounts of money. But signs of the next crisis are already evident, due to the addition of so many new parks and the effects of inflation, and the cost of rehabilitating a system of more than 330 parks will be astronomical. Most of the older parks have been waiting for years for repair or replacement of their deteriorating facilities. Many of the newer areas have failed to receive any of the funds needed to provide basic visitor services. The period of rapid expansion of the park system has probably ended, and the Park Service seems to have entered a new era in which money, rather than land, will be the scarcest commodity.

The parks would survive without funds.

Money does not really buy wilderness preservation, but it is needed to restore historic settings. Most of the Park Service budget (exclusive of new park acquisition costs) goes to build, repair, and maintain roads and trails, water and sewage systems, historic structures, museums, and campgrounds, as well as to hire administrative, maintenance, and ranger employees. Lacking these requisities, the parks would be more like scientific preserves.

So money is vital to the quality of park use. A performance of the Metropolitan Opera, no matter how inspired, would be sadly tarnished if the audience had to pick its way down the aisles through potholes and litter and be greeted by seats that were slashed and stained. The effect of this kind of shabbiness was aptly described by Boyd Evison, one of the more reflective park superintendents (now at Sequoia), when he testified in 1975 at House committee hearings on the budget shortfall:

> Any decline in the quality of visitor services and resource management (which includes maintenance) has an insidious effect extending far beyond what is immediately visible. In parks, the medium most assuredly is the message. Rotting historic structures, rampant exotic species, rutted trails, and littered roadsides tell the public that America doesn't care enough to husband its most distinctive natural and historic resources. Why then should the recipients of such messages treat those resources with care? Neglect begets neglect. Perhaps the most serious costs are in terms of resources irretrievably impaired, and of experiences forever lost.

The public will not support energy exploration in the parks.

In the past, especially during wartime shortages, parks have been targeted by commercial interests. However, in World War I stockmen achieved only token sheep and cattle grazing in a few of the western parks, and the aircraft industry turned to other and equally satisfactory construction materials in the early days of World War II after making a bid to lumber the Sitka spruce trees in Olympic National Park. No one, of course, can predict how desperate the need may become for new energy sources. In a worst-case circumstance, Congress would certainly authorize mining and drilling operations in the parks—or anywhere else on the public lands.

Recent applications to the Forest Service from 143 mining firms for permission to develop the geothermal lands adjacent to the western boundary of Yellowstone were denied, however, after vigorous public response when it was learned that drilling could take place only a few miles from Old Faithful, with totally unpredictable results on the park's thermal features. Appearing on the "Today" television program in 1981, Superintendent John Townsley of Yellowstone was asked whether he expected the parks would be safe from energy development. "This is very much the watershed time for our parks," he replied. "If we want to have places where we can find beauty and serenity, we must be willing to pay for them."

Air pollution, principally from the burning of fossil fuels, poses the greatest threat to the parks.

In 1982 the Clean Air Act, which has been under strong criticism from industry leaders who complain of excessive costs and reduced production, is scheduled for reauthorization. President Reagan has indicated he will look favorably on industry requests for relaxing existing controls. Certainly, energy production is an urgent national priority.

There is a critical relationship between energy development and the national parks, essentially a battle over trade-offs: clean air and unscarred land versus strip-mining of domestic coal to fuel power plants that will replace foreign oil imports. The damage to parks has already begun. Plumes from the Four Corners plant (built before enactment of the Clean Air Act) have been traced for hundred of miles. Grand Canyon has visibility problems an average of 100 days a year. The superintendents of most Rocky Mountain parks are no longer able to assure visitors of clean air and good visibility. Smog from the Los Angeles basin rolls into Death Valley, clouding vistas that were once crystal clear.

The success of energy conservation measures may be a factor in protecting parks. The outcome of the current battles between conservationists and developers over the proposed construction of massive power projects planned by electrical utility companies in the Southwest may be decided on a separate issue: with significant decline in the use of power, much of the electricity to be generated by the new plants may not be needed.

If directors continue to come and go as rapidly as they have recently, the trend toward the politicizing of the Park Service may be irreversible.

The Park Service has a well-earned reputation as one of the more spirited agencies in government. It has had unusually competent leadership. "There have been no half-timers among the Directors of the Park Service," one historian has noted. They have been devoted to the parks that they have stubbornly, and skillfully, defended from political horsetrading. They have also been highly respected by Park Service people who have looked to them for direction and a sense of purpose.

The revolving-door treatment of directors since 1972 has seriously shaken the stability and confidence of the entire organization. It is the function of the director to assure that the national parks receive due process whenever important policy determinations are being made at the departmental level. The parks deserve an experienced professional in charge of the agency, one who is assured of continuity and is free to be an advocate for the parks and to make policy recommendations to the Interior secretary.

With few exceptions, the management of the park system is not a matter of partisan politics. The parks would suffer at the hands of a politically selected director whose tenure was dependent upon the enthusiasm he could generate for the faddish goals of a new administration. If this becomes the norm, the Park Service will surely begin to lose those precious qualities that have made it, in the judgment of some, a different kind of government organization.

There will be another secretary of the Interior after James Watt.

No other department of the government can rival Interior for the widely divergent ideological convictions of its secretaries: from Douglas McKay to Stewart Udall, Walter Hickel, Cecil Andrus, and finally James Watt. The choices reflect the contradictory responsibilities of Interior: from preserving endangered species to building dams, from protecting Civil War battlefields to encouraging oil exploration on the intercontinental shelf. Secretaries come and go fairly quickly. Since World War II their tenure has averaged a little over three years, less for assistant secretaries, or about the amount of time it takes a park ranger to become familiar with his district.

Ten years ago, when the first edition of this book was being written, Walter Hickel was Interior secretary. The controversy over his appointment matched the brouhaha that followed Watt's selection, for much the same reasons. A self-made millionaire who became governor of Alaska, Hickel had denounced Udall and the Interior department for interfering with the God-given right of Alaskans to make their fortunes from the public lands. Conservationists gave Hickel a hard time at his confirmation hearings; there may even have been charges that appointing Hickel chief at Interior was like putting the fox in the chicken coop. He lasted less than two years, mellowing considerably on the job, and had only minimal long-term impact on departmental enterprises.

When one has been an Interior insider for nearly thirty years and has watched the uninterrupted parade of Interior secretaries and assistant secretaries, arriving with such fanfare and departing so discreetly, what stands out most of all is that there were so many of them. The critics of Mr. Watt and his thumb-in-the-eye treatment of the "greenies" (the conservation crowd) can therefore take heart. Sooner or later another Stewart Udall or Cecil Andrus will set up shop in that spacious paneled office on the sixth floor of Interior, although waiting for the Watt regime to run its course could require the patience of a fisherman.

APPENDIX A

THE ORGANIC ACTS OF THE NATIONAL PARK SERVICE

The Yellowstone Act, signed by President Ulysses S. Grant on March 1, 1872:

> . . . the tract of land in the Territories of Montana and Wyoming, lying near the head-waters of the Yellowstone river . . . is hereby reserved and withdrawn from settlement, occupancy, or sale under the laws of the United States, and dedicated and set apart as a public park or pleasuring-ground for the benefit and enjoyment of the people. . . . regulations shall provide for the preservation, from injury or spoilation, of all timber, mineral deposits, natural curiosities, or wonders within said park, and their retention in their natural condition.

Establishment of the National Park Service, signed by President Woodrow Wilson on August 25, 1916:

> . . . The service thus established shall promote and regulate the use of the Federal areas known as national parks, monuments and reservations hereinafter specified by such means and measures as conform to the fundamental purpose of the said parks, monuments, and reservations, which purpose is to conserve the scenery and the natural and historic objects and the wildlife therein and to provide for the enjoyment of the same in such manner and by such means as will leave them unimpaired for the enjoyment of future generations.

APPENDIX B

THE NATIONAL PARK SYSTEM

The national park system (see Table B.1) contains more than 330 parks covering some 80 million acres, an area larger than Colorado. Located in all but one of the fifty states, the parks extend from Alaska, Hawaii, and Guam to Puerto Rico and the Virgin Islands. The equivalent of a second system was created by the 1980 Alaska Lands Bill that added, among other areas, eight new national parks, of which six were larger than Yellowstone (see Table B.2). Although the president can proclaim national monuments on federal lands, this authority is rarely used; every new park is established by an act of Congress. Over the years, various attempts have been made to reduce the confusion caused by the ever-growing number of titles coined by Congress for the parks, but the list continues to grow (Park Service people make no attempt to memorize the classifications; they call them all parks). An *Index to the National Park System and Related Areas,* containing data and descriptions for each park, can be purchased from the Government Printing Office.

TABLE B.1. Statistical Summary of the National Park System in 1981

Classification	*Number*	*Acreage*
National Parks	48	46,688,505
National Monuments	79	8,650,580
National Preserves	12	19,640,550
National Lakeshores	4	196,456
National Rivers	10	522,691
National Seashores	10	597,655
National Historic Sites	65	18,020
National Memorials	22	7,943
National Military Parks	12	34,748
National Battlefield Parks	3	6,762
National Battlefields	8	10,479
National Battlefield Sites	1	12
National Historical Parks	24	109,854
National Recreation Areas	17	3,661,542
National Parkways	4	160,852
National Scenic Trails	1	52,034
Parks (other)	10	31,986
National Capital Parks (of Washington, D.C.)	1	6,470
White House	1	18
National Mall	1	146
National Visitor Center	1	000
Total	334	80,397,303

TABLE B.2. Areas Included in the 1980 Alaska Lands Bill

Designation	*Acreage*
Aniakchak National Monument	350,000
Aniakchak National Preserve	160,000
Bering Land Bridge National Preserve	2,457,000
Cape Krusenstern National Monument	560,000
Denali National Park	4,366,000
Denali National Preserve	1,330,000
Gates of the Arctic National Park	7,052,000
Gates of the Arctic National Preserve	900,000
Glacier Bay National Park	3,328,000
Glacier Bay National Preserve	57,000
Katmai National Park	3,960,000
Katmai National Preserve	308,000
Kenai Fjords National Park	570,000
Kobuk Valley National Park	1,710,000
Lake Clark National Park	2,440,000
Lake Clark National Preserve	1,210,000
Noatak National Preserve	6,460,000
Wrangell–St. Elias National Park	8,147,000
Wrangell–St. Elias National Preserve	4,171,000
Yukon-Charley National Preserve	1,720,000
Total	51,256,000[a]

[a]Includes carry-over acreage from Katmai National Monument (2,792,000), Glacier Bay National Monument (2,805,000), and Mt. McKinley National Park (1,939,000). These three parks, plus Klondike Gold Rush National Historic Park (13,000) and Sitka National Monument (108), were established before the 1980 act.

BIBLIOGRAPHY

Abbey, Edward. *Desert Solitaire: A Season in the Wilderness.* New York: Ballantine Books, 1968.

Albright, Horace M. *Origins of National Park Service Administration of Historic Sites.* Philadelphia: Eastern National Park and Monument Association, 1971.

Darling, F. Fraser, and Eichhorn, Noel D. *Man and Nature in the National Parks.* Washington, D.C.: Conservation Foundation, 1969.

Elliot, Sir Hugh, ed. *Second World Conference on National Parks.* Morges, Switzerland: International Union for Conservation of Nature and Natural Resources, 1974.

Haines, Aubrey L. *The Yellowstone Story.* 2 vols. Yellowstone Library and Museum Association in cooperation with Colorado Associated University Press, 1977.

Hampton, H. Duane. *How the U.S. Cavalry Saved Our National Parks.* Bloomington: Indiana University Press, 1971.

Hendee, John C.; Stankey, George H.; and Lucas, Robert C. *Wilderness Management.* Washington, D.C.: Government Printing Office, 1978.

Hosmer, Charles B., Jr. *Preservation Comes of Age: From Williamsburg to the National Trust, 1926–1949.* 2 vols. Charlottesville: University Press of Virginia, 1981.

Ise, John. *Our National Park Policy: A Critical History.* Baltimore: Johns Hopkins Press, 1961.

Kuuvanmiit Subsistence: Traditional Eskimo Life in the Latter Twentieth Century. Washington, D.C.: National Park Service, 1977.

Lee, Ronald F. *Family Tree of the National Park System.* Philadelphia: Eastern National Park and Monument Association, 1972.

McPhee, John. *Coming into the Country.* New York: Farrar, Straus and Giroux, 1976.

Marshall, Robert. *Alaska Wilderness: Exploring the Central Brooks Range.* 2nd ed. Berkeley: University of California Press, 1970.

Nash, Roderick. *Wilderness and the American Mind.* Rev. ed. New Haven: Yale University Press, 1973.

National Parks for the Future. Washington, D.C.: Conservation Foundation, 1972.

Quirk, Patrick J., and Fise, Thomas F. *The Complete Guide to America's National Parks.* Washington, D.C.: National Park Foundation, 1979.

Runte, Alfred. *National Parks: The American Experience.* Lincoln: University of Nebraska Press, 1979.

Sax, Joseph L. *Mountains Without Handrails: Reflections on the National Parks.* Ann Arbor: University of Michigan Press, 1980.

Schneider, Bill. *Where the Grizzly Walks.* Missoula, Mont.: Mountain Press Publishing Company, 1977.

Shankland, Robert. *Steve Mather of the National Parks.* 3rd ed. New York: Alfred A. Knopf, 1970.

Swain, Donald. *Wilderness Defender: Horace M. Albright and Conservation.* Chicago: University of Chicago Press, 1970.

Tilden, Freeman. *The National Parks.* Rev. ed. New York: Alfred A. Knopf, 1976.

———. *Interpreting Our Heritage.* Rev. ed. Chapel Hill: University of North Carolina Press, 1967.

Udall, Stewart. *The Quiet Crisis.* New York: Holt, Rinehart & Winston, 1963.

United Nations List of National Parks and Equivalent Reserves. Prepared by the IUCN International Commission on National Parks for the United Nations Economic and Social Council. Brussels: Hayez, 1971.

Wirth, Conrad L. *Parks, Politics, and the People.* Norman: University of Oklahoma Press, 1980.

INDEX

About the Book and Author

The National Park Service
William C. Everhart

Since the first edition of this book was published ten years ago, the U.S. national park system has more than doubled in size, and the National Park Service (NPS) has been subjected to more political manipulation than at any time since the agency was established in 1916. Before 1972, no NPS director had ever been removed for political reasons; since 1972, there have been five directors, four of whom were fired. This book analyzes the complex problems and conflicting demands encountered by the organization responsible for protecting the national parklands while making them available for public use and enjoyment.

William Everhart describes the activities of special interest groups—from concessioners to conservationists—who seek to influence NPS decision making. A former assistant director for interpretation, he examines such questions as whether (as many have charged) the parks are indeed being "loved to death" and such favorites as Yellowstone and Yosemite have been turned into "rural slums" by overuse, whether the new urban parks in San Francisco and New York are diluting the traditional high standards of the park system, and whether recent interventions by the White House and Congress have politicized the Park Service.

Everhart devotes a chapter to the long, acrimonious—and successful—battle to establish the equivalent of a second national park system in Alaska. Speculating on the future, he notes that Park Service directors to date have been experienced, dedicated professionals, and comments that if new administrations appoint primarily political henchmen to this key post, the Park Service will inevitably lose its distinctive qualities and our national heritage may suffer irreparable damage.

William C. Everhart, according to current NPS director Russell Dickenson, has credentials for commenting on the NPS that "are as good as a man can have." He began his career in the NPS in 1951 as park historian, and after his retirement in 1977 from the position of assistant to the director for policy, he has been a visiting professor at Clemson University and a consultant to the Arizona–Sonora Desert Museum in Tucson.